T0392758

# INTERACTIVE DOCUMENTARY

Interactive documentary is still an emerging field that eludes concise definitions or boundaries. Grounded in practice-based research, this collection seeks to expand the sometimes exclusionary field, giving voice to scholars and practitioners working outside the margins.

Editors Kathleen M. Ryan and David Staton have curated a collection of chapters written by a global cohort of scholars to explore the ways that interactive documentary as a field of study reveals an even broader reach and definition of humanistic inquiry itself. The contributors included here highlight how emerging digital technologies, collaborative approaches to storytelling, and conceptualizations of practice as research facilitate a deeper engagement with the humanistic inquiry at the center of documentary storytelling, while at the same time providing agency and voice to groups typically excluded from positions of authority within documentary and practice-based research, as a whole. This collection represents a key contribution to the important, and vocal, debates within the field about how to avoid replicating colonial practices and privileging.

This is an important book for practice-based researchers as well as advanced-level media and communication students studying documentary media practices, interactive storytelling, immersive media technologies, and digital methodologies.

**Kathleen M. Ryan** is a documentary filmmaker and an associate professor of journalism at the University of Colorado Boulder. Her hybrid work focuses on transformations in storytelling due to shifting media technologies. Specifically, she explores the intersection of theory and praxis within evolving media forms such as interactive documentary. Her projects deal with issues of gender, self-identity, visuality, and user/participant agency.

**David Staton** is an associate professor at the University of Northern Colorado where he teaches in the Department of Journalism and Media Studies. His areas of research include visual communication, ethics, and sports journalism. He has been involved in the production of three feature-length documentary films, which have been screened internationally. *Ghost Resort*, his first experimental documentary short, is now at festival.

# INTERACTIVE DOCUMENTARY

## Decolonizing Practice-Based Research

*Edited by Kathleen M. Ryan
and David Staton*
*(With editorial assistance from
Tammy Rae Matthews)*

Routledge
Taylor & Francis Group

NEW YORK AND LONDON

First published 2022
by Routledge
605 Third Avenue, New York, NY 10158

and by Routledge
4 Park Square, Milton Park, Abingdon, Oxon, OX14 4RN

*Routledge is an imprint of the Taylor & Francis Group, an informa business*

© 2022 selection and editorial matter, Kathleen M. Ryan and David Staton; individual chapters, the contributors

The right of Kathleen M. Ryan and David Staton to be identified as the authors of the editorial material, and of the authors for their individual chapters, has been asserted in accordance with sections 77 and 78 of the Copyright, Designs and Patents Act 1988.

All rights reserved. No part of this book may be reprinted or reproduced or utilised in any form or by any electronic, mechanical, or other means, now known or hereafter invented, including photocopying and recording, or in any information storage or retrieval system, without permission in writing from the publishers.

*Trademark notice*: Product or corporate names may be trademarks or registered trademarks, and are used only for identification and explanation without intent to infringe.

*Library of Congress Cataloging-in-Publication Data*
A catalog record for this book has been requested

ISBN: 978-1-032-00511-9 (hbk)
ISBN: 978-1-032-00131-9 (pbk)
ISBN: 978-1-003-17450-9 (ebk)

DOI: 10.4324/9781003174509

Typeset in Bembo
by Apex CoVantage, LLC

# CONTENTS

# ILLUSTRATIONS

# CONTRIBUTORS

**Rania Al Namara (Elhelo)** worked as media and communications professional in the Middle East, particularly in the West Bank and Gaza, for the past 14 years. Her research interest focuses on the role of human-interest stories in reporting humanitarian crises in conflict zones with contents and textual analysis within nonprofit organizations. She is a PhD student at the University of Colorado Boulder, United States.

**Diego Cerna Aragon** is a media and technology researcher based in Peru. He holds a BA in Communication from the University of Lima (Peru) and an SM in Comparative Media Studies from the Massachusetts Institute of Technology (USA).

**Judith Aston** is co-founder of i-Docs and Associate Professor in Film and Digital Arts at UWE Bristol, United Kingdom. Her background is in anthropology, geography, interaction design, and creative media practice. At the heart of her work is the desire to put evolving media technologies into the service of promoting multiperspectival thinking and understanding.

**Joel Kachi Benson** is a Nigerian documentary filmmaker and virtual reality (VR) content creator. Benson is the creative director for JB Multimedia Studios and VR 360 Stories. He received his degree in filmmaking from Central Film School in London.

**Gino Canella** is a documentary filmmaker and assistant professor of journalism at Emerson College, United States. His research and creative works explore activist media, journalism, and the framing of race and labor, produced with grassroots organizers. He is interested in how media production and exhibition complement local organizing and promote civic participation.

**Isabelle Carbonell** is a Belgian-Uruguayan-American sci-fi nonfiction filmmaker who holds a PhD in Film & Digital Media from the University of California, Santa Cruz, United States. Her research and practice lies at the intersection of expanded documentary, environmental justice, and the Anthropocene, while striving to develop new visual and sonic approaches and methods to rethink documentary filmmaking and create a multispecies cinema.

**Jeb J. Card** is an assistant teaching professor in anthropology at Miami University, United States. His work includes study of colonial transformations in Central America, such as *Hybrid Material Culture* (2013) and the history of archaeology in light of broader public and intellectual interests in the past with *Lost City, Found Pyramid* (2016), and *Spooky Archaeology* (2018).

**Felipe Carrelli** received his Master's in the Creative Media Postgraduate Program (PPGMC) at Federal University of Rio de Janeiro (UFRJ), Brazil, in 2021.

**Anita Wen-Shin Chang** is an artist/scholar and assistant professor of communication at California State University East Bay, United States. Her award-winning films are screened internationally, including at the Whitney Museum, Walker Arts Center, and the National Museum of Women. She is the author of *Third Digital Documentary: A Theory and Practice of Transmedia Arts Activism, Critical Design and Ethics*, and has published in *American Quarterly*, *Verge*, *positions*, *Concentric*, and *Taiwan Journal of Indigenous Studies*.

**Paolo Silvio Harald Favero**, a visual anthropologist and image-maker, is currently Professor in Visual and Digital Culture at the University of Antwerp, Belgium. His main interest is in the role of images in human life. He is the author of *Image-Making-India* (Routledge, 2020) and *The Present Image* (Palgrave Macmillan, 2018).

**Alexandra Sophia Handal** is a Palestinian artist, filmmaker, and essayist with a transnational upbringing. Based in Europe since 2004, Handal continues to spend extended periods of time in Palestine.

**Leonie Jones** is a filmmaker and associate head of film and screen production at the University of Southern Queensland, Australia. As a writer and director of documentary films, Leonie's practice includes oral history as an important part of post-conflict storytelling. Leonie's documentaries include *Long Tan: The Soldier's*

*Story* (2006), *The Battle of Milne Bay '42* (2008), *The Battle of Fire Support Base Coral* (2016), and the i-doc *26 days: The Battle of Coral Balmoral* (2020).

**Adrian Kahgee** (Saugeen First Nation), founding member of *Odeimin Runner's Club*, is an artist and community arts educator based in Canada. She is the co-producer of Saugeen Takes on Film, a community-based film program working with artisans, youth, and knowledge keepers. Her research is centered around her Afro-Indigenous relations, as a member of Saugeen and as a freedom seeker/ Black Canadian descendant.

**Anandana Kapur** is founder-director Cinemad India, a startup working on media literacy and storytelling. Her documentary films focus on gender, social change, and culture. As a Fulbright Fellow and Shastri Indo-Canadian Institute grantee, she studied co-creation and interactive documentary media at the Open Doc Lab, MIT, and DMRC, Ryerson University. Anandana also curates nonfiction media and has served on the jury at several film festivals. She is currently a Mason Fellow at the Harvard Kennedy School (USA).

**Aashish Kumar** is Professor of Radio, Television, Film and Immersive Media at Hofstra University, United States. He is interested in emerging media forms that use innovative storytelling strategies to help people become more aware of internal diversity and the margins of communities. To him, such an empathic understanding is key to forming broader solidarities and bridging the gap with "the other."

**Tammy Rae Matthews** is a doctoral candidate at the University of Colorado Boulder, United States, who unites her passions – sport, media, language, and gender – in her primary research, which includes historical and contemporary representations of transgender athletes in sports media. Her additional interests are in education, global and domestic culture, new media, interpersonal relationships, travel, art, technology, and business.

**Stefano Odorico** is a reader in Contemporary Screen Media at Leeds Trinity University, United Kingdom, where he directs the International Research Centre for Interactive Storytelling. He is a co-founder and member of the editorial team of *Alphaville: Journal of Film and Screen Media* and has published numerous works on film, media theory and practice, documentary studies, and interactive documentaries.

**André Paz** is Professor at the Federal University of the State of Rio de Janeiro (UNIRIO), Brazil, and at the Creative Media Graduate Program (PPGMC) at the Federal University of Rio de Janeiro (UFRJ).

**Leighton C. Peterson** is Associate Professor of Anthropology at Miami University, United States. A linguistic and media anthropologist, Leighton has published numerous works on emergent practices in Native media, Indigenous film, and Navajo language use in media. As a public television producer, his works include *Weaving Worlds* (2008), *Columbus Day Legacy* (2011), and *Metal Road* (2017).

**Matt Peterson** is an organizer at Woodbine, an experimental space in New York City. He directed the documentary film *Scenes from a Revolt Sustained* (2015), and is a co-director (with Malek Rasamny) of a multiplatform project *The Native and the Refugee*, which documents the lives of American Native Americans living on reservation land alongside stories from the Palestinian refugee camps.

**Malek Rasamny** is a researcher, writer, and a filmmaker who grew up in New York, and is now based between Paris and Beirut. Along with *The Native and the Refugee*, he is working on a multimedia research project on reincarnation in post-war Lebanon.

**Tessa Ratuszynska** is a practice-based PhD student at the University of West Scotland Immersive Media Academy, and during 2020 was a Bristol and Bath Expanded Performance Pathfinder fellow (both UK). Visit www.tessaratuszynska. com to learn more.

**Debbie Ebanks Schlums** (Jamaica/Canada) is a PhD student and Vanier Scholar in Cinema and Media Studies at York University, Toronto, Canada. Her research explores methodologies of Caribbean diasporic archiving in the Jamaican Diaspora through storytelling and media installation. As a visual artist, Debbie has exhibited work in public galleries and festivals in Canada in sculpture, performance, and social practice.

**Carles Sora-Domenjó** is an interdisciplinary scholar whose creative and critical research explores the intersections of technology, audiovisual, culture, and arts. He is Associate Professor and Academic Director of CITM (Center for Image and Multimedia Technologies), a digital creativity center at Universitat Politècnica de Catalunya (UPC), Terrassa, Spain. He has worked on more than 25 interactive projects for visual arts, performance, and scientific dissemination.

**Eva Theunissen** is a PhD candidate at the Visual and Digital Cultures Research Center, University of Antwerp, Belgium. Her research addresses the relationship between digital/visual technologies, embodiment, and social in/visibility. Methodologically, she combines online and offline ethnographic fieldwork and is a proponent of in-depth, embodied research methods.

**Rebeka Tabobondung** (Wasauksing First Nation), a media and story creator, is the founder and editor-in-chief of MUSKRATMagazine.com, a leading digital Indigenous arts and culture magazine based in Canada. She is also a filmmaker, writer, poet, and Indigenous knowledge researcher. Her current collaboration, with Montreal-based Rezolution Pictures and APTN, is the *Spirit of Birth* web series and interactive mobile App/digital platform.

# PREFACE

A number of terms have been suggested to describe the hybridized digital innovations that have become widespread in the first part of the twenty-first century. Multi- or cross-platform. Transmedia. Convergent storytelling. "The Snow Fall Effect."[1] All refer to a type of cross-pollination between "old" and "new" media, where, borrowing from Henry Jenkins (who coined the term "convergence culture"), "the power of the media producer and the power of the media consumer interact in unpredictable ways."[2]

Of course, Jenkins was considering how content spreads *across* media platforms, which is not the intent of this book. Instead, the authors herein are looking at a site of specific transformation: interactive documentary storytelling, regardless of platform(s) used. For us, the term "interactive documentary" (or i-doc) offers the most satisfactory descriptor for transformations in the relationships between creator, subject, and audience found in documentary's digital turn; a space, too, in which conversations about this evolving practice, its processes, and its products might be interrogated. This book argues that the implications of a push toward co-creation transform the i-doc into a specific type of practice-based research (PBR), one which facilitates the breaking down of traditional hierarchies and opens up spaces for voices often left powerless in more traditional academic formats. PBR is "an original investigation undertaken in order to gain new knowledge, partly by means of practice and the outcomes of that practice."[3] It is less interested in the hypothesis/research question model, instead privileging creative practice to understand what we don't know about our world. For i-docs, that creative practice manifests in nonfiction, nonlinear community-based storytelling, providing an active voice and research authority for those often left outside the margins. The i-doc, in this collection, offers scaffolding that may queer the narrative, accord intersectionality a platform, and question privilege.

Foremost, this volume's 18 chapters pose a reconsideration of this relatively young approach to nonfiction storytelling. Like the founders of the i-docs biennial symposium "our definition . . . is deliberately open ended. We embrace any project that starts with the intention to engage with the real, and that uses digital interactive technology to realize this intention."[4] While this of course includes immersive technologies such as web-based documentaries, virtual reality, and augmented reality, it also allows space for things that may not be considered "traditional" documentaries, such as social media, video gaming, or arts projects.

At the same time, we take seriously the charge to not just simply assert an effort toward "decolonizing" the field but to encourage work "that challenges colonial structures underpinning academia."[5] In so doing, we want to be cautious not to add to the "long and bumbled history of non-Indigenous peoples making moves to alleviate the impacts of colonization."[6] Decolonizing, in our understanding, does not, and should not, merely provide lip service for those from traditional positions of power (cisgendered, White, male, traditionally abled) to somehow get a "pass" for past marginalizing behavioral practices. Rather, it should seek ways to provide space for difficult discussions and exhibit a willingness to cede privilege to and share authority with those often marginalized.

The book thus is organized into five broad sections or key concepts. Each section includes research interrogating the theory and practice of the i-doc form as well as interviews with practitioners using immersive and interactive technologies as a part of their creative process. As Janet Murray has suggested, the two are reinforcing constructs; interactivity is more about agency and immersion is more about presence, a suspension of disbelief.[7] As editors, what we find especially encouraging is how the expansiveness of the i-doc definition seems to *demand* geographic and cultural diversity. While some contributors are drawn from what has been defined as the "Global North" (Australia, Canada, Europe, United States), others are drawn from regions or countries newly industrialized or those with a history of colonialism, such as Brazil, Chile, India, Jamaica, Nigeria, and Taiwan. Contributors are also members of diasporas or identify as queer, neurodivergent, and other "othered" identities.

In the first section, Potentials, the authors consider how applying collaborative processes to i-docs provides a powerful site for deconstructing the authority of the director and providing agency to those who are traditionally considered a documentary's "subjects." In Chapter 1, we discuss the implications of a creative practice that engages in production approaches grounded in shared authority and co-creation. Judith Aston and Stefano Odorico look back in order to look forward in Chapter 2, considering the promise polyphony holds for i-doc as collaboration. In Chapter 3, filmmaker and scholar Aashish Kumar in conversation with Tammy Rae Matthews talks about his work with often-invisible diasporas – specifically LGBTQ+[8] individuals from Southeast Asia and how the i-doc format offers insights not found in more traditional narrative forms. Finally, Carles Sora-Domenjó and Anandana Kapur (Chapter 4) propose a potential approach to assess engagement with audiences, community-based collaborators, and the larger community itself through emerging immersive formats.

Collaborations, the second section, puts theory into action, with strategies for successful transformations using interactive technologies to expand some of the best practices of traditional documentaries and academic disciplines such as oral history or ethnography in decentering the filmmaker and embracing shared authority within production and storytelling. Specifically, the authors and interviewees discuss how "outsiders" can employ specific strategies to both recognize and then decenter their own positions of privilege in order to provide spaces for voices often not provided access, from Gino Canella's (Chapter 5) work using Facebook as a type of collaborative filmmaking platform with a Sufi theater group in Senegal to Leonie Jones' (Chapter 7) use of what she dubs "oral history interactive documentary" as a tool to help Australian veterans negotiate memories of war and trauma. The two chapters bookend an interview (Chapter 6) with filmmakers Malek Rasamny and Matt Peterson on their multi-platform project *The Native and the Refugee*, which attempts to tie together the experiences of Ogala Lakota living on a reservation in the United States and Palestinians living in a refugee camp in Bethlehem.

Poetics uses specific case studies to understand how the i-doc explodes traditional narrative boundaries and even the video documentary form itself. Isabelle Carbonell (Chapter 8) describes her evocative i-doc *The River Runs Red*, as challenging who should be privileged as narrators within the storytelling process, seeking ways where non-human subjects can have an equal voice in understanding the aftermath of disaster. Similarly, Alexandria Handal (Chapter 9) uses imagined narratives to reclaim the history of Palestinians in the occupied West Bank in *Dream Home Property Consultants*, which she discusses with Rania Al Namara. Explorations in sound in the i-doc *Tongues of Heaven* – with the guiding concept of how to collaborate with communities that frequently don't have a voice within the process – is the focus of Chapter 10 by Anita Wen-Shin Chang.

In Technologies, the authors consider the i-doc form, arguing how emerging – or even long-established – technologies and platforms can be understood as a part of the genre. Paolo Silvio Harald Favero and Eva Theunissen (Chapter 11) explore their own embodied experiences in two virtual reality projects. Their discussion is followed by an interview (Chapter 12) with award-winning Nigerian 360-pioneer Joel Kachi Benson, who views the technology as a way to allow Africans to tell their own stories. André Paz and Felipe Carrelli (Chapter 13) are similarly working in Africa, documenting their own experiences working in partnership with GalileoMobile and the Saharawi people in Western Sahara in the creation of a transmedia project that challenges both political and scientific boundaries.

Finally, in Expanding Boundaries, the authors ask the question: what exactly is a "decolonized" digital documentary? As they demonstrate, when the real is engaged in digital spaces, the boundaries of documentary – and co-creation – become increasingly (and provocatively) fuzzy. In Chapter 14, Leighton C. Peterson and Jeb J. Card explore the ramifications of documentary becoming unhinged from traditional historical, academic, or media gatekeepers via YouTube channels. The result is not only participatory and interactive but also, they argue, potentially damaging. The section's interview with Tessa Ratuszynska (Chapter 15) explores how the i-doc can be used as a way to bridge the gap between mainstream and "othered" communities and asks if the format can be a way to help build understanding. Next, Diego Cerna Aragon (Chapter 16) explores digitally based temporary street projection in Peru to challenge the conceptions and definition of the form and function of the medium. The projections, the subsequent social media photographs archiving them, and the participation of the audience all are embedded with interactivity and serve to deconstruct traditional linear documentary formats, becoming what he posits could be a "nontraditional" form of i-doc. The section ends with a challenge to the very notion of decolonization from Debbie Ebanks Schlums, Adrian Kahgee, and Rebeka Tabobondung (Chapter 17). They use their own positionality as members of an Indigenous/Caribbean collective to reject the term in favor of a-coloniality, where the i-doc becomes a space to explore and imagine collaboration disassociated from the settler mentality.

In moving away from dominant power structures and dominant voices, this collection calls for a redistribution of (potential) power toward a more egalitarian expanse as found within the i-doc. This territory, then, is gently contoured as a site for ongoing discussion and debate. It is the exclusive province of no one and is an ideal in progress. The authors of this volume add their voices to these already existing conversations and extend these frameworks to complicate economic, financial, geographical, and sociocultural underpinnings, as well as the outcomes, of practice-based research.

David Staton and Kathleen M. Ryan

## Notes

1. "Snow Fall; The Avalanche at Tunnel Creek" (*New York Times*, 2012) was a Pulitzer Prize- and Peabody Award-winning multimedia presentation. It popularized the use of the parallax scroll, which added a faux 3-D effect that colloquially became known as the Snow Fall Effect. See: www.nytimes.com/projects/2012/snow-fall/index.html#/?part=tunnel-creek.
2. Henry Jenkins, *Convergence Culture: Where Old and New Media Collide* (New York: New York University Press, 2006), 2.
3. Linda Candy and Ernest Edmunds, "Practice-Based Research in the Creative Arts: Foundations and Futures from the Front Line," *Leonardo* 51, no. 1 (2018): 63.
4. Judith Aston, Sandra Gaudenzi, and Mandy Rose, "Introduction," in *i-docs: The Evolving Practices of Interactive Documentary* (London: Willdflower Press, 2017), 1.
5. Nayantara Sheoran Appleton, "Do Not 'Decolonize' . . . If You Are Not Decolonizing: Progressive Language and Planning Beyond a Hollow Academic Rebranding," *Critical Ethnic Studies Journal Blog* (February 4, 2019), http://www.criticalethnicstudiesjournal.org/blog/2019/1/21/do-not-decolonize-if-you-are-not-decolonizing-alternate-language-to-navigate-desires-for-progressive-academia-6y5sg.

6. Eve Tuck and K. Wayne Yang, "Decolonization is Not a Metaphor," *Decolonization: Indigeneity, Education & Society* 1, no. 1 (2012): 3.
7. See: Janet Murray, *Inventing the Medium: Principles of Interaction Design as a Cultural Practice* (Cambridge: MIT Press, 2011).
8. LGBTQ+ stands for lesbian, gay, bisexual, transgender, queer and/or questioning, intersex, and asexual and/or ally. Seek https://outrightinternational.org/content/acronyms-explained.

# PART ONE
# Potentials

# 1

# AGENCY THROUGH CO-CREATION

## Interactive Documentary as Decolonizing Practice

*Kathleen M. Ryan and David Staton*

A few years ago on a trip to Paris, we made a point of heading to la Cinémathèque Française in the city's 12th arrondissement. The film museum is housed in a Frank Gehry-designed building in the Parc de Bercy, and the permanent collection includes sets from films by Georges Méliès and cinematic innovations by the Lumière brothers and Thomas Edison. While the collections intrigued us, a large reason for our visit was the gift shop. Inspired in part by the writings of Johnathan Crary,[1] we were hunting for proto-cinematic toys to use as tools in visual communication and media history classes: modern recreations of things like zoetropes or praxinoscopes that were small, inexpensive, and portable.

We didn't find the modern zoetropes or praxinoscopes we were looking for in the museum's gift shop. But inside the museum's exhibit spaces, we watched short "films" on a device far too heavy and burdensome to bring home in our carry-on luggage: the mutoscope. The crank-driven machine flipped through illuminated cards – the subject less important to us than the experience of our physical engagement with the technology and by extension the story. The mutoscope demands interactivity: our physical actions were required to advance the narrative.

The mutoscope is a concrete, physical example of how interactivity is embedded in filmic (and by extension documentary) history. But equally embedded are practices of colonization by documentary filmmakers, of "othering" or silencing groups who do not wield political or social power.[2] In this chapter, we argue that the i-doc, as a type of practice-based research (PBR), provides an opportune sphere for decolonization. It offers what can be described as a "shared authority" with narrators, audiences, and filmmakers. Due to the i-doc's flexible and fungible form, it proves to be an ideal host to increase agency for traditional documentary "subjects" as well as audiences.

DOI: 10.4324/9781003174509-2

## The I-doc: A Brief History

While André Almeida and Heitor Alvelos trace the concept of interactive documentary to the 1967 Montreal World Expo[3] and the MIT Docubase cites *Moss Landing* in 1989 as one of the first digital projects to be called an interactive documentary,[4] the history of the term in academic scholarship is a bit more recent.[5] Carolyn Handler Miller describes – but does not specifically define – interactive documentary projects in her 2004 book on digital storytelling.[6] Three years later, Dayna Galloway, Kenneth B. McAlpine, and Paul Harris attempted to define the interactive documentary via four broad categories of interaction:

- *Passive Adaptive*, where the computer interface makes on-screen changes based upon the viewer's unconscious responses;
- *Active Adaptive*, where the user consciously makes choices to story direction via direct input;
- *Immersive*, or fully participatory formats; and
- *Expansive*, or community-based documentary experience.[7]

Similarly, Kate Nash proposed four "dimensions of interactivity": technology, relationships, audience experience, and, importantly, discourse. She argues, "The discursive dimension asks us to consider the relationship between user actions and the voice of the documentary, exploring user agency and the rhetorical potential of interaction,"[8] crucial "to capture the significance of interactivity."[9]

At roughly the same time, the Digital Cultures Research Centre at the University of West of England (Bristol) began a series of symposia considering the emerging practices of i-docs. The symposia brought together international scholars in this emerging practice,[10] and developed into a website,[11] social media presence,[12] and, eventually, a book. The open-ended definition the Bristol team uses, requiring merely a grounding in the real and a use of interactivity in digital technologies, is "as much about process as about product."[13] But then Judith Aston, Sandra Gaudenzi, and Mandy Rose, add a crucial caveat: "it is first and foremost about people as opposed to machines."[14]

The term, i-doc, is an intentional one, different from "webdoc" which implies a specific platform and audience. Pat Aufderheide notes that while some see the i-doc's taxonomy as being rooted in user experience, others differentiate between the i-doc, web documentary, and transmedia. In the former, "user participation [is] built into their action and typically features databases as integral to their actions."[15] By contrast, web documentary features "traditionally static material" available online, and transmedia projects use a variety of analog and digital platforms, usually featuring "only a selection of material rather than contributions" and limited interactivity.[16] But she also notes that often these boundaries blur, "complicated not only by the level of interactivity but also by the fact that the interactivity takes place, potentially, across so many spaces and platforms in a user's life."[17] In other words, not all transmedia projects or webdocs may be i-docs, but i-docs may employ transmedia and webdoc strategies. As Siobhan O'Flynn observes, "no single critical," or disciplinary/theoretical, "practice can adequately address the diverse and idiosyncratic components that each new project may present."[18]

Thus, hybridity and interdisciplinarity are at the heart of the practice. It is grounded in co-creation, a collaboration between documentarians, audiences, and subjects. The i-doc is "an open space of thinking," as Hanna Brasier observes, "a space where maker and user select individual elements, thereby changing and producing multiple relations between these elements."[19] Its form is only limited by the imagination of its co-creators.

## Mapping the Interactive Documentary

So, if an i-doc can be anything, what exactly is an i-doc? Aufderheide, citing personal communication with former head of the National Film Board of Canada, Tom Perlmutter, posits the i-doc may be a "new art form."[20] It is tangentially related to Cheryl E. Ball's model for "new media scholarship," or a form of interconnected web-based images, video, and hyperlinks that work with the website's text to create meaning in different ways than the traditional academic journal or book.[21] But at the time of our writing, the i-doc remains "a form that still has yet to attain its distinctive shape and attendant expectations" a form that "is a stimulating and creative arena for producers and is equally rich for scholars."[22]

Baker Alkarimeh and Eric Boutin propose a model where "interactive technology is employed . . . to potentially convey an interactive communication with the user."[23] While there is room for *user* agency in their model, no mention is given to collaboration with narrators. Insook Choi argues that the i-doc is composed of author, user, and contributor, with the assumption that the user will be modifying established paths (in other words, changing the *meaning* of the content but not necessarily contributing new content or collaborating with the author in content creation).[24] These are models of a documentary storytelling form that are mobile, flexible, and public, "characterized by interdeterminacy, community, and risk"[25] engaging producers and the public in ways that are fluid and experimental, united only in the digital aspects of the chosen platform.

The i-doc can be a web-based platform, virtual reality, augmented reality, dome-based screenings, or 360° video – or in some cases a transmedia combination of all of the above. In Aston, Gaudenzi, and Rose's edited collection, live performances, hackathons, and social media stalking on Facebook are also explored as part of the i-doc's oeuvre.[26] In some cases, the interactivity can be tied to traditional media. The Catalan production *Guernika, Pintura de Guerra* used Windows Media Center technology to embed bonus content within the televised broadcast of the documentary, accessed through the remote control. Other television viewers who had an interactive digital terrestrial television decoder and multimedia home platform could similarly access interactive content.[27]

The i-doc can also be made up of amateur content, such as the vernacular videos found in places like YouTube, either through curated channels or webcam responses to post provocations.[28] YouTube pieces such as *The Message* (2006) or *Life in a Day* (2010) as examples of work that is "shaped by the affordances of digital video and participation" where the line between "director" and "audience" is intentionally blurred.[29] In *Guernika*, users were invited to incorporate their own digital artistic additions to the famous Pablo Picasso painting and share it in an online repository.[30]

For many scholars and practitioners, social media offer a natural sphere for the i-doc. Patrick Kelly says that on Instagram, in particular, "curated moments . . . are carefully selected by the filmmaker, reimagined as a new creative project, and presented in a way that demonstrates that a critical distance has been observed by the filmmaker."[31] The resulting content is public, demands reactions by the audiences, can be searched via hashtags, and can provide a story or narrative. In one of our projects, *Pin Up! The Movie: An Interactive Documentary*, we've taken this curation one step further, turning the project's Instagram page over to members of the subculture for collaboration. We place few limits on these guest curators and encourage them to tag themselves in the posts.

During the recent COVID-19 global pandemic, Gaudenzi and Sandra Tabares-Duque created a collaborative Facebook space called "Corona Haikus." The haikus, three photos and a short piece of text, were initially designed as a way to document time during lockdown. Participants were encouraged to use the photos and text from the site to create their own remixes, shared with the community or posted as pop-up exhibits.[32] An open-source collaborative audio project, *Corona Diaries*, was similarly inspired by the pandemic. It offers occasional content prompts, asking people globally to share their experiences during the pandemic. The testimonies would be then used under a Creative Commons license by journalists, artists, and other creators.[33]

These examples and others, such as interactive docugames[34] or journalistic applications of 360, VR, AR, and interactivity in short-form storytelling,[35] point to what we would argue are the exciting potential of the i-doc: its flexibility. John Pavlik, citing what he calls the "Snow Fall" revolution (referring to the *New York Times* Pulitzer Prize-winning 2012 story), says "i-docs represent a compelling story form that can blend excellence in reporting – based on quality audio, video, and data – with user experiences designed to highlight the complexity of many of the world's most vital issues."[36] The fact that the i-doc isn't any *single* thing offers room for experimentation, innovation, and, potentially, erosion of colonial practices.

## Practice Makes Research

Like the traditional analog documentary film, the i-doc is a form of creative practice, albeit one with slightly more permeable boundaries. Kim Munro argues, unlike textual analysis, "making documentary as a way of testing out a methodology is a way to apply the filmmaking as research in an iterative dialogue between the theory and the practice."[37] PBR is "a process of constant navigation, experimentation and error . . . within a scholarly paradigm, it is this process which is constantly spotlit rather than the artefact itself." In other words, PBR is not simply the creative act but instead research which uses the creative act as its method or point of study.

PBR can be defined as "an original investigation undertaken in order to gain new knowledge, partly by means of practice and the outcomes of that practice."[38] It's often used in the medical field,[39] but creative examples include creating comic book illustrations to discuss "identity, representation and power,"[40] using narrative and interactivity to contextualize the murder of a Black British teenager,[41] re-appropriating orphan films (films abandoned by the copyright holder),[42] and a video mapping of Los Angeles' film noir history with the viewer/user as a mobile *flâneur*.[43] Michael A.R. Biggs and Daniela Büchler argue for "rigor" in PBR, while acknowledging that the exact definition of "rigor" is discipline-dependent.[44] As Sophie Hope argues, "It is not enough to practice; it requires justifying in order for it needs to be considered rigorous."[45]

Documentary filmmakers frequently engage PBR as part of their creative research practice. For instance, the documentary *600 Mills* becomes a springboard to understand how documentary film can help audiences become involved not merely in "the acquisition of knowledge in the rational/cognitive sense but involved a broader concept of sensory and embodied knowledge."[46] Nicola Black's work with Roma in Scotland combines reflexivity with communication collaboration. It offers insights not only into the tensions between power and agency but also when "combined with sustained critical thinking, greater nuance is given to an understanding of Roma self-inscription."[47] Key here is the notion of praxis, or experiential learning. When the community is considered as intrinsic to knowledge as traditional "experts" (i.e., medical doctors and researchers), the resultant networks formed and knowledge gained, "is significantly more broad and inclusive."[48]

Roshinin Kempadoo makes a similar argument. Her digital art project, *Future Belonging*, attempts to query the relationship between culture gatekeepers (museum curators, historians), marginalized or misrepresented groups, and the way data are gathered and validated. As such, it "consciously posits the user into a relational space with digital technology and a networked process of 'data' circulation and information flow and within a networked process . . . by positioning and implicating the user through active engagement."[49] This points to us the strengths of PBR as a "cyclical and iterative process"[50] demanding both reflexivity into and attempts to erode traditional power structures. This becomes possible through a ceding of power to – and co-creation with – both community "subjects" and audiences.

## Doing Decolonizing

"Decolonizing" itself is a loaded term, especially so when used by non-minority scholars working in a university setting in traditional places of privilege such as North America, Western Europe, or Oceania. The dictionary definition, "to free from colonial status,"[51] does not begin to tease out the political and cultural complications that are inherent in the process; epistemic and literal violence ravaged by the colonizers against the colonized is similarly ignored in this definition's clinical language nor does it hint at the diversity of marginalized communities and the need for intersectionality in any decolonial moves. Or, as Linda Tuhiwai Smith notes in her call to decolonize research, "deconstruction is part of a much larger intent."[52] For our purposes, it includes undermining two related types of othering. First is *settler colonialism* against Indigenous populations, where "settlers come with the intention of making a new home on the land, a homemaking that insists on settler sovereignty over all things in their new domain."[53] Second is the recognition that other groups can also experience marginalization from those in positions of privilege due to race, gender orientation, different physical abilities, and other forms of "othering."

Eve Tuck and K. Wane Yang say the act of decolonization must focus on "how the invisibilized dynamics of settler colonialism mark the organization, governance, curricula, and assessment of compulsory learning" and "how settler perspectives and worldviews get to count as knowledge and research and how these perspectives – repackaged as data and findings – are activated in order to rationalize and maintain unfair social structures."[54] These two positions are interrelated and thus require equal attention. Smith elegantly demonstrates this in her call to decolonize methodologies. She speaks about the move by outsiders (often, but not limited to, anthropologists) to "research" and "interpret" Indigenous communities, often with little input from the people being studied. Rather than the outside "expert" translating what a culture means, she sets a goal of self-determination within research: "Self-determination in a research agenda becomes something more than a political goal. It becomes a goal of social justice, which is expressed through a wide range of psychological, social, cultural and economic terrains."[55] By nature, this is a process of decolonization, of recognizing that research becomes richer when it is "dynamic and open to different influences and possibilities."[56]

At this point, it is useful to consider *Nanook of the North* (Flaherty, 1922). The groundbreaking film laid the template for "what would be documentary film . . . present[ing] real people and their everyday lives on screen."[57] The film not only served as a foundation for the traditional documentary but was also very influential in the history and development of ethnographic filmmaking.[58] However, the film is also embedded with what Faye D. Ginsburg calls "the history of colonial looking relations"[59]: the Inuit "family" was actually cast by Robert and Frances

Flaherty,[60] and at times did things on screen that they actually didn't do in real life. Instead, it was a construction:

> Nanook and his fellow actors knowingly craft themselves into the kind of stock characters characteristic of turn of the 20th century popular culture. In so doing, they can barely contain their hilarity as they perform the "happy-go-lucky Eskimo," a satire on the Western fantasy of Arctic peoples.[61]

The work was done with the complicity of the Flaherty's Inuit subjects. He screened daily rushes of the film for them and collaborated with them on the recreations and other daily-life sequences seen in the film. Nonetheless, it was created by a white filmmaker and can be seen to have supported the audience's colonial ideology (i.e., the Arctic North is "desolate" and its people "primitive" and, thus, is ripe for "settlement and exploitation").[62]

This is not an attempt to diminish the value of *Nanook* within documentary history. But the narrative it follows (intentionally or not) can be seen as conforming to a type of settler colonialism. In *Nanook*, the North is nearly uninhabited (ignoring Inuit communities, which existed), which Olivia Michiko Gagnon argues is a deployment of the concept of *terra nullius*, or empty land, "displacing both Inuit voices and more complex renderings of Northern-ness" and perpetuating stereotypes about both the people and the land itself as " 'empty' landscapes have been used across the Americas in service of devastating colonial land theft."[63] For Gagnon, remediations offer one way to decolonize *Nanook*, such as the performance of Inuk throat-singer Tanya Tanuk as a live soundtrack for a screening of the silent film.[64] The performance becomes "its own kind of historiographic practice with the ability to reorient the present's relationship to the past in order to open up other kinds of futures."[65]

The remediation – as well as its subsequent analysis in an academic journal – is part of what Smith calls "a long-term process involving the bureaucratic, cultural, linguistic, and psychological divesting of colonial power"[66] – including a revision of what is "scholarship" itself. The addition of new voices to an archival text points out not only what is missing from the film itself (Indigenous voices unfiltered by the settler's gaze) but also our understanding of the text itself. It can therefore be seen as an act of decolonization.

## A Shared Authority

So how can the i-doc actively avoid the more colonial practices of documentary's past and avoid simply being video evidence of an artistic form of tourist drive-by decolonization with little actual and sustained collaboration? Oral history introduces the term "shared authority," or the idea that the person telling the oral history (the narrator) holds equal footing to and understands the meaning of the individual's life experiences as the oral historian.[67] Similarly, Rose uses the term "shared authority" to explain how PBR in general, and i-doc in specific, uses participatory design processes where the producer is a facilitator in the creation of "a media system that works on behalf of the subjects rather than representing them."[68] She is advocating co-creation as an alternative to the "dominant extractive ethos of the knowledge generation" power dynamic found in the traditional documentary,[69] such as the colonial paradigm seen in *Nanook*.

This co-creation ethos extends to "people formerly known as audiences."[70] In their touchstone work for the MIT Media Lab, Cizek, William Uricchio, and Sara Rafsky attempt to operationalize the shift that happens when the user is considered an active participant in the creation of meaning in the i-doc. This is a careful ontological move: filmic "audiences," which implies a passive viewing experience, are transformed into an engaged and active "user" and "participant." As they warn, "nothing is cut and dry," but the shift points out that "community-based values and practices live at the core of co-creation."[71] Nash suggests answers or possibilities that fundamentally indict "users." This term has specificity: "The user performs the database, engaging in a relationship with the database and the subject of the documentary. She engages not just with the specific content chosen, but equally with the paths not chosen which nevertheless constitute the discursive field."[72] This is the move from viewer to user that creates the possibility space Hayles defines as an "emergent adaptive system."[73] Filmmakers ignore those values at their own peril.

Paola Bilbrough observes that the self-reflexivity demanded by PBR allows her to consciously interrogate "the continuum of give and take and shifting power dynamics between participants and myself" in her documentary filmmaking process.[74] Thus, PBR via film can create scholarship "in ways that are visible and that matter."[75] For Jorge Vasquéz-Herrero and Gisela Moreno, this is part of the DNA of i-docs, specifically in Ibero-America, where projects such as *Calles Perdidas* (2015),[76] *Pregoneros de Medellín* (2016),[77] or *Proyecto Quipu* (2011)[78] provide potential for social change and transformation within communities.[79] Liz Miller and Martin Allor take this one step further. Citing practices by i-doc producer Cizek in her multiyear project *Highrise*, "as a cultural animator, she is orchestrating and articulating collaboration and connections at every stage of production. The individuals and communities that form around each initiative often instigate a series of ripple effects or unforeseen engagements."[80] This demonstrates the potential of engaging local partners at every stage of development and sharing co-creation and co-ownership of a project.

This may be a somewhat idealistic goal. Cizek's work, for example, has been underwritten by major media organizations, including the National Film Board of Canada and *The New York Times*. But by "activating the media complex," Miller and Allor argue "a strategy of engagement is in essence a strategy of configuration within the media complex between users, the media, partners and players which gives rise to online and on-ground connections, initiatives and actions."[81] There is both a phenomenological *and* ontological shift being made here: not only is the traditional viewer now a "user" (with its attendant associations to gaming) but also the subject has now become a "partner" (assuming co-ownership in the project).

We argue that the i-doc's privileged position as a sphere for decolonization plays out in three ways; access, authority, and audience.

- *Access.* A traditional filmic documentary demands professional videography equipment for shooting and editing, and showings may be limited if a director is not connected to film festival programmers, theatrical distributors, or home media content providers. Other voices can become silenced, or forced to tell their stories only through the voice of a person who is often an outsider: the director. The expansive definition of the i-doc upends these notions. While there are barriers to some technologies, social media platforms such as Instagram, Facebook, TikTok, and SnapChat can serve as i-doc storytelling using nonprofessional smartphone-based cameras and simplistic editing.
- *Authority.* Even experimental nonlinear documentaries bear the imprint of their director, the person who determines the story structure and content. When authority is shared with documentary subjects, the director – or in many cases the distributor or funder – determines the content and tone of the final cut. I-docs have the potential to upend this paradigm, through collaborative storytelling, and production practices. This includes things like crowdsourcing or privileging user-created content. Borrowing from oral history, the i-doc can be an exercise in shared authority, where community narrators and the project director have an equal say in the form and content of the story being told.
- *Audience.* Just as the i-doc eases access, transforming "subjects" to "narrators," so too can the format allow for audiences to be more directly engaged in the form and shape of the story being told. Unlike the feature film where audiences watch in the order intended by the filmmaker, the nature of the i-doc disrupts content linearity. There is no guarantee that the audience member will watch the story in the order intended by the director(s). Ceding story control is an epistemological transformation of documentary and provides a way to decenter the notions of auteurs and authorship.

The i-doc can thus provide a shift in what Gaudenzi calls "the power balance in meaning construction"[82]: the creator knows the user's end experience is unpredictable and adjusts accordingly. This envisions the i-doc as a form that has the potential to "rework . . . documentary's historic role in the public sphere" and "engage counter publics – groups contesting hegemonic discourse or power structures – as co-creators."[83]

We say this not to uncritically or blindly laud *technology* as transformative – as Nash warns there is "no necessary connection between interactivity and . . .

empowerment."[84] However, specific practices can be enhanced by interactivity. Consider the *Los Sures* project, grounded in a 1984 documentary about a Brooklyn immigrant neighborhood, that was later updated by Collaborative Studios into short i-docs by twelve different emerging artists. Its success lies less in the animated oral history or the gamification approach that reveals content based on user choices; rather, the project works because of "the relationship that the [original] filmmakers established with the longstanding community-based organization, El Puente,"[85] which opened doors to other community members, who then collaborated with the new version of the project.

At the same time, audiences may be ambivalent to interactive participation. Nonetheless, Nash observes they "may attach meaning to *the ability to participate*" (emphasis added),[86] even if the individual declines to personally add to the story via discussion posts or contribution of content. This in itself can be transformative. The rhetorical shift due to the technological advances that led to the emergence of the i-doc upends the traditional relationships and roles of audience, producer, and subject. We argue here that this in turn creates an ontology and phenomenology, which are baked into the DNA of interactive documentary.

## Interactive Decolonization

The ontology of the i-doc thus offers the potential to "break the relentless structuring"[87] of colonial and marginalization practices through projects that "facilitate multi-faceted processes of dialogue through a combination of digital and material platforms and methods,"[88] and which insist that audiences, narrators, and producers are on equal footing with each other. In the academic sphere, decolonization can come through the people who are invited to the proverbial table. Consider how Will Straw and Janine Marchessault navigate their roles as gatekeepers of a sort, editors of an academic handbook on Canadian film. They recognize that the community is shaped by both collaboration and individual "community-based cultures,"[89] and insist that this community must take a central role in "the effort to decolonize all aspects of Canadian life."[90] For their part, this means highlighting Indigenous, feminist, POC, and LGBTQ filmic practices – and the work of scholars from those intersections – not as an add onto "traditional" or "mainstream" work but instead as *an intrinsic part of the Canadian film community*. They use their position to insist upon cultural change.

The creative space similarly offers ways to cement a shared authority as an essential part of the filmic process. Documentarians, of course, have attempted to do this in the past. The Navajo Film Project is a case in point. White visual ethnographers provided Diné would-be filmmakers with 16 mm cameras as well as film, editing equipment, and, most importantly, technical instruction. The original research project (and subsequent book, *Through Navajo Eyes*) has been critiqued for its colonial perspective, including referring to the seven filmmakers as "the sheep" and framing the Navajo people in general as living apart from modernities such as film cameras.[91] Nonetheless, the subsequent films (seven in total), over which the filmmakers had complete editorial and creative control, demonstrate what Leighton C. Peterson calls "a uniquely Navajo filmic grammar."[92] Peterson says that while non-Indigenous audiences "are always looking for the 'Indigenous' in these films,"[93] subsequent community screenings and reappropriations demonstrate how the films can allow the Diné to reassert their visual sovereignty:

> The films – the underpinnings of sustained community benefit that had been products of the project – had been there all along. With the return of the films, resignification, and renewed community involvement, what was once thought of as simultaneously a groundbreaking and patronizing experiment finds new articulations and new uses.[94]

Ignoring this reaction of "the sheep" to their self-produced narratives is part of the practice of colonialism.

A similar example can be found in the *Los Sures* project. One community member described the original 1984 documentary as "that film we hate."[95] But the same community member, after rewatching the film, agreed to help the community production company Union Docs in creating an updated project. Christopher Cekay Allen, co-founder of Union Docs, describes the intricacy of the collaborations

> I knew we couldn't count on people to take the time and effort required to contributed details that would actually be worthy of sharing. We would have to do the groundwork ourselves to provide early exciting examples of the kind of content we were seeking, and we would have to add significant incentives.[96]

At the same time, he says, "As our investment in the interview process grew, and as we started to get better and better stories"[97] the project itself improved. Part of the investment included inviting local politicians and other community members, such as the "film we hate" community member, to critique and enrich the project, including fixing issues from the original documentary.[98]

It can be profoundly disconcerting – and difficult – to do work that decenters the creator or author. The singular authority is ceded in favor of a shared voice. But it's also profoundly important. Eesaha Pandit calls this type of work "the only way," adding that any inevitable mistakes made provide opportunities for learning.[99] In our Instagram collaborations,[100] where we allowed members of the pin up/vintage subculture to take over our feed for a month at a time, we hoped that the guest curators would bring their own perspectives to the forefront. Yet many of the guest curators, even those who are people of color, replicated the patterns of our feed from the past, such as a Taiwanese pin up whose curation didn't include pin ups from Asia but rather those who were mostly white and from the United States.

A more productive example comes from Miss Sweet Black, a Black Parisian pin up, living at the time in French Guiana. She focused her efforts on showcasing only women of color, without any direction from us. In one, she wrote about the "forgotten women of vintage retro culture," Muslim women, praising their merger of pin up style with traditional religious values, and pointing out the fashion history of Islamic countries. The pin up she featured, The Veiled Vintage, responded, in a heart emoji-laden comment: "What a beautiful post. Thank you for your support. We Muslim women are really forgotten in the vintage community, but I'm working hard to change that."[101] The post promoted several responses discussing the importance of visibility in the community with other subcultural members.

Sweet Black described her guest curation (during July 2020, as anti-racism protests spread internationally) as a way to "fight against racism in our community."[102] The pin up subculture supports feminist ideals and gives lip service to intersectionality, but thin, White women are often considered the "norm" and racist ideology is present in parts of the scene.[103] To push against this, she posted sharp critiques and commentary, including some directed at the page itself. In one, she promoted the owner of another Instagram page that is dedicated to pin ups of color (POC) saying, "As you know I'll not stay here forever so if you want to continue to see, support and follow poc into the pin up community, you must follow her page ASAP."[104] She did something similar when posting about another page that focuses only on Asian pin ups.

This is a discomforting critique. As producers, we like to *think* we're doing the right thing. We've dedicated previous months or weeks to POC or other marginalized groups (including Black, LGBTQ+, and Asian pin ups). Other months feature a mix of pin ups of different body types, races, ethnicities, genders, and sexual orientations. But it's obvious that even with these efforts, for pin ups from marginalized groups, it may not be enough. Our lived experiences are different from theirs, and our attempts to "do the right thing" still seem as lesser-than, especially when compared to an all-Black or all-Asian space.

We often tell our narrators that our job is to be a curator of sorts. That's not to imply the cultural gatekeeping associated with the archive. Rather, we see our roles as taking the 30,000-foot view, identifying patterns, themes, and trends that our subcultural collaborators may not recognize themselves. We need to be open to both seeing these patterns and realizing there may be unintended ways we still, even with best intentions, support hegemonic norms. It's the only way we can use our creative practice "as an enquiry that is validated, trustworthy and 'useful' beyond the benefits of the practice/practitioner themselves."[105]

As i-doc producers, it's important that we recognize that the story isn't about us. Rose notes, "within a context of interactive documentary, co-creation can be a route to convening dialogues that can provide significant resources in those ongoing processes of change."[106] I-docs are characterized by what Patricia Zimmermann and Helen De Michiel characterize as "movement," or "open-source" transformations as i-docs "adapt to the ebb and flow of participatory modalities located in changing geographic specificities."[107] Co-creation demands flexibility. It is through collaboration that we discover revelations which assist in these ongoing processes of change and that reinforce the importance of our commitment to a shared authority: openness, flexibility, and shared authority. It is only through embracing and enhancing these principles can i-docs fully live us to the possibilities inherent in decolonization.

## Notes

1. See: Jonathan Crary, *Techniques of the Observer: On Vision and Modernity in the Nineteenth Century* (Cambridge, MA: MIT Press, 1992).
2. See: Peter G. Bloom, *French Colonial Documentary: Mythologies of Humanitarianism* (Minneapolis: University of Minnesota Press, 2008); Lee Grieveson and Colin MacCabe, eds., *Film and the End of Empire* (New York: Palgrave Macmillan, 2011); Ella Shohat, *Unthinking Eurocentrism: Multiculturalism and the Media* (New York: Routledge, 2014).
3. André Almeida and Heitor Alvelos, "An Interactive Documentary Manifesto," in *Interactive Storytelling: Third Joint Conference on Interactive Digital Storytelling Proceedings*, eds. Ruth Aylett et al. (Berlin: Springer, 2010), 123.
4. Docubase, "Moss Landing," MIT Open Documentary Lab, accessed August 11, 2020, https://docubase.mit.edu/project/moss-landing/.
5. This scholarship coincides with an increase in i-docs being produced. Docubase includes 388 projects in the database, sortable by year. Four of the listed projects were created in 1995 or earlier, none from 1996 to 2000, and nine from 2001 to 2006. See: https://docubase.mit.edu/project/.
6. See: Carolyn Handler Miller, *Digital Storytelling: A Creator's Guide to Interactive Entertainment* (Amsterdam: Taylor and Francis, 2004), 349–74.
7. See: Dayna Galloway, Kenneth B. McAlpine and Paul Harris, "From Michael Moore to JFK Reloaded: Towards a Working Model of Interactive Documentary," *Journal of Media Practice* 8, no. 3 (2007): 325–39.
8. Kate Nash, ' "Clicking on the World: Documentary Representation and Interactivity," in *New Documentary Ecologies: Emerging Platforms, Practices and Discourses*, eds. Kate Nash, Craig Hight, and Catherine Summerhayes (New York: Palgrave Macmillan, 2004), 51.
9. Nash, 58.
10. i-Docs is the only academic gathering to focus specifically on interactive documentary, broadly defined. Other organizations, such as the academic group Visible Evidence, feature both traditional and emerging (including interactive) documentary practices.
11. See: http://i-docs.org/.
12. Including Facebook (www.facebook.com/groups/153942381346236/), Twitter (https://twitter.com/i_docs), and Vimeo (https://vimeo.com/dcrc).
13. Judith Aston, Sandra Gaudenzi, and Mandy Rose, "Introduction," in *i-docs: The Evolving Practices of Interactive Documentary*, eds. Judith Aston, Sandra Gaudenzi, and Mady Rose (London; Willdflower Press, 2017), 2.
14. Aston, Gaudenzi, and Rose, 2.
15. Pat Aufderheide, "Interactive Documentaries: Navigation and Design," *Journal of Film and Video* 67, no. 3–4 (Fall/Winter 2015): 69.
16. Aufderheide, 69.

17. Aufderheide, 70.
18. Siobhan O'Flynn, "Designed Experiences in Interactive Documentaries," in *Contemporary Documentary*, eds. Daniel Marcus and Selmin Kara (New York: Taylor & Francis Group, 2015), 73.
19. Hannah Brasier, "Moments of Noticing: 'I See You' as a Speculative Work Towards an Essayistic List Practice for Interactive Documentary," in *Digital Media and Documentary: Antipodean Approaches*, ed. Adrian Miles (Cham, Switzerland: Palgrave MacMillan, 2018), 21.
20. Aufderheide, "Interactive Documentaries," 71.
21. See: Cheryl E. Ball, "Show, Not Tell: The Value of New Media Scholarship," *Computers and Composition* 21 (2004): 403–25.
22. Aufderheide, "Interactive Documentaries," 78.
23. Baker Alkarimeh and Eric Boutin, "Interactive Documentary: A Proposed Model and Definition," *French Journal for Media Research* 7 (2017): 17.
24. Insook Choi, "From Tradition to Emerging Practice: A Hybrid Computational Production for Interactive Documentary," *Entertainment Computing* 1 (2010): 106.
25. Helen De Michiel and Patricia R. Zimmermann, "Documentary as an Open Space," in *The Documentary Film Book*, ed. Brian Winston (London: British Film Institute, 2020), 356.
26. See: Aston, Gaudenzi, and Rose, *i-docs*.
27. Arnau Gifreu Castells, "The Case of *Guernika, Pintura de Guerra*, the First Catalan Interactive Documentary Project," *Studies in Documentary Film* 6, no. 2 (2012): 231.
28. See: John Dovey and Mandy Rose, "'This Great Mapping of Ourselves': New Documentary Forms Online," in *The Documentary Film Book*, 366–75. See note 25.
29. Dovey and Rose, 371.
30. Castells, "The Case of *Guernika, Pintura de Guerra*," 238–39.
31. Patrick Kelly, "Instagram as Archive: Constructing Experimental Documentary Narratives from Everyday Moments," in *Critical Distance in Documentary Media*, eds. Gerda Cammaer et al. (New York: Palgrave Macmillan, 2018), 216.
32. See: www.facebook.com/groups/226094118756231/.
33. See: https://coronadiaries.io/about.html.
34. See: Galloway, McApine and Harris, "From Michael Moore."
35. See: Francesco Marconi and Taylor Nakagawa. *The Age of Dynamic Storytelling: A Guide for Journalists in ta World of Immersive 3-D Content* (New York: The Associated Press, 2017).
36. John Pavlik, *Journalism in the Age of Virtual Reality: How Experiential Media Are Transforming News* (New York: Columbia University Press, 2019), 130.
37. Kim Munro and Paola Bilbrough, "An Ecology of Relationships: Tensions and Negotiations in Documentary Filmmaking Practice as Research," *Media Practice and Education* 19, no. 3 (2018): 262.
38. Linda Candy and Ernest Edmonds, "Practice-Based Research in the Creative Arts: Foundations and Futures from the Front Line," *Leonardo* 51, no. 1 (2018): 63.
39. See: Ann C. Macaulay and Paul A. Nutting, "Moving the Frontiers Forward: Incorporating Community-Based Participatory Research Into Practice-Based Research Networks," *Annals of Family Medicine* 4, no. 1 (January/February 2006): 4–7; James J. Werner and Kurt C. Stange, "Praxis-Based Research networks: An Emerging Paradigm for Research that is Rigorous, Relevant and Inclusive," *HSS Public Access*, published in final edited form as: *Journal of the American Board of Family Medicine* 27, no. 6 (2014): 730–35, doi:10.3122/jabfm.2014.06.140034.
40. Martha Newbigging, "What do Comics Want? Drawing Lived Experience for Critical Consciousness," *Journal of Illustration* 5, no. 2 (2018): 266.
41. See: Tahera Aziz, "Shifting the Frame: From Critical Reflective Arts Practice to Practice-Based Research," *Journal of Media Practice* 10, no. 1 (2009): 69–80.

42. Jo Clements, "*Time Out*: An Exploration of the Possibilities for Archived Time-Based Media as a Tool for Exploration within a Fine Art Practice-Based Research Enquiry," *Journal of Media Practice* 13, no. 3 (2012): 239–53.

43. Sean Mather and Susan Kerrigan, "*Noirscapes*: Using the Screen to Rewrite Los Angeles Noir as Urban Historiography," *Journal of Writing in Creative Practice* 9, no. 1–2 (2016): 89.

44. See: Michael A. R. Biggs and Daniela Büchler, "Rigor and Practice-Based Research," *Design Issues* 23 (Summer 2007): 62–69.

45. Hope, "Bursting Paradigms," 84.

46. Leo Berkeley, Martin Wood, and Smiljana Glisovic, "Creative Destruction: Screen Production Research, Theory, and Affect," *Journal of Writing in Creative Practice* 9, no. 1–2 (2016): 26.

47. Nicola Black, " 'Technologies of the Self' – Bridging Academic Theory and Practice-Based Research Through Creative Documentary Enquiry," *Media Practice and Education* 20, no. 2 (2019): 191.

48. Werner and Stange, "Praxis-Based Research," 4.

49. Roshini Kempadoo, "*Future Belonging* – A Case Study in Practice-Based Research," *Journal of Media Practice* 2, no. 3 (2002): 143.

50. Macaulay and Nutting, "Moving the Frontiers," 4.

51. "Decolonize," Merriam Webster (1999), www.merriam-webster.com/dictionary/decolonize.

52. Linda Tuhaiwai Smith, *Decolonizing Methodologies: Research and Indigenous Peoples* (London and New York: Zed Books, 1999), 3.

53. Eve Tuck and K. Wayne Yang, "Decolonization is Not a Metaphor," *Decolonization: Indigeneity, Education & Society* 1, no. 1 (2012): 5.

54. Tuck and Yang, 2.

55. Smith, *Decolonizing Methodologies*, 116.

56. Smith, 116.

57. Betsy A McLane, *A New History of Documentary Film* (New York: Bloomsbury Academic, 2012), 27.

58. McLane, 36.

59. Faye D. Ginsburg, "Screen Memories: Resignifying the Traditional in Indigenous Media," in *Media Worlds: Anthropology on New Terrain*, eds. Faye D. Ginsburg, Lila Abu-Lughod, and Brian Larkin (Berkeley: University of California Press, 2002), 39.

60. McLane, *A New History*, 30.

61. Anna Grimshaw, "Who Has the Last Laugh? Nanook of the North and Some New Thoughts on an Old Classic," *Visual Anthropology* 27, no. 5 (2014): 433.

62. See: Olivia Michiko Gagnon, "Singing with *Nanook of the North*: On Tanya Tagaq, Feeling Entangled, and Colonial Archives of Indegeneity," *ASAP/Journal* 5, no. 1 (January 2020): 45–78.

63. Gagnon, 55.

64. The performance was originally commissioned as part of the Toronto International Film Festival in 2012 and later toured across Canada and to New York City. See: Holly Gordon, "Inuk throat singer Tanya Tagaq on Reclaiming Nanook of the North," *CBC News* (January 25, 2014), www.cbc.ca/news/indigenous/inuk-throat-singer-tanya-tagaq-on-reclaiming-nanook-of-the-north-1.2508581.

65. Gagnon, "Singing with *Nanook*," 50.

66. Smith, *Decolonizing Methodologies*, 98.

67. See: Susan E. Chase and Coleen S. Bell, "Interpreting the Complexity of Women's Subjectivity," in *Interactive Oral History Interviewing*, eds. Eva McMahan and Kim Lacy Rogers (Hillsdale, NJ: Lawrence Erlbaum Associates, 1994), 63–82.

68. Mandy Rose, "Not Media About but Media With: Co-Creation for Activism," in *i-docs*, 62. See note 13.

69. Rose, 52.
70. Katerina Cizek, William Uricchio, and Sara Rafsky, "Part 4: Media Co-Creation with On-Line Communities and New Technologies," in *Collective Wisdom: Co-Creating Media Within Communities, Across Disciplines, and with Algorithms*, eds. Katerina Cizek and William Uricchio (Cambridge, MA: MIT Open Documentary Lab and Co-Creation Studio, 2019), https://wip.mitpress.mit.edu/pub/collective-wisdom-part-4/release/1, doi:10.21428/ba67f642.f7c1b7e5.
71. Cozen, Uricchio, and Rafsky.
72. Kate Nash, *Interactive Documentary: Theory and Debate* (New York: Routledge, 2022), 22.
73. N. Katherine Hayles, "Narrating Bits: Encounters Between Humans and Intelligent Machines," *Comparative Critical Studies* 2, no. 2 (2005): 28.
74. Munro and Bilbrough, "An Ecology of Relationships," 260.
75. Munro and Bilbrough, 267.
76. See: www.inter-doc.org/indice/indice-6/.
77. See: https://pregonerosdemedellin.com.
78. See: https://interactive.quipu-project.com.
79. See: Jorge Vázquez – Herrero and Gisela Moreno, "Documental Interactivo Iberoamericano, Proximidad y Transformación Social," *Doc On-line* 2017SI (December 2017): 123, http://dx.doi.org/10.20287/doc.esp17.dt05.
80. Liz Miller and Martin Allor, "Choreographies of Collaboration: Social Engagement in Interactive Documentaries," *Studies in Documentary Film* 10, no. 1 (2016): 59.
81. Miller and Allor, 64.
82. Sandra Gaudenzi, "User Experience Versus Author Experience: Lesson Learned from the *UX Series*," in *i-docs*, 123. See note 13.
83. Rose, "Not Media About but Media With," 52.
84. Nash, "Clicking on the World," 51.
85. Christopher Cekay Allen, "Living Collaborations in Los Sures, Brooklyn: 1984 and Today," in *i-docs*, 80. See note 13.
86. Nash, "Clicking on the World," 54.
87. Tuck and Yang, "Decolonization is Not a Metaphor," 31.
88. Rose, "Not Media About but Media With," 62.
89. Will Straw and Janine Marchessault, "Introduction," in *The Oxford Handbook of Canadian Cinema*, eds. Janine Marchessault and Will Straw (New York: Oxford University Press, 2019), xvi.
90. Straw and Marchessault, xxii.
91. Leighton C. Peterson, "Reclaiming Diné Film: Visual Sovereignty and the Return of *Navajo Film Themselves*," *Visual Anthropology Review* 29, no. 1 (2013): 32.
92. Peterson, 32.
93. Peterson, 33.
94. Peterson, 37.
95. Allen, "Living Collaborations," 80.
96. Allen, 68.
97. Allen, 69.
98. Allen, 80.
99. Eesha Pandit "Making Movement Mistakes: What to Do When You F@*k Up," in *The Crunk Feminist Collective*, eds. Brittney C. Cooper, Susana M. Morris, and Robin M. Boylorn (New York: The Feminist Press at the City University of New York, 2017), 164.
100. The i-doc is made up of a web site with interactive content (video and textual), social media (Facebook, Instagram), and a paywall-protected streaming feature-length film.

101. Pin Up! The Movie, "Among the Forgotten Women in Vintage Retro Culture are Muslim Women," *Instagram Post* (2019), www.instagram.com/p/CC8UNSNnGH6/?igshid=1fdij5noylgmb.

102. Pin Up! The Movie, "See this Gorgeous Woman," *Instagram Post* (2019), www.instagram.com/p/CC1NMk_HVYa/?igshid=b7f5mb0grdws.

103. See: Kathleen M. Ryan, *Pin Up! The Subculture: Negotiating Agency, Representation, and Sexuality with Vintage Style* (New York: Peter Lang, 2020).

104. Pin Up! The Movie, "@MissVelvetWren is the Owner of the Official @pinupsof colour page," *Instagram Post* (2019), www.instagram.com/p/CC5kQTbHmwE/?igshid=yxbxqd9s70dq.

105. Sophie Hope, "Bursting Paradigms: A Color Wheel of Practice Based Research," *Cultural Trends* 25, no. 2 (2016): 84.

106. Rose, "Not Media About but Media With," 63.

107. Patricia R. Zimmermann and Helen De Michiel, *Open Space New Media Documentary: A Toolkit for Theory and Practice* (New York: Routledge, 2018), 99.

# 2

# INTERACTIVE DOCUMENTARY

## Its History and Future as a Polyphonic Form

*Judith Aston and Stefano Odorico*

## Introduction

This chapter picks up on the editors of this volume's assertion that interactive documentary is in a constant process of becoming and that it is not so much a genre as a set of possibilities and practices that are constantly evolving in response to not only technological developments but also the cultural specificities within which these technologies unfold. This refusal to allow the term to be pinned down to precise definitions or boundaries is in the spirit of what Paolo Favero has aptly described as "interactive documentary practices,"[1] abbreviated here to i-docs. At the heart of this is the intention "to generate interdisciplinary exchange across academia and industry, platforms and genres."[2] As Favero has stated, "the transcultural space of creative practices is perhaps the one we need to monitor in the future, in order to discover the leading trends in the field."[3] In so doing, we can approach i-docs as "a direction, an inspiration for creating more inclusive participatory and multi-modal experiences capable of responding to the changing world that surrounds us."[4] This book, with its focus on decolonizing practices, builds on this transcultural spirit, with this chapter looking more specifically at the decolonization of i-docs through the lens of polyphony.

We see polyphony as being a key component of what i-docs have to offer in a way that is not dependent upon – but certainly aligns well with – concepts of co-creation, participation, and collaboration. As a key part of this, we propose that polyphonic approaches offer a way of thinking about narrative that can help to decolonize our understanding of "story" by questioning our received ontological assumptions and opening up perspectives that challenge essentialist ideas. We also see polyphonic approaches to i-docs as being helpful with combating fear of the "other," offering us tools and perspectives that can help to embrace diversity and

DOI: 10.4324/9781003174509-3

move away from the tendency toward ideological polarization. As part of this, we argue for the relevance of polyphony within i-docs to eco-narratives which give agency to the more-than-human,[5] helping us to compose or co-create collective, non-anthropocentric, and sustainable approaches to the future. In this sense, we see polyphony within i-docs as contributing toward the development of multimodal literacies that promote our ability to engage with complexity, navigate uncertainty, and celebrate diversity both within and across species, all key skills that we believe to be necessary for negotiating the challenges of the twenty-first century.

Building primarily on Mikhail Bakhtin's work on polyphony – and also referring to Michel Foucault's work on heterotopias – we argue that a dialogic approach is central to this, as a means of generating "new social relations and new forms of participation in the material, physical and social exigencies of everyday life."[6] This places i-docs as a tool for understanding "local contexts and the times in which we live," in order to "better grasp (and possibly intervene in) the lived world that surrounds us."[7] With this in mind, we reference our current collaborative *Polyphonic Documentary* project,[8] which has recently developed into a working group composed of over 70 people across several continents. We explain how this project is focusing on the potential of polyphony as an approach for multiperspectival thinking within an i-docs context. While polyphony can be clearly found across a number of documentary forms, we explain that our main focus at this point is around reframing earlier debates within i-docs around narrative/non-narrative/anti-narrative and its relationship to storytelling and database aesthetics.

## Key Terms, Definitions, and Research Questions

Patricia Zimmermann has noted that

> polyphony emerges from music history and theory. It describes the layering of different melodies and voices to create new resonances, a combinatory art depending on both vertical and horizontal vocal movements . . . polyphony is a common organizing structure in Renaissance and Baroque music, as well as in other types of music such as Indonesian gamelan, West African drumming, and Estonian and Ukrainian polychoral folk music.[9]

Moving away from a musical context, she also makes the point that historiographers have "criticized linear causal history as reductive of historical complexity, and have advocated for the explanatory power of polyvocal forms so that other voices and experiences can dislodge power relations."[10] Our work with polyphony builds on this approach to historiography and on the proposition that, when applied to the documentary form, "polyphonic structures can generate heterotopias through assemblages of difference, diversity, and interdisciplinarity."[11]

Heterotopia was first mentioned by Foucault in a limited way in 1966,[12] but our preference is to reference one of his more expansive talks from 1967.[13] Unlike utopia, heterotopia describes a potentially real space (in time) in which we can see and hear what is going on around us from different perspectives. Heterotopias can function in diverse ways, and their use can change over time. They are, however, always spaces where incompatible or contradictory kinds of space converge, including cinemas, festivals, asylums, and prisons. They are dependent on the particularities of history, geography, and society, offering spaces to talk and reflect on our contemporaneity, and they are also connected to the entire world that surrounds them. We are exploring heterotopias and their relevance to polyphonic thinking through practice-led research. This enables us to use interactive documentary to get "our hands dirty again"[14] and to learn through an interactive process of studying and making. While our focus to date has been primarily on Bakhtin's work on the polyphonic novel, we will come back to Foucault's work on heterotopias as our *Polyphonic Documentary* project progresses.

In relation to Bakhtin, we propose that there is value in interrogating his ideas about the polyphonic novel to examine their relevance to decolonizing i-docs. Questions that relate to this within our research project include: What is the ongoing relevance of ideas about polyphony developed within the specificities of ideological frameworks from past times and cultures to a contemporary transcultural context? Can the approaches to polyphony, which offer an alternative to the binary and overly empirical thinking of the Enlightenment, still serve this purpose? How do Bakhtin's ideas about polyphony as a single-authored construct fit with current debates about co-creation which work in opposition to this construct? Can digital, nonlinear interactive forms be developed as a place for using documentary to help work out new modes of interrelationship which are fit for navigating the challenges of the twenty-first century? Where do the limits of an expanded and decolonized notion of "story" lie? As we write this chapter in 2021, the i-Docs Research Group, of which Aston is one of the convenors[15] and from which this collaboration on polyphony has emerged, is 10 years old. This offers an opportunity to look back in order to look forward to consider where the field has come from, where it is going, and how this is playing out within the context of decolonization and polyphony.

## Looking Back to Look Forward

Though not explicitly articulated as such at the time, the principles of polyphony were very much what lay behind the motivation in co-convening the first i-Docs symposium in 2011 and have remained a central interest within the i-Docs Research Group ever since. Resonating with prior work on ethnographic archives and computer-based spatial montage,[16] the French collaboration between Arte and Upian for their 2008 interactive documentary (i-doc) project *Gaza/Sderot* was a key moment (see Figure 2.1). This now classic piece of professionally

**FIGURE 2.1**  *Gaza/Sderot: Life in Spite of Everything.*

*Source:* gaza-sderot.arte.tv

produced work explores everyday life across two cities in Israel and Palestine. It was co-produced with six filmmaking teams in each country, who collected video material of everyday life across a 40-day period, and it was designed as a split-screen i-doc to enable direct comparison of everyday life across the two cities.

Viewers could explore the material by date, people, themes, or specific locations on a map, to build up a picture of what could bring people together and not just divide them. The split-screen approach showed two different versions of the subjects' everyday truth, their "realities" in two different countries that share the same, permanent war context. This multiplication of windows on screen points to a multiplication of points of view: "Although most people generally are aware of documentary as having an association with truth rather than truth itself, when you exhibit on more than one screen you make that association more transparent."[17] The project's executive producer, Alexander Brachet, gave a keynote on *Gaza/Sderot* at the first i-Docs symposium in 2011,[18] and the project has been written up as a comprehensive case study by Ella Harris.[19] It was an example of web-based i-doc work that lent itself to polyphony as a form of multiperspectivalism because it could be engaged with in several different ways. This soon became a well-established approach in the i-doc field, including through Canadian projects such as *Out My Window* (2009),[20] *A Journal of Insomnia* (2019),[21] and *Sputnik Observatory* (2009).[22]

As technologies have continued to develop, the field has expanded to incorporate a wider range of approaches, which includes among others virtual and augmented reality. As part of this, the term "immersive" and issues relating to "presence" have become popular in many academic and industry circles, moving the focus away from the term "interactive" and its associated issues relating to "agency." Rose writes that this offers some "welcome relief from the challenge of distraction inherent in browser-based work,"[23] and the i-Docs Research Group has responded more generally by expanding the "i" in i-docs to incorporate both immersion and interactivity.[24] In addition to this, pioneering projects such as *Gaza/Sderot* (2009)[25] are no longer widely available because the Adobe Flash software that they were developed in is no longer being updated to accommodate the fast pace of change with computer operating systems and internet search engines.

While the aggressive nature of "upgrade culture" is clearly an ongoing problem, there is also growing evidence to suggest that interest in the computer-based aesthetic of multiple windows and nonlinear navigation is experiencing somewhat of a revival. Multi-window interfaces such as that of Zoom have become ubiquitous, high-profile interactive narrative projects have started to emerge on channels such as Netflix (who have developed their own bespoke software tool for interactive narrative production), and many of us are engaged with using interactive tools for online learning. A major conference on interactive narrative in August 2021 was convened in response to this,[26] Kate Nash's recent book on interactive documentary[27] reflects on this, too, and interest in how this intersects with developments in artificial intelligence is building momentum.[28] We see this as evidencing the ongoing need to bring interactivity and immersion into dialogue with each other, to not lose sight of the one in favor of the other, whilst at the same time being mindful of the pitfalls of technological determinacy.[29]

This builds on Janet Murray's point that interactivity and immersion should be seen as two mutually reinforcing concepts.[30] Furthermore, Murray brings attention to three aesthetic principles, which combine in new ways through interactive narrative: immersion, agency, and transformation.[31] She describes *immersion* as being the feeling of being present in another place and engaged in the action therein, relating it to Samuel Taylor Coleridge's "willing suspension of disbelief."[32] With this in mind, Murray describes the computer as an "enchanted object," which creates "a public space that also feels very private and intimate."[33] *Agency* is described as being the feeling of empowerment that comes from being able to take actions. This is more than interface activity, as the actions need to influence the experience for there to be agency.[34] *Transformation* is then related to the shapeshifting that can be achieved by being able to switch perspectives or points of view within an interactive narrative.[35]

Murray explains that by experiencing "interwoven stories as one unit, we can enhance the kaleidoscopic capacity of our minds, our capacity to imagine multiple points of view."[36] We see this as offering a transformative process that is key to the way in which we think about polyphony within an i-docs context. The spatial composition of multiple windows in the screen creates what Murray describes as a "virtual space" that can be navigated around.[37] In digital projects, this virtual space is negotiated through the human–computer interface, which gives participants, users, or viewers some agency in deciding how to explore this space. This makes it quite different from the split-screen aesthetic seen in more traditional documentary formats, which uses multiple windows in a more fixed way, as part of the documentary's sequential progression. As part of this, we are also interested in how this can play out in the hybrid space between the digital and non-digital, as i-docs can incorporate both.

## Bakhtin, Dostoevsky, Polyphony, and Decolonization

A key aim behind looking at the relevance of Bakhtin's work on polyphony to i-docs is our thinking around the need to decolonize storytelling and indeed, as a key part of this, to keep working on decolonizing our own minds. This links to Bakhtin's ideas about polyphony in the novel as being the consequence of a dialogic, as opposed to monologic, sense of truth. Using Fyodor Dostoevsky's work as his example, Bakhtin argued that the polyphonic novel has the potential to unsettle absolute truths, drawing the authoritative into question and helping us to embrace multiple perspectives and points of view.[38] In so doing, that which might otherwise have been considered to be certain becomes debated and open to interpretation. Bakhtin argued that this was achieved in Dostoevsky's novels in that the author put himself into a dialogic relationship with his characters, giving them autonomy to speak with their own voice and point of view without any explicit judgment from the author. In so doing, Bakhtin showed how Dostoevsky, as an explorer of ideas and systems of belief, was enabling his readers to explore important societal themes (such as suicide, poverty, human manipulation, and morality) from a variety of different perspectives.

This still plays out in Dostoevsky's novels as story but in a way that is not based on the principles of drama[39] and that gives autonomy to the reader. While the author maintains a privileged role in terms of structuring the overall narrative, there is no explicit attempt to make the characters subservient to an overarching authorial point of view. Instead, the author's role is to enter into dialogue with the characters, and, in a quite distinct way, to participate in that dialogue. In so doing, Bakhtin sees Dostoevsky as being "one of the interlocutors in the 'great dialogue' that he himself has created."[40] This enables the novel to use story as a site for debating ideas about how society should be constructed which are not fixed but which highlight the ongoing interaction of ideas, emphasizing fluidity, and change rather than rigidity.[41] For Bakhtin, the polyphonic novel could help to "renounce our monological habits so that we might come to feel at home in the new artistic sphere that Dostoevsky discovered . . . in that incomparably more complex *artistic model of the world* which he created."[42] Given that openness, fluidity, dialogue, and multiperspectivity are values that we consider to be core to i-docs, this is our motivation for taking the time to consider what Bakhtin's work can teach us about polyphony.

A clear difference behind Bakhtin's work with the novel and contemporary i-docs, however, is that Bakhtin was writing about single-authored and generally fixed texts, whereas i-docs can be co-authored and more fluid in terms of their duration. This begs the question as to the ongoing relevance of his ideas to the contemporary landscape of computer-mediated communication, which many have argued looks more to oral traditions of storytelling than it does to the more fixed conventions of print culture. Amelia Winger-Bearskin, for example, draws on her own Indigenous traditions to write about "decentralized storytelling,"[43] and the Co-creation Studio at MIT's Open Documentary Lab[44] is also doing wider work on Indigenous storytelling traditions.

Our argument is that Bakhtin's critical thinking on polyphony brings additional insights and perspectives that are complementary to this work on Indigenous storytelling traditions. Core to this is the way in which Bakhtin offers a framework through which different ideas, approaches, and cultural traditions can be discussed alongside each other. Although his focus was on the single-authored, print-based novel, his thinking opens perspectives and approaches that can also be applied to more contemporary mediatized contexts. Key to this is his dialogic approach that facilitates multiperspectivity, as opposed to being focused on one way of thinking and acting. Through dialogue (which is participative and not unduly provocative), human beings are facilitated to understand themselves in relation to "others," learning to negotiate the "I" with the "we," discovering the differences that characterize all of us and learning to accept them. Embedding this dialogue, within our media production processes (as in co-creation) and/or within the media texts that we create (as in polyphony), is an approach that we see as being helpful on many levels, from the local through to the global. We have collective problems to address, such as climate emergency and ideological polarization, which would benefit from multiperspectival understanding. This can draw on the range of tools and techniques that are available to us and, there is no reason why the principles of polyphony within i-docs cannot draw on oral storytelling as much as on other forms such as the novel.

In this sense, there is a strong alignment between co-creation and polyphony,[45] although it is important to also acknowledge that one can still be enacted without the other. By this we mean that co-creative i-docs do not always need to lead to polyphonic outcomes and, likewise, polyphonic outcomes do not always need to be co-created. As with polyphony, co-creation strives toward greater inclusivity and awareness of methodological biases,[46] and it has been acknowledged that it is naive to suggest that power structures can be completely overcome.[47] Bakhtin's ethics acknowledges these points in relation to polyphony, with his interest in carnival being confined to certain spaces and structures that can be created to facilitate an atmosphere of openness through which different perspectives and opinions can potentially find common ground. Within the privileged space of the novel, Bakhtin also acknowledges the responsibility of the author or what we might call within a co-creation context the orchestrator/s of the dialogue.

Though heavily influenced by Albert Einstein's writing on relativity, particularly in his later writing, it is also important to acknowledge that Bakhtin was not an advocate of relativism.[48] He was rooted in Russian culture and was a clear advocate of the philosophy of pluralism within that culture. This is an essential point when looking at the relevance of his ideas to i-docs, it being important to acknowledge one's own rootedness. In this instance, ours is within Western democratic culture, which is inevitably influencing our writing about polyphony, no matter how open we may be to other transcultural contexts.

## Decolonizing Story and the Mind Through I-docs

Roger Lundin shows how, when Bakhtin first published about Dostoevsky in 1929,[49] Dostoevsky could see that Western thought had come through the Enlightenment to be dominated by monological thinking and the idea that truth could be contained within a single system (i.e., Newton, Hegel, Marx) or lodged securely within a single consciousness (i.e., Descartes).[50] This led to the idea of dualism and binaries, and it was the basis for the rationalism of science and European thought that has played out through colonialism and beyond. Dostoevsky could see how the monological thinker does not need to know other persons or points of view to complete their own understanding of the truth, and that a monological system requires neither correction nor development, for it has already grasped the truth in its totality.[51] Bakhtin has argued that Dostoevsky's novels used polyphony to create an alternative vision for society in which things are accepted as being more complex and far less certain. Although the binary thinking of the Enlightenment has been brought into question by many thinkers since,[52] we argue here that it is still present in many of the systems and structures of contemporary Western society, including the dominant way in which we continue to tell and receive stories.

One might say, in fact, that debates about what constitutes democratic values – for example, multiculturalism versus monoculturalism – are at the heart of ideological polarization within our society today and are a key reason democracy is said to be "in crisis."[53] One can also say that the Enlightenment placed humans in a position of superiority over our environment, leading to a culture of extraction that is now manifesting as climate emergency. While contemporary scientific thought does recognize the need to embrace complexity and to consider our place alongside the "more-than-human,"[54] we are still seeing these debates playing out in politics through tensions between democracy and authoritarianism, plurality and monoculture, sustainability and ongoing extraction. Our interest in the multiple relates to plurality and diversity, as opposed to a multitude of voices that coalesce around conformism, sameness, or unity. That said, we would not wish this conception of the multiple to deny the power of collective action through which seemingly diverse groups and individuals can find commonality through a defined interest or goal, such as class struggle or identity politics.[55]

Our provocation is that we need to understand and reflect on this, in order to think through the assumptions that we bring to the storytelling methods and tools that we use. Indeed, we would go as far as to suggest that many of the dominant tools for interactive storytelling work against this kind of reflection despite their potential to do otherwise. This is partly because, although these tools promote nonlinear and interactive mind-mapping as means of conceptualizing story ideas, their workspace for putting content together is often organized around the principles of sequential editing, in a comparable way to traditional film editing systems. While this is helpful, in that it makes the software more accessible to noncoding filmmakers, it also tends to push authors back toward preconceived ideas about how we construct narratives or tell stories. These preconceived ideas are often based on dramatic approaches centered around conflict, which all too often leads authors back to binary tropes such as good/evil, heroes/villains, and us/them to help drive the narrative forward. While the storyboarding and mind-mapping systems that accompany these software tools do allow for a broader range of approaches to narrative, it requires extra effort to do this because the actual editing workspace is not conducive to it. Indeed, Murray herself speaks about "dramatic agency"[56] within interactive narrative, thus promoting the idea that narrative within interactive digital formats is still fundamentally about drama.

Our argument is that, building on the work of the Modernists and postmodern artistic movements, and on wider insights gained from folk and non-Western cultures, we need to take a more expansive understanding of narrative and story, to incorporate a wider range of approaches. In this sense, decolonizing our approach to storytelling, and hence our minds, is not just about bringing in a greater diversity of voices but is also about taking collective and personal responsibility for looking at the ways in that we construct and tell stories. This needs to include awareness raising and critique around the tendency to look for universal tropes across all cultures, both in narrative structure and in themes. While we fully accept that dramatic narrative is not unique to Western culture, being found for example in myths and legends across a whole host of cultural contexts, we are questioning the tendency toward monological thinking about story as drama within contemporary media culture. This can be seen as a form of neocolonialism in its own right, dictated by the drive toward profit and satisfying the preconceptions of mainstream audiences. While Bakhtin's work on polyphony is our starting point for this, it is by no means our end point, as many of his ideas were indeed embraced by twentieth-century movements such as the Modernists and postmodernism.[57] It is by returning to his thinking in relation to these movements and to ongoing societal tensions, that we intend to explore what resonates with interactive documentary practices and how this can be put into dialogue with other thinkers such as Foucault and beyond.

Building on Bakhtin's thinking, if we are genuinely going to embrace, and indeed learn from, what has more recently been called "the ontological turn,"[58] which tells us that there are different ways or modes of being, we need to continue to open up (as opposed to close down) what we mean by "story." We see this as being particularly important to documentary making in a context of ideological polarization and climate emergency, in which dramatic narrative, and its associated link to causality, may not always be the most productive way to help us to think through the problems that we are facing. At the i-Docs 2016 symposium, this issue of "story" was raised in the "tools for thought"[59] strand, through keynotes from Alisa Lebow and Florian Thalhofer. Lebow has subsequently gone on to collaborate with Alexandra Juhasz and convene an important dialogue under the title of "Beyond Story."[60] While this dialogue does not explicitly seek to expand our idea of what "story" is, there is still strong alignment with our approach, through their direct critique of the monologism of contemporary documentary commissioning circles. Their argument is that these circles are becoming even more obsessed with the dramatic narrative of "story", in so doing closing the door on other approaches which have always been integral to the rich tradition of documentary making. Thalhofer continues to explore these other approaches outside of the commissioning context. He is taking an expanded idea of what "story" is, through his ongoing work as the designer of Korsakow and in collaboration with our *Polyphonic Documentary* research project.

In our context of polyphonic i-docs, authority does not reside in one single voice, but it is often characterized by a polycentric and decentralized approach in which various narrative lines are available. While we are not saying that this is the only approach worth taking, we wish to explore its potential within a wider landscape of possibilities. This is to build on Bakhtin's point that "the development of the polyphonic novel is a huge step forward not only in the development of novelistic prose . . . but also in the development of the *artistic thinking* of humankind."[61] In making "new demands on aesthetic thought," he also points out that when "raised on monologic forms of artistic visualization, thoroughly steeped in them, aesthetic thought tends to absolutize those forms and not see their boundaries."[62] Going back to Murray's concept of "virtual space,"[63] these boundaries can indeed be explored on a computer, where audiovisual material held in a directory or database can be called and edited into several windows within the screen using interactive authoring tools. The composition of multiple windows can also change based on the author's decision or allocated randomly. In the creation tool Korsakow, for example, each piece of audiovisual material can be assigned to a different interface and multiple window compositions developed.

This relates to the idea of "open" versus "closed," as Korsakow puts all elements of the film into dialogue with each other, opening it up to a plethora of multiple perspectives. This has the potential to help the author to decolonize the way we talk (and think) about our lived experience, by focusing on footage, shots, and sequences that might otherwise have been neglected. Engagement with a software tool like Korsakow can, therefore, help to broaden our understanding of narrative and story in documentary. It can help with presenting lived experience in a different, alternative, and hopefully more democratic way, moving away from the general obsession for dramatization and sensationalism that is all too prevalent in the documentary industry today. As the inventor of Korsakow, Thalhofer, has called this type of sensationalism "extreme storytelling,"[64] adding:

> I myself (and I think more and more people), don't think any more that the extremes are interesting. Why? Real life lives in the middle, not in the extremes. Extremes, at least in my life, are not very common. And, solutions for problems often exist in a middle ground. The problems of climate change will not be solved in the extremes . . . Extremes are usually irrelevant, totally boring.[65]

## Further Reflection on Tools

It is important to stress that, as a tool, Korsakow is likely to be useful in some contexts but not in others. By exploring its potential alongside that of other tools, we are aiming to discover where it can have most impact and where other tools are more useful. For example, Korsakow is not intuitive to many, as the author(s) need to reach a satisfactory level of understanding of the software and of its transformative potential to use it effectively. Another tool, Stornaway, breaks from a film editing logic by logic enabling those working with it to organize and edit content through "story maps" and "story islands." These can be predetermined and easily visualized to help authors to plan out pathways and patterns, as a way of organizing thoughts and presenting them to others (see Figure 2.2). Korsakow, on other hand, is based on the principle of smallest narrative units (SNUs) and points of contact (POCs) in which anything can be connected to anything by allocating keywords (see Figure 2.3). Though less provisional and emergent than Korsakow, it does perhaps mean that Stornaway is a better tool for communicating the results of research, whereas Korsakow can help to find new patterns and connections as part of the research process itself. That said, within the field of eco-narratives, for example, it may be that Korsakow is an effective means through which to de-anthropomorphize the way in which we tell stories. This relates to its potential to move us away from a human-centered focus to a "storytelling framework flexible enough to co-create with nonhumanity, even during an environmental moment characterized by crisis."[66]

This idea of co-creation relates to the fact that, as a research method, Korsakow has potential as a practice for analyzing our behavior in the way that we produce documentaries and in the way that we tell stories. This builds on insightful PhD research with Korsakow practitioners from the anthropologist, Franziska Weidle,[67] who is also part of our *Polyphonic Documentary* project. Building on her work, we are proposing that Korsakow is a good research tool for decolonizing the mind and how we think about stories because it enables us to find unexpected

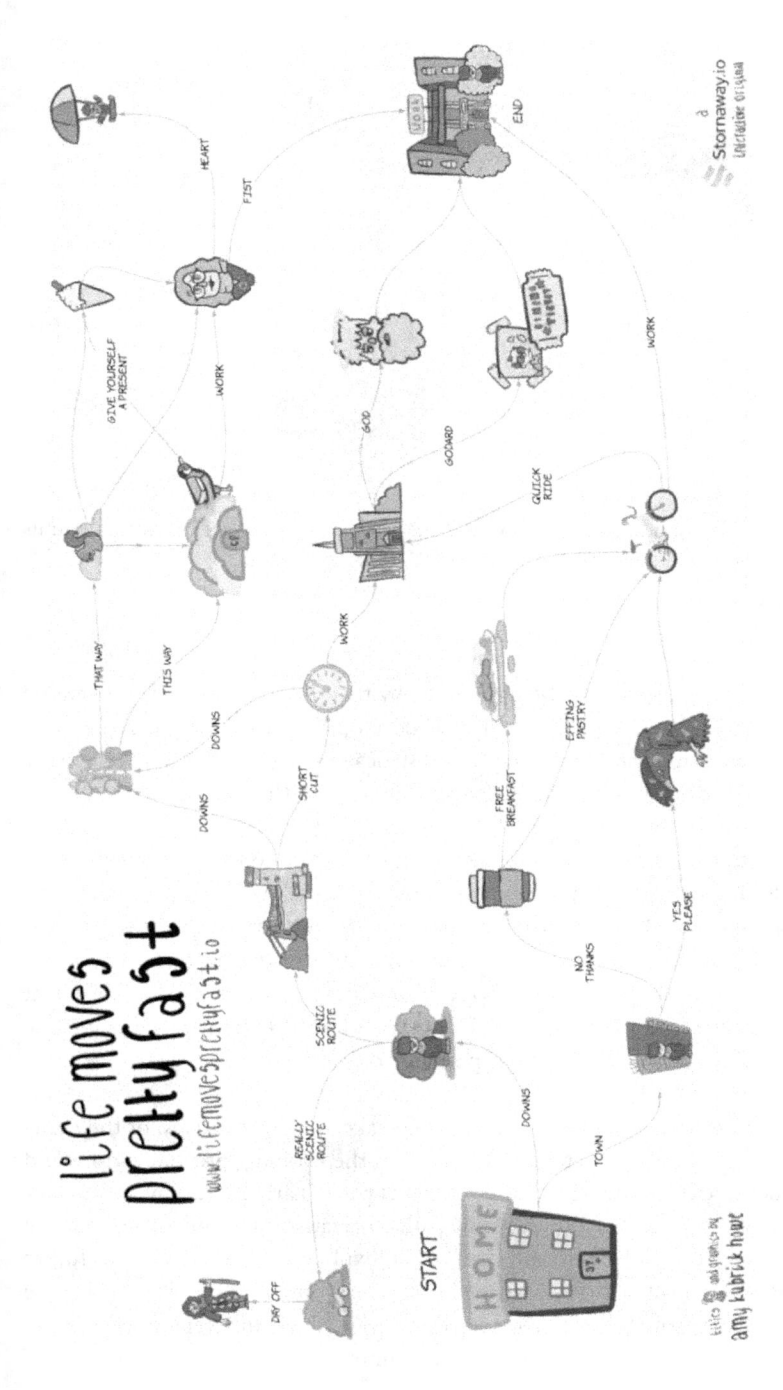

**FIGURE 2.2** The organizing principle of Stornaway based on story maps and story islands.

*Source:* Figure by Amy Kubrick Howe

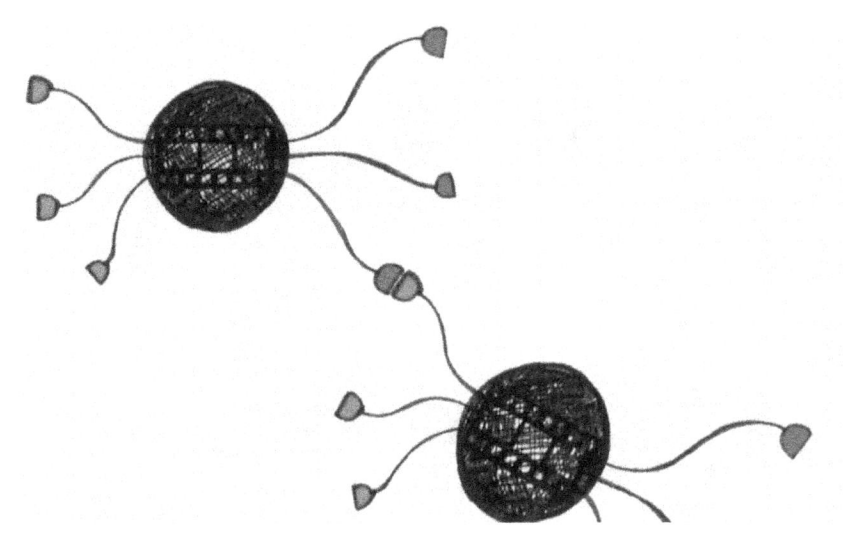

**FIGURE 2.3**   The organizing principle of Korsakow based on smallest narrative units (SNUs) and points of contact (POCs).

*Source:* Figure by Florian Thalhofer

patterns and encourages us to be challenged by that. Korsakow could, indeed, be used as an auto-ethnographic or personal development tool for the subsequent creation of more uni- and multi-sequential structures,[68] which are not necessarily dependent on Korsakow for their delivery. It may be that, for Korsakow to be accessible as a communication tool for documentary makers, one first needs to understand how it works and what it is trying to do. Key to this is the fact that, as with Bakhtin's ideas about the polyphonic novel, Korsakow refuses to dramatize. It does not provide all the information of the story but instead allows those who engage with it to fill in the gaps and create alternative stories. In this sense, if one brings preconceived expectations about what a story is, based on the dominant paradigm of dramatic narrative, to a Korsakow project, then one is likely to be disappointed and frustrated by the experience of using it.

Our intention with the *Polyphonic Documentary* project therefore is to build our collective understanding, initially through Korsakow and Stornaway, of the communicative potential of different tools based on the evolving preconceptions and understanding that we bring to them. What is particularly important in interactive documentaries is that the different paths, narratives, or sub-stories that are not selected by the viewer are still there to be explored, used, remixed in future experiences, in another time, perhaps in another context. The viewer is aware of that, as a key component of i-docs that makes them different from linearly presented documentaries with only one beginning, middle, and end. It is there, at the back of our minds, that material is still always available even if we have not used it yet:

> The text appears to fragment, to atomize, into constituent elements (into lexias or blocks of text); and these reading units take on a life of their own as they become more self-contained, because they become less dependent on what comes before or after in a linear succession.[69]

Stornaway, through its use of mind maps, gives the author(s) the facility to decide how much to make this additional material explicitly evident to the reader and how much to make this something that has to be discovered through ongoing interaction with the material. Korsakow, on the other hand, does not have this option, as all the different connections are algorithmically generated, meaning that there will always be an element of serendipity and surprise.

This approach allows us to become actively aware of what is happening around us and in the story in a way that is as much about interaction as it is about immersion. We believe that it creates a process of awareness or subjectification, whereby creating structures (using Korsakow) can help us to decolonize the way we tell stories, offering a more democratic and "aware" process. For Wiehl, who also has a good understanding of Korsakow and is part of our project, "the issue of (distributed) authorship in Korsakow and the issue of user experience – are entwined: the always implied subjectivity of any configuration is laid open and becomes decisive for the experience."[70] In order to build our collective under-standing, we are creating experimental projects that will enable us to reflect upon the way in which we use digital technology to think about and tell stories. In so doing, we are less interested at this point in how these projects communicate out to a wider audience than in how these projects can help to transform our own awareness and understanding. As with all forms of experimentation, this does require a degree of commitment that may or may not translate into projects which can be understood by a wider audience beyond those with an explicit interest in what the different software tools have to offer.

## Conclusion

To sum up, in line with an increasing number of scholars across a variety of disci-plines, our proposition is that an over-alignment of dramatic narrative with story structure is an example of monological thinking and that this works against the principles of polyphony. As we both work in a film department, we are familiar with having this debate with colleagues, many of whom believe, as practicing filmmakers, that dramatic narrative is central to their craft and that conflict is needed to produce engaging stories. While we are not against dramatic narrative, our concern is to challenge its centrality, which we link to wider debates about decolonization, to contribute to an ongoing opening up of what storytelling is and how it can continue to evolve.

Though aligning with Murray's ideas about kaleidoscopic narrative, we wish to extend the debate beyond her focus on the conventions of dramatic narrative, with a view to helping us to move us beyond the binary thinking of the Enlightenment, which still pervades many of our thought processes to this day. We argue that we need to develop literacies which lead us away from a constant desire for resolution to problems that are in fact ongoing and which require a different approach to narrative and complexity if they are to be adequately addressed. We have chosen ideological polarization and climate emergency as our core themes to explore, in the belief that monological thinking and an overemphasis on the hierarchical supremacy of humans need to be challenged and countered. We see this as being essential if we are to successfully navigate our way through the challenges that lie ahead.

We are aware, however, that we can all too easily labor under the illusion that we are open-minded and accepting of polyphony when in fact our version of what this is may be more monovocal and reinforcing of power structures than we may care to admit. We are also aware that, by looking at polyphony through the lens of i-docs, we are by no means offering a comprehensive study of possibilities. Additionally, we understand that dramatic narrative has its part to play within i-docs and that this is by no means being confined to Western culture. We do, however, wish to challenge the way in which it continues to be used to reinforce the binary and empirical thinking of the Enlightenment, which is not always helpful. We are, therefore, keen to explore areas where a different approach to story might be more helpful and to make the point that, in some cultures such as the Hollywood film industry, the importance of dramatic narrative is overemphasized. We also wish to consider where the limits of an expanded and decolonized notion of story might lie, considering circumstances in which i-docs do not need to engage with narrative and story at all. These are challenges that require a degree of honesty, dialogue, reflection, and openness. This is not to stop us from acting but to keep ourselves in constant check around our own biases and understanding of the problematics, as well as the possibilities, of polyphony as it relates to interactive documentary practices and to society.

## Notes

1. Paolo S. H. Favero, "The Travelling i-Doc: Reflections on the Meaning of Documentary-Based Image-Making Practices in Contemporary India," in *i-doc: The Evolving Practices of Interactive Documentary,* eds. Judith Aston, Sandra Gaudenzi, and Mandy Rose (London and New York: Wallflower Press, 2017), 237.
2. Judith Aston, "Interactive Documentary: What Does It Mean and Why Does It Matter?" *i-Docs website,* March 2016, http://i-docs.org/interactive-documentary-what-does-it-mean-and-why-does-it-matter/.
3. Favero, "The Travelling i-Doc," 250.

4. Favero, "The Travelling i-Doc," 251.
5. See: Donna J. Haraway, *Staying with the Trouble: Making Kin in the Chthulucene* (Durham, NC: Duke University Press, 2016); Hayden Lorimer, "Cultural Geography: Non-Representational Conditions and Concerns.," *Progress in Human Geography* 32, no. 4 (February 8, 2008): 551–59.
6. Favero, "The Travelling i-Doc," 237.
7. Favero, "The Travelling i-Doc."
8. See: https://polyphonicdocumentary.com/.
9. Patricia R. Zimmermann, "Polyphony and the Emerging Collaborative Ecologies of Documentary Media Exhibition," *Afterimage* 47, no. 1 (2020): 63, https://doi.org/10.1525/aft.2020.471011.
10. Zimmermann, "Polyphony and the Emerging Collaborative."
11. Zimmermann, "Polyphony and the Emerging Collaborative."
12. See: Michel Foucault, *The Order of Things: An Archaeology of the Human Sciences* (Paris: Éditions Gallimard, 1966).
13. Michel Foucault, "Of Other Spaces, Heterotopias," *Architecture, Mouvement, Continuité* 5 (1984): 46–49, trans. Jay Miskowiec, https://foucault.info/documents/heterotopia/foucault.heteroTopia.en/.
14. Favero, "The Travelling i-Doc," 237.
15. See i-docs.org for further details.
16. See Judith Aston, "Spatial Montage and Multimedia Ethnography: Using Computers to Visualise Aspects of Migration and Social Division Among a Displaced Community," *Forum Qualitative Sozialforschung / Forum: Qualitative Social Research* 11 no. 2 (2010), https://doi.org/10.17169/fqs-11.2.1479.
17. Cahal McLaughlin, "Freedoms and Accountabilities," in *Truth or Dare: Art and Documentary* eds. Gail Pearce and Cahal McLoughlin (Bristol and Chicago: Intellect Books, 2007), 39.
18. See: Judith Aston and Sandra Gaudenzi, "Interactive Documentary: Setting the Field," *Studies in Documentary Film* 6, no 2 (2012): 125–39, doi:10.1386/sdf.6.2.125_1.
19. See: Ella Harris, "Introducing i-Docs to Geography: Exploring Interactive Documentary's Nonlinear Imaginaries," *Area* 49, no. 1 (2016): 25–34, https://doi.org/10.1111/area.12275.
20. See: www.nfb.ca/interactive/highrise_out_my_window_en.
21. See: www.nfb.ca/interactive/a_journal_of_insomnia/.
22. See: https://vimeo.com/sputnikobservatory.
23. Mandy Rose, "The Immersive Turn: Hype and Hope in the Emergence of Virtual Reality as a Nonfiction Platform," *Studies in Documentary Film* 12, no. 2 (2018): 147, https://doi.org/10.1080/17503280.2018.1496055.
24. See: i-docs.org.
25. See: http://gaza-sderot.arte.tv/.
26. IFM: Interactive Film and Media Conference 2021: New Narratives, Racialization, Global Crises, and Social Engagement, https://interactivefilm.blogspot.com/.
27. See: Kate Nash, *Interactive Documentary: Theory and Debate* (London: Routledge, 2021).
28. See, for example: the workshop organized by The Space in 2019 on artificial intelligence and next generation storytelling: www.thespace.org/resource/artificial-intelligence-and-next-generation-storytelling.
29. See: Aston, *Interactive Documentary,* online.
30. See: Janet H. Murray, *Inventing the Medium: Principles of Interaction Design as a Cultural Practice* (Cambridge, MA: MIT Press, 2012).
31. Janet H. Murray, *Hamlet on the Holodeck: The Future of Narrative in Cyberspace* (Cambridge, MA: MIT Press, 1997), 181.
32. Murray, *Hamlet on the Holodeck,* 110.

33. Murray, *Hamlet on the Holodeck*, 99.
34. Murray, *Hamlet on the Holodeck*, 128–29.
35. Murray, *Hamlet on the Holodeck*, 154.
36. Murray, *Hamlet on the Holodeck*, 160–61.
37. Murray, *Hamlet on the Holodeck*, 83.
38. See: Mikhail Bakhtin, *Problems of Dostoevsky's Poetics*, trans. Caryl Emerson (Minneapolis: University of Minnesota Press, 1984).
39. Bakhtin, *Problems of Dostoevsky's Poetics*, 17, 34.
40. Gary Saul Morson and Caryl Emerson, *Mikhail Bakhtin: Creation of a Prosaics* (Stanford, CA: Stanford University Press, 1990), 239.
41. Julia Kristeva, "Word, Dialogue and Novel," in *The Kristeva Reader*, ed. Toril Moi, trans. Alice Jardine (New York: Columbia University Press, 1986), 39–40, originally published as "Bakhtin, le Mot, le Dialogue et le Roman," *Critique* 239 (1967): 38–65.
42. Bakhtin, *Problems of Dostoevsky's Poetics*, 272.
43. Amelia Winger-Bearskin, "What is Decentralised Storytelling?" *Guild of Future Architects Review* (August 2021), https://medium.com/guild-of-future-architects/what-is-decentralized-storytelling-7f136704c0fe.
44. https://cocreationstudio.mit.edu/.
45. As acknowledged by Zimmermann in "Polyphony."
46. See: Reece Auguiste et al., "Fifty Speculations and Fifteen Unresolved Questions on Co-creation in Documentary," *Afterimage* (May 2020), https://doi.org/10.1525/aft.2020.471012.
47. See for example: Namaan, "When is Co-Creation Possible," 42; Rose, "Not Media About but Media With," 62–63.
48. See: Caryl Emerson, "Isaiah Berlin and Michail Bakhtin: Relativistic Affiliations," *symplokē* 7, no. 1/2 (1999): 139–64.
49. See: Mikhail Bakhtin, *Problems of Dostoevsky's Creation* (Leningrad: Priboi, 1929).
50. Roger Lundin, *Believing Again: Doubt and Faith in a Secular Age* (Cambridge, MI: Wm. B Eerdmans Publishing Co., 2009), 163.
51. Lundin, *Believing Again*, 163.
52. See: Jeffrey Alexander, *The Dark Side of Modernity* (Cambridge: Polity Books, 2013).
53. The topic, for example, of the Visible Evidence XXVII conference: www.visibleevidence.org/conference/visible-evidence-xxvii/.
54. See for example: Lorimer, "Cultural Geography"; Haraway, *Staying with the Trouble*.
55. Michael Hardt and Antonio Negri, *Multitude: War and Democracy in the Age of Empire* (New York: Penguin Books, 2004), 105–6.
56. Janet H. Murray, "Dramatic Agency: The Next Evolution of Storytelling," talk given at the 2015 *Future of Storytelling Summit*, https://inventingthemedium.com/tag/dramatic-agency/.
57. For more on why Bakhtin himself did not explicitly engage with the Modernists, see: Stacy Burton, "Paradoxical Relations: Bakhtin and Modernism," *MLQ: Modern Language Quarterly* 32 no. 4 (February 2008): 519–43.
58. See: Martin Holbraad and Morten A. Pederso\en, *The Ontological Turn: An Anthropological Exposition* (Cambridge: Cambridge University Press, 2017).
59. Building on Harold Rheingold, *Tools for Thought : The History and Future of Mind Expanding Technology* (Cambridge, MA: MIT Press, 1986).
60. Alexander Juhasz and Alisa Lebow, "Beyond Story," *World Records* 5 (Spring 2021), https://vols.worldrecordsjournal.org/05/01?index=1."
61. Bakhtin, *Problems of Dostoevsky's Poetics*, 270.
62. Bakhtin, *Problems of Dostoevsky's Poetics*, 270.
63. Murray, *Hamlet on the Holodeck*, 83.
64. Florian Thalhofer, "The Way We Tell Stories," *I-Docs Symposium Keynote* (2016), www.youtube.com/watch?v=KEnBYi2HY5c.

65. Jennifer Proctor and Bridgid Maher, "Emotional Multiplicities in Multi-sourced Work," *Database | Narrative | Archive* 1, no. 1 (January 2013): 11, http://dnaanthology.com/anvc/dna/emotional-multiplicities-in-multi-sourced-work.

66. Corrine Donly, "Toward the Eco-Narrative: Rethinking the Role of Conflict in Storytelling," *Humanities* 6, no 2, Special Issue on Animal Narratology (April 2017): 1, https://doi.org/10.3390/h6020017.

67. See: Franziska Weidle, *Of Trees and Clouds: Software-mediated Visions in Documentary and Ethnographic Filmmaking Practices* (Gottingen: V and R Unipress, 2020) for a full analysis of this work.

68. Murray, *Inventing the Medium*, 43.

69. George P. Landow, *Hypertext 2.1: The Convergence of Contemporary Critical Theory and Technology* (Baltimore, MD: The Johns Hopkins University Press, 1997), 64.

70. Anna Wiehl, "Beyond 'Toolness': Korsakow Documentary as a Methodology for Plurivocal Interventions in Complexity," *Alphaville: Journal of Film and Screen Media* 15 (Summer 2018): 44, www.alphavillejournal.com/Issue15/ArticleWiehl.pdf.

# 3

# CHOOSE YOUR OWN GENERATION

## Interactive LGBTQ+ Narratives From South Asian Families

### Aashish Kumar in conversation with Tammy Rae Matthews. Edited by Tammy Rae Matthews

In this conversation with Tammy Rae Matthews, Aashish Kumar (he/him) discusses the potential for exploring identity and sexuality through i-docs, which he believes create an innovative site for collaborative deconstruction and provide opportunities for insights not available through the more traditional narrative forms of storytelling. Through his work, Kumar explores and documents visible intergenerational narratives through innovative platforms to explore and address challenges confronting the South Asian community.

In this interview, he details his process and project *Body, Home, World: South Asian American LGBTQ+ Journeys.*[1] As of summer 2021, two family journeys are available on the platform. Each journey is told over five episodes – four from the perspective of queer-identifying and family participants and a convergent fifth episode that brings these journeys together. The project's outreach strategy has successfully connected with LGBTQ+ advocacy organizations in the United States and South Asia. The inaugural story features the journey of the Mehta family from Texas as told by Parag Mehta, a prominent *desi* activist, and his father Vijay Mehta. The second story follows the transnational journey of Vaibhav Jain, who came to this country as a public health graduate student and met a gay Indian American (Parag Mehta) but had to encounter the complexity of bringing along his Indian family on their journey of acceptance and celebration. Kumar plans include adding two additional stories to the North American edition, expanding the portal to include stories from the subcontinent and other parts of the diaspora, and creating a section that will feature stories submitted by members of the South Asian queer diaspora.

TRM: In terms of your work, how would you describe "decolonization"?

AK: At the broadest level decolonization can be seen as a practice that seeks to intervene and disrupt cultural, political, and intellectual traditions deriving

DOI: 10.4324/9781003174509-4

from a settler-colonized or a colonizer-colonized relationship. Within the context of my creative work and teaching, I would describe it as:

1. an effort to foreground texts, authors, and cultural artifacts that precede the colonial take-over and erasure; a persistent questioning of the implicit acceptance of Eurocentric or western canons, and a centering of pre-colonial AND post-colonial intellectual traditions;

2. a reworking of a decades-old humanities curricula that privilege the white male perspective and the introduction of texts – both written and cinematic – that center narratives and creators of color in the telling of their stories, honoring the dictum "No Stories About Us Without Us";

3. a collaborative approach in documentary storytelling whether traditional or interactive, that privileges co-creative or shared authorship over auteur-informed tradition; and a rethinking of contemporary frameworks of distribution that are dominant in determining funding, production, and access to stories and audiences.

More specifically, in the context of my present work on sexual and gender diversity in South Asia and its diaspora, it consists of undoing a colonial-era suppression and erasure of centuries-old symbols, mythology, and religious texts that provided expression to gender-fluid and queer identity in that part of the world. Queer-rights movements in the west have successfully created touchstones by which we recognize the lineage of these movements. However, they need to be deepened and globalized through the highlighting of stories that constitute the pre-modern and ancient history of queerness. Such a reckoning can serve two functions. For those living in South Asia or its diaspora who have inherited the colonial narrative of queerness as abhorrent and criminal, it can serve to acknowledge and normalize the existence of a long history of queer identity in their culture. In the primarily white cis male queer spaces of the west, it can help broaden and diversify queer discourse, especially emphasizing the longstanding presence of queer and trans voices of color in other parts of the world.

TRM: How would you define an i-doc?

AK: Over this past decade, the term i-doc has come to be defined variously and has been used loosely for projects ranging from simple websites featuring video content to websites where coding, design, and interactivity work together to communicate a theme, experience, or story. In my view i-docs are best approached not as a simple repurposing of nonfiction or documentary storytelling for the web but as a new medium with its own evolving grammar, viewing modes, creative intentions, and methods of distribution and reception. Gene Youngblood presciently offers the following quote in his *Expanded Cinema* (1970): "The accumulation of facts is no longer of top priority to humanity. The problem now is to apply existing facts to new conceptual wholes, new vistas of reality."[2] Indeed, i-docs aspire toward new vistas of reality and therefore represent a paradigm shift in the field of nonfiction storytelling.

Increasingly, many have sought to include emerging media forms such as VR/AR within the field of i-docs. I have mixed feelings about such an umbrella usage of the term, especially since each of these newer forms is device-specific and as such offers unique ways of accessing and experiencing stories. VR and AR also offer a distinct departure from web-based forms of nonfiction storytelling in the way they explicate "presence" and create a "frameless point of view experience" as the primary viewing mode. I tend to think of i-docs as browser-based forms of storytelling that live in the hyper-connected space of the internet utilizing its computational affordances. But beyond posing a technical definition of i-docs, I have found the following values of "responsive" storytelling to be a useful way to guide my own research and creative practice in this field. These are inspired in large part by the pioneering work of Canadian documentarians from the early days of the Fogo Island "participatory video" projects to the latest iterations of NFB's i-doc series *Highrise*.[3] According to this framework, which is by no means an exclusionary one, i-docs:

- should strive toward a participatory relationship with individuals and communities who make up its subjects
- should allow for personalization
- should respond to and register viewer interactions in unique ways
- should derive their design, navigation, and user experience from the culture, context, and texts relevant to its target audience
- should deepen our research into and understanding of patterns of human behavior but should also question, refine, and provide transparency to the manner in which viewers'/users' data are used for such research

TRM: What is the value of exploring identity and sexuality through i-docs?

AK: One of the reasons that I gravitated toward i-docs is because I saw them as a great space for particularized narratives. In such a space, identity-based storytelling can be supported by resonant visual, aural, and experiential design elements. Designing the ecosystem that cradles these narratives in a meaningful and resonant way *is* telling the story. In this context iconography, color, and sound rise beyond being non-diegetic filmic elements on the site and become part of the interactive diegesis. In the case of *Body, Home, World* the digital *mandala* is not simply an attractive design interface; it visually conveys the history, universality, humanistic essence, and purpose of the story. Borrowing from the Tibetan sand *mandala's* ritualistic role as a transformative and healing practice, the digital *mandala* doubles as a visual story interface *and* as a space that invites introspection through narrative empathy. In viewing stories that represent the journeys of LGBTQ+

individuals and their family members, the user is invited to journey with the participants. These journeys provide the possibility of transformative reflection among those who may be struggling in isolation and affirm their identity through visible representations.

In addition, i-docs can circumvent one of the primary dilemmas that confront traditional documentary storytelling – the compulsion toward a story arc that may require the juxtaposition of multiple characters and competing identities. Often such a dialectical montage has the net effect of neutralizing or posing a false equivalence of viewpoints. In *Body, Home, World* it was important to me to be able to center the viewpoint of queer-identifying participants and to trace their unique journey as *separate* from that of their family or loved ones. I accomplished this by using branching narratives which allow the viewer/user to trace their journeys individually through unique pathways. Offering the user an interactive choice to select from among the various unique journeys portrayed on the site preserved the centrality of these experiences.

TRM: I loved the story of the gay Indian wedding intentionally designed to be both a traditional Indian wedding and a space of activism. From your perspective, what are the project's main themes and objectives?

AK: *Body, Home, World* was created to promote cohesion, to change familial and community attitudes among South Asian-Americans regarding their LGBTQ+ identifying members, and to share visible queer narratives among members of the South Asian diaspora. It is a recognition that in many immigrant communities of color, the family dialogue on sexual and gender identities is fraught with tension and risk, and that the spaces for safe inquiry, consultation, and advocacy are few and far between. The narratives on the site are offered with the hope that they will help create a sense of shared experience through an empathic "stepping-in-the-shoes," and aid in the shaping of a community that is inclusive and respectful of its internal diversity.

As a cis heterosexual brown male who had worked on films about bias crime and mental health stigma among immigrant South Asians, I was relatively less connected to queer brown spaces. Back in 2010, I read about an incident at Rutgers University that resulted in the tragic suicide of a gay student Tyler Clementi. Tyler's suicide was triggered by a betrayal of trust by his South Asian roommate Dharun Ravi. A lot was said in the courts about Dharun's complicity and lack of respect for the gay community. For me this wasn't just about Dharun. It made me think about all the young South Asians who may be growing up in homes where LGBTQ+ issues were never brought up or were diminished or erased when encountered. At the time, my son was 10 years old, and even though ours was a progressive academic household, we weren't discussing gay rights in the context of the South Asian or Indian community. Families are an essential part of the South Asian-American diaspora. As a parent and as a filmmaker, it was clear that the path to bringing LGBTQ+-rights in a visible way to our living rooms had to start with families like ours.

As immigrants from a post-colonial society, South Asians came to this country with deep disruptions and distortions in their understanding of gender and sexual diversity. Colonial-era anti-sodomy laws had succeeded in erasing representations of sexuality and gender fluidity in our art, mythology, sculpture, and public discourse, replacing it with a rigid hetero-patriarchal framework of the "normal." Not to say that there weren't already fertile grounds for such a framework among many sections of Indian society. Second, as immigrants who came into this country cherry-picked by a narrowly permissive immigration act in the 1960s, we were defined largely by our status as a successful, professionalized model minority. If your self-perception cages you into performing that identity, any suggestion of deviation from this norm – whether to do with mental health, sexual, or gender diversity, or as we are increasingly seeing, caste hierarchies – can be seen as diminishing that identity and is responded to with denial or erasure. Finally, as immigrants we live in a media environment which for the last 50-odd years has seen very little representation of people of color. It is only now – and largely due to the streaming revolution – that media representations of Black and brown people are slowly becoming more available. In such an environment it is even harder to imagine, discuss, debate, reflect, and engage in difficult dialog – processes that all communities need to undergo as they evolve and experience generational changes.

By documenting visible intergenerational narratives and presenting them within a creative and innovative platform, my hope is to address the challenges mentioned earlier that confront the South Asian community.

TRM: What challenges did you experience while creating and building *Body, Home, World?*

AK: The challenges were threefold: creative, financial, and organizational. Creatively I had to unlearn old ways of storytelling, planning, and execution that were designed for linear documentaries. It wasn't easy to find places where a mid-career academic could learn more about the processes by which i-docs are planned and created. I eventually found an amazing initiative in Europe called !F Lab (Interactive Factuals Lab) which proved to be a great fit. Run by Sandra Gaudenzi, co-editor of *i-docs: The Evolving Practices of Interactive Documentary*,[4] and an academic with an impressive practice-based research in i-docs, !F Lab provided incubation and proto-typing workshops for creatives who had a work-in-progress project. Over a period of two 5-day workshops, I was able to ideate and prototype the first iteration of *Body, Home, World*. It would undergo two major redesigns over the next 3 years before the current version emerged.

During the fundraising phase, I realized that a majority of grant funding is directed at broadcast or festival-ready works. If the funding was for emerging media projects, they were expected to be VR/AR projects. I am a strong proponent of webdocs or i-docs, and I feel that in a relatively short span of the last 15 years, i-docs have matured greatly with improvements in compression, HTML5, and innovative APIs like WebGL. However, much of the emerging media economics has tended to favor device-dependent, narrow-access, and expensive technologies such as VR/AR. Much of the early work on *Body, Home, World* was accomplished through small research grants from Hofstra University's Lawrence Herbert School of Communication and the Provost's LGBTQ+ Research grant. The final impetus came through a small grant from the Department of State for Alumna of the Fulbright program.

The final organizational challenge was putting together a team comprising a graphic designer, creative technologist, and sound designer. Visual design for i-docs is a balancing act, serving the aesthetic, functional, and storytelling functions all at once. I was lucky to assemble a team that understood these priorities and worked supportively with each other. Without doubt, the most radical creative breakthrough happened when I met Ali Tan Ucer, the Creative Director/ Technologist of the WebGL design that *Body, Home, World* is currently presented in. This key relationship between documentarian and visual coder is central to all i-docs. I was fortunate to have a collaborator who could take my vision and give it the interactive lift that made it into a compelling work, blending design, coding, and storytelling.

TRM: How can digital participatory techniques – such as those developed in *Body, Home, World* – expand LGBTQ+ oral histories?

AK: *Body, Home, World* is an effort to bring a relational dimension to queer stories – a dimension that emphasizes the participation of allies. These may include families, friends, advocates, and researchers – all essential transmitters and sharers of an expanded and inclusive vision of gender and sexual diversity seen in these stories. The platform builds on the work of PV (participatory video) experts who reliably showed the value of including stakeholders in the process of creating community narratives. What is new about the way it conceptualizes "participation" is that it extends it into funding and distribution. Using a combination of social media networks and organizational hubs with queer-led or ally organizations at the center, the project anticipates a community-resourced and community-led dissemination of these stories.

While the first phase of *Body, Home, World* consists of stories produced and curated by the filmmaker (me) working in close concert with participants who were invested in creating a multivocal platform, the subsequent expansion of the platform will build on the community that has formed around this platform. Inspired by the stories of those who are currently featured, queer voices from the subcontinent and its diaspora will lead the second wave of storytelling on the platform in the form of contributed narratives. This model of shared creation, distribution, and use of community stories in an online networked world has the advantage of limitless expansion as a living history platform for the digital diaspora. As a project that promotes reconciliation, healing, and inclusivity, this model could potentially be used in the context of queer storytelling in any community

TRM: To what extent do i-docs offer access to the lives of others, particularly South Asian-American LGBTQ+ people. What are the benefits and the limits?

AK: Due to the fluid distribution methodology and the participatory and networked modes of contributing and sharing, the i-doc platform offers an alternative to the highly gate-kept mainstream media networks. South Asian-American representation in the media is relatively scant and of recent vintage. The prospect of widely seen queer narratives from this community is nowhere on the horizon. Queer "influencers" and social media personalities have successfully built a following of hundreds of thousands of LGBTQ+-identifying South Asians in alternative social spaces. These spaces are cherished by POC[5] queer communities for what they offer − a safe and visible platform for them to share, view, and celebrate visible queer experience. The real value of i-docs is in bringing these narratives to parts of the diaspora that would otherwise not have encountered them for reasons stated earlier.

I-docs continue to face the challenge of limited or "light" engagement with video/film content which is symptomatic of online browsing behavior. The intergenerational audience profile of *Body, Home, World* ranges widely in technical competencies. Many in this community of users may face difficulties negotiating the innovative interface of i-docs. In terms of familiarity, i-docs are relatively unknown among audiences outside of the usually vested communities of creators and users. This increases the likelihood of (especially) older immigrants being excluded from participation. The problems are not insurmountable. For *Body, Home, World* I am working to create a simpler, low-graphics, low-bandwidth version that can allow easier access to internet users who are more accustomed to reading text and use limited mouse or touch controls.

## Notes

1. See: http://bodyhomeworld.com/.
2. Gene Youngblood, *Expanded Cinema* (New York: Dutton, 1970).
3. See: Katerina Cizek, director, *Highrise* (Montreal: National Film Board of Canada, ongoing), Highrise.nfb.ca.
4. Judith Aston, Sandra Gaudenzi, and Mandy Rose, eds., *I-Docs: The Evolving Practices of Interactive Documentary* (New York: Wildflower Press, 2017).
5. People of color.

# 4

# DOCUMENTARY IMPACT

## A Framework for Analyzing Engagement Strategies Used in I-docs

*Carles Sora-Domenjó and Anandana Kapur*

### The World of I-docs

With our lives increasingly being defined by virtual play and engagement, the choice of web-based i-docs (referred herein as i-docs) as the focus of our discussion evolved organically. To this we bring a few threads – (i) There is today an established body of work on interactive documentaries[1] that is concerned with understanding the choice structures that shape digital documentary experiences. (ii) Impact in i-docs, unlike other genres of documentaries, is a vector of discussion and interest. But its digital nature, production contexts, as well as distribution and exhibition platforms can be markedly different. Discussions on impact frameworks are also relevant to how we think about i-docs and their ability to facilitate autonomy, mobility, and expression. (iii) Not all i-docs may be advocacy focused but the range of outreach/distribution models can provide opportunities to identify best practices/interventions for makers.

We think of i-docs and the study of impact as an exploration of how creative and platform-based choices influence social participation. To do so, we shall first re-introduce i-docs as sites of community engagement, followed by a discussion of the implications of "decolonizing" this documentary genre. A review of existing approaches to impact and impact design shall highlight how discourse on web-based documentaries rubs shoulders with profit-based metrics. In this light, we shall propose a framework that prioritizes participation over metrics.

The past decade has seen the emergence of a sub-genre of documentary that straddles documentary practice, multimedia, and interaction design.[2] Among these, web-based i-docs host interactive nonfiction on the internet made accessible via a digital interface. I-docs often crowdsource content and participation even though they can also be highly designed and controlled environments. The

DOI: 10.4324/9781003174509-5

former type requires users to interact with the content through varying degrees of digital performativity and gamification. Gestures such as switching on audio/ video, answering prompts, voting for outcomes, navigating digital spaces, etc. are invoked to seek participation and/or collaboration of viewing publics and communities. Experimental and traditional approaches intertwine in i-docs and narrative structures are often discarded for more fragmented experiences. Cross-platform and paratextual features allow i-docs to invite audiences to play with and perhaps even evolve the content.

Given their multilinear, poly-vocal aesthetic,[3] i-docs are able to "destabilize quests for 'totalizing meaning; by emphasizing interactivity, contestation and multiplicities of meanings,' especially with regard to controversial issues."[4] I-docs exhibit diverse research protocols, technological innovation, and strategies for circulation/engagement that combine learning from traditional documentary with new media frameworks. As platforms for discussion, and archives of subaltern and minority views, they invite analyses of identities that are rehearsed in public life by intervening and disrupting hierarchies of knowledge [and ways of knowing] by encouraging discovery through juxtaposition and relativization. I-docs create affective impact by renegotiating the rules of interaction between distanced cultures and communities. By bracketing them as users within its own ideological matrix, an i-doc then functions as evidence (or the possibility) of alternate social and cultural orders. To understand their impact, therefore, it becomes imperative to examine more closely how they conceive of the user:

> Is user content conceived of as an addition to the documentary database or are users given scope to modify the structure of the documentary? To what extent are contributions foregrounded or, alternatively, situated in a separate space away from the "real" documentary content? In other words, what is the relationship between user contributions and the voice of the webdoc?[5]

## Decolonizing Documentary Interventions

The line of thinking discussed earlier also anticipates another vital question – Is the labor of the user being appropriated? Alessandro Gandini suggests that there are extant three critical categories concerning digital infrastructure in contemporary discourse – i. "audience labor" that considers users passive commodities, ii. "digital labor" where users are unpaid content producers, and iii. "platform labor" where users partake of a digital gig economy as paid workers.[6] These can also be applied to the digital ecology that i-docs operate in. Users can have largely passive, personally involved, or incentivized engagement with the i-doc across stages of its production and reception. These degrees of participation can be outcomes of choice or deliberate design and persuasion. So, while the "democratic potential" of an i-doc lies in its capacity to draw upon "vernacular literacies – skills and competencies . . . built up through everyday experience, especially experience as a mass media consumer,"[7] it is important to understand the (in)visible tensions behind creating and sustaining web-based documentaries. Calibrating whether working with(in) communities translates to agency in co-authoring the final product or has lapsed into appropriation of their labor is also aimed at identifying and encouraging creative strategies which redistribute power between communities and makers.

The manner and stage at which the category "community" is invoked is also extremely significant. Communities can be "physical, political, social, psychological, historical, linguistic, economic, cultural, and spiritual spaces."[8] In colonized cultures, these communities sometimes arise from "deliberate policies" that ghettoize and commit people to the margins where they are physically and culturally constrained and kept "out of sight."[9] The power and impact of being part of a digital community can then be manifold. Not only does the invitation to participate invoke the possibility of creating community but it also makes the possibility of organizing around common and historically neglected concerns tangible. Impact then also becomes a reflection of the social mobility that communities might acquire. In this regard, framing who is or can be part of a community is critical because it has a direct causal effect on the terms of co-creation (upskilling/anonymity/consent and consensus building), platforms (hybrid/low-fi/high-tech), and the format of the creative artifact (public facing/policy-maker facing/conditional or open access). The category "community" may also be an impact goal itself when working with fragmented narratives and dispersed individuals or family's dependence in creating demands for justice and access.

I-docs may also be considered successful as critical interventions if their makers are able to negotiate the regulatory and commercialized aspects of the internet. Even as we are aware that capitalist metrics of impact such as numbers of likes, shares, and hits reveal nothing about the quality or depth of engagement, these data points are used repeatedly to direct/misdirect attention. They have acquired normative status and i-doc makers tread a tricky terrain when they have to adopt or entirely reject this worldview. Temporality, noise, and disruptions can thus overwhelm more sustained, patient, and empathetic connections. "Participation and content creation do not just happen organically. Understanding how to prompt engagement beyond the 'Like' button is a central concern of the digital producers who build i-docs and webdocs."[10] David Dufresne, maker of the i-doc *Fort McMoney*, shares,

> There are no rules. And certainly, no targets! The common base for viewers of interactive works is not age, culture, or lifestyle. It's curiosity and time, two rarities in today's world. The famous 1% rule states that 80% of Internet users only view content, 19% have very little involvement and 1% are very active. All our work and much of our time go to that . . . 1%! That's both the craziness and beauty of the genre.[11]

In all this, the implications of digital inequity must not be left out of discourse on the scope and impact of i-docs. Those operating on the margins of societal, economic, and now digital frontiers may not even have the tools or literacy to be considered. Even as the increasing ubiquity of smartphones has enabled access to the internet in ways that would have been difficult to predict at the turn of the century, the degrees of engagement and participation are varied and uneven. There exists acute time-poverty divides (women, underserved classes, underdeveloped economies) as well lack of ownership/access to devices. Disparities in people's information and communications technologies abilities and uses augment social inequalities rather than alleviate them.[12] Consequently, "even after people gain access to the internet and cross the so-called digital divide, differences will remain in how they use the medium, namely, how skilled they are at it, how free they are to use it in different situations and toward what purposes they put it."[13] Additionally, sociopolitical realities such as internet shutdowns and state-imposed sanctions jeopardize the architecture within which an i-doc may strategically or unwittingly be situated. "The political horizon for decolonization thus remains quite open. Decolonization constitutes a process where communities and individuals experiment with and evaluate different strategies for relating to the state and global market."[14]

The internet operates in a real-time cycle of non-ending content. Commercialized and regulated aspects of the internet should be considered while considering impact and using private services as documentary platforms for sharing and unfolding partially or totally the content of an i-doc. Since social media networks are focused on connecting users only momentarily by pushing a model of perpetual-now communication,[15] we can assert that this model does not fit coherently with digital media productions (like i-docs) aiming to facilitate long-term horizons for social good, advocating for real-world change, or creating deep relations within the members of a community. Social debates fostering long discussions, in fact, collapse due to the micro-dynamics of social networks.

The always-on dynamic of social platforms impedes more in-depth debate, which means the connections and ties between people and users of the i-doc that emerge at a particular moment in time (especially within social debates) tend to quickly disappear. Although they are highly effective at helping cover particular actions, social networks may not be the best tools for complex discourses. "In social media-dominated online environments, processes of togetherness are always ephemeral, always already on the point of giving way to the next set of trending topics and related sentiments."[16]

## Decoding Impact

Impact is defined variously as "an experience (either real or perceived)"[17] or "declared intention or purpose."[18] Despite the myriad definitions available to a practitioner/researcher, it is challenging to separate real-world outcomes (usually mapped post a release) and the strategies used in (co)creating the artifact. This is because creative choices of i-doc makers often encompass thoughtful engagement, informed consent, knowledge-sharing, and data-gathering (anecdotes/evidence). Each of these processes shapes both the documentary maker and the community whose life experiences are being archived or narrated. Several practice-based researchers, in fact, document the profoundness of these processes for their craft.[19] Self-awareness for the filmmaker, however, does not always address anxieties about how their work may be received or understood. It is also not necessary that this awareness shall translate to a schema or directions for users to audit their experience of interacting with the artifact.

When practice-based research is regarded as "an original investigation undertaken in order to gain new knowledge, partly by means of practice and the outcomes of that practice,"[20] then evaluating the outcome of the practice of making an i-doc also merits consideration. This aspect of the practice would include sharing the means of creation with a community and the experiences encompassed during this process, participatory design (such as workshops and interviews), knowledge transfers to/from participants, sharing power (including right to veto), and the final audiovisual outcomes. In that regard, the impact of the i-doc should also consider the documentation of the practice process on itself.

The idea of impact also has origins in the principles of accountability and transparency. It helps map, understand, share, and therefore, improve upon existing approaches. If practice-based research can be considered a critical interrogation in order to develop one's practice through the making of an artifact, then impact is a critical interrogation of the creative artifact in the social world. Even as this may be read as a tendency to return to knowledge as artifact, seeking to study impact does nuance and expand the meanings and relationships associated with a work. Posteriori working by way of analyzing impact can enable the documentary maker to leave the observer's "ivory tower . . . by a strange road of initiation, to the heart of knowledge itself."[21] This exercise could be undertaken by the makers themselves or by stakeholders chosen by the community. So, we persist with the endeavor of defining impact because "to know the world better with art, we need definitions."[22]

## Impact Design Conversations

Offline too, in immersive environments, the question of impact remains topmost. In their study on the relationship between "technological platforms" and "viewer response to VR," the Media Impact Lab (Norman Lear Center, USC Annenberg) found that, "the novelty of the medium creates incentives to explore the space rather than absorb information, and provides enormous potential for distraction from complex narratives or information-dense sequences."[23]

Marcus and Kara suggest that i-docs might be assessed in terms of "experience design,"[24] that is, how the documentary is perceived and consumed in terms of functionality, aesthetics as well as resulting physical and emotional affective responses. Impact would then be defined as a measure of "the user experience in every aspect of a given work (cinematic, game, participatory, creative) and in the cohesion and integrity of the whole."[25] This approach enables one to challenge/transcend the metrics of "number of visitors" because the amount of time spent engaging with and exploring an open site is variable and subjective. With i-docs being created with underlying "metaphors," it may be easy for users to work out the creative message at an early stage. It is only if they have an informational need is the exploration sustained. Impact merits reformulation as a longer-term effect because "just the availability of resources is not enough; the users should also be able to feel that they are able to use these resources."[26]

When defined as an "intentional change creation process,"[27] impact design can begin as a structured path leading to an "ideal." In praxis, this may involve creating your own "theory of change,"[28] that is, a progressive action map where iterative testing of your hypothesis with one set of stakeholders informs subsequent inter/co-dependent steps and so on. Context would shape any theory of change; and, hence, each articulation would vary with each maker. "Theories of change come in all shapes and sizes. We like to think of them as game boards that represent the moves you must make to win."[29] Here impact is an interplay of choice of media/format (like creating an i-doc) and methods of deployment that are able to address a problem (social/political change) as an aggregation. Impact design is then an iterative evaluation of micro-decisions such that result course corrections lead to macro-level gains.

## Impact Production Conversations

"The Impact Field Guide and Toolkit" of the Doc Society classifies documentary impact as both "top-down" and "bottom-up."[30] The former is considered a policy or legislative level shake-up, and the latter is regarded as being able to influence practical realities like relationships, behaviors, and norms. The guide further elaborates the idea of impact as a dynamic of "changing minds, changing behaviors, building communities, changing structure."[31] Here, the framework for impact is a "total ecosystem approach" where the documentary maker and their work is positioned as a subset of existing advocates such as legislators, activists, non-for-profits, communities, funders, allies in mainstream media, and academia. Then mapping impact necessarily becomes a multi-stakeholder exercise that potentially yields insights about gaps and further interventions, including ideas for new documentaries.

The guide also references revenue generation as an important factor in evaluating impact. Impact models are therefore also about economic viability.

> To be blunt, for the creators of i-docs and transmedia documentaries, the goal of community-building is often directed simultaneously towards activism and revenue generation, as traditional business models often no longer

apply. Both goals exist as intertwined, necessary components in what contributes to success. As such, the determination as to where power and agency ultimately reside, with the documentary maker, audiences and/or subjects of a given documentary project remains unstable.[32]

Written from an investor's point of view, The Fledgling Fund's Impact Report suggests that impact culminates in "action and collaboration."[33] Impact design is presented as shifting gears from revenue-oriented film promotion to social change via outreach and community engagement.

The metrics of evaluation hinge not just on eyeballs but being able to estimate "how many people better understand the issue because the film was made."[34] The report further nuances its approach to impact by underlining that reaching out to diverse audiences is critical to energizing public debate. This is significant because it signals that the social position of the maker(s) should not determine or limit the outreach. The case for multiplicity of points of view is again reiterated when the question of metric arises.

> We believe it's important to look at a variety of data sources, such as survey results, case studies and anecdotal data that when taken together can provide a nuanced picture of a project's impact. In addition to different data sources . . . tracking can be done through a film's website where people can report the impact the film has had on their own lives and, in turn, the impact they are making on their community.[35]

Impact, however, can be both positive and negative. The internet is a dynamic and disruptive space. Impact design/strategies should therefore also consider contingencies, technology obsolescence, and potential harms to users, protagonists, or themselves. These harms could include surveillance, campaigns to discredit, intimidation, loss of privacy/over-exposure, cyberbullying, and even incarceration. It is inevitable that as i-docs incorporate real-time content/make dynamic changes to the experience like other internet-based media, mimicking of larger internet behaviors and norms will also kick in.

## Impact-as-a-Phased-Process: A Proposal

Change is never accepted uniformly. Various segments of a population will either embrace or adopt with delays, accept with evidence, or resist till it is normative behavior. Others are likely to outrightly reject a new idea/proposal for change including actively discouraging it. Yet others may appropriate and reshape it. Interest, intent, and conviction are abstract and subjective terms that guide such choices and should be studied longitudinally. Opinion leaders who operate offline offer substantive counterweight to digital metrics of impact, even those steered by artificial intelligence. In fact, algorithmic and digital metrics may prove to be unreliable given that they can be confounded by unanticipated changes.

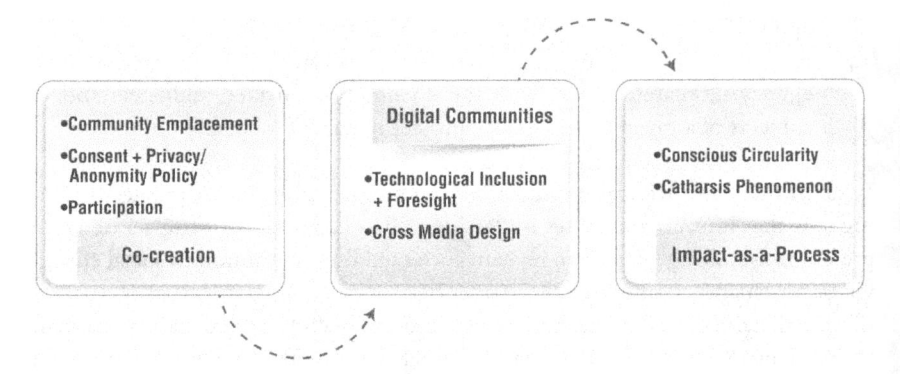

**FIGURE 4.1** Framework for understanding and analyzing impact and engagement in i-docs.

*Source:* Figure by the authors

"Machine-learning models are . . . also fragile; they perform badly when input data differs too much from the data they were trained on."[36] So, we need a model of metrics that is grounded in deeper attention to the anecdotal, the real/physical/offline implications, and relations generated with the i-doc experience.

We believe that impact is also hard to replicate per se because the experiential possibilities of i-docs are many. A one-size-fits-all approach with conventional, quantitative metrics is unable to account for "more subtle dimensions of social change – like long-term impacts of a participatory media making process rather than the final media product – as well as a variety of hard-to-measure institutional impacts, such as innovations in artistic forms or organizational process."[37]

As a contribution to this discussion, we propose a rubric, if not a model, to assess the impact that i-docs might have on the communities and audiences that they seek to engage (see Figure 4.1). The approach places, "plurality of voices and intertextual references" above "celebratory or affirmatory reproduction."[38] The relevance of such a rubric lies in being able to identify and document best practices at the modular level such that they can be replicated, studied, or evolved depending on the context of another artistic work.

While this is an open framework for future work, it may also be applied to the study of existing i-docs and/or ongoing impact plans. This framework is also inspired and oriented by our own professional experiences as documentary makers and interactive designers. We believe there are seven qualitative but essential aspects that should be considered while planning impact.

## Co-Creation

The current era of networked digital media – characterized by a paradigm of shared authorship and distribution of content (creator(s) + user(s)) – has led to a renewed interest in co-creation. In comparison to traditional documentaries, i-docs have the comparative advantage of engaging with communities longer-term and across time and place.

> Co-creation is a very broad term that implies a thoughtful process, which involves a collaboration with the intent to make quality media with partners instead of just about them, to make media as a media-maker together with people that aren't media-makers: citizen, academics, professionals, technologists, organizations.[39]

In the i-doc *Hollow* (2013), directed by Elaine McMillion and designed by Jeff Soyk, the co-creation process centered on continuous community consultations (offline + online). The webdoc itself became a vehicle of the voices, and representational aspirations of a community wanting to reinvent itself.[40]

Realizing co-creation in letter and spirit can scaffold impact if we unpack the prefix "co" at the outset – Do we create with people or for people?[41] And who are these people – Makers? Audiences/Users? Communities? Protagonists?

> In this regard, it is essential to bear in mind how co-creation is managed in terms of establishing the rules of participation, the space for negotiation, and the ownership of the results. Such issues are so crucial that the success or failure of co-creation initiatives depend on a process of negotiation between both parts in a sense that "one must look at the polarities of power and control that determine the context in which the co-creative processes take place."[42]

Who has the authority to initiate and negotiate the process of co-creation? Do co-creators need digital media literacy and technological resources in order to lead a co-creation practice? Who will be the primary mobilizer of this process? What steps can we take to translate the concept and intention to online and hybrid interactive audiovisual productions? How do we archive and protect the voices that have aggregated from digital disruptions (i.e., software/hardware discontinuance)?

## *Community Emplacement*

The modes of involving communities in the design, strategy, and implementation of a documentary are increasingly being studied through the prism of co-creation. The paradigm of value generation through collaborative and inclusive practices has also led to conversations about how a documentary intervention can be sustained beyond a fleeting or immediate encounter. For instance, Rachel Falcome and Michael Premo's *Sandy Storyline* (2013) has been encouraging/inviting stories of the aftermath of hurricane Sandy for the past 8 years.[43]

Even as co-creation is complex and dynamic and might vary with context, it is universally agreed that the terms of engagement and the ability to critique or disagree with the process should be available at all times. Further, it should be reinforced at all times that the community is not only being represented but also is fashioning its own self-image through such processes. Feedback on whether this goal is being achieved would be a valuable cornerstone in the journey toward impact.

## Participation

Our idea of participation is in direct resonance with Henry Jenkins' statement:

> I object to calling it participation if the people involved have no sense of themselves as belonging to something bigger than the individual. For me, participation starts at that moment when we see ourselves as part of a group that is seeking to achieve some shared goals through collective effort.[44]

The practical realization of "belonging to something bigger than the individual" is crucial for the development of impactful conversations. This can be tested through stakeholder interviews, focus-group discussions, and reassessment of goals based on community-level feedback. This allows the impact plan/design to accommodate unanticipated real-world events or critical pushback.

So, if we understand participation as a way to engage and create links and relationships among "the voices" of a community,[45] the project may begin by inviting community members to consider participation by reflecting on whether and how the processes of a collaborative media work might be useful or even transformative for them. Participation shall be addressed not only in final stages of the project, that is, in terms of final users or User-Generated Content, but also from the perspective of the voices that are amplified through the co-creative process and how their future interactive contributions will redistribute the power to shape narratives and outcomes. Co-creative practices may even contribute to creating tangible/longer-term/consistent grassroots relations through the process of development of the project and its potential use as a tool for discussion or political action within a community.

## Consent + Privacy/Anonymity Policy

Informed consent acquires more complex dimensions when virality enters the picture. Not only are points of origin lost very quickly but also creators may have little-to-no control on the material being reappropriated or even misappropriated. Decontextualized readings and fabrications lend to the danger of exacerbating existing fault lines in society and culture.

> Furthermore, there is also an ongoing debate about whether the internet and social media offer any real anonymity, as users are increasingly mapped,

tracked, and watched by governments, as well as corporations, who use the data for purposes ranging from surveillance to marketing.[46]

When working with vulnerable groups (children, survivors of violence, witnesses/whistleblowers, etc.), this becomes especially critical because the very palpable risk of retraumatization via online harassment can only be addressed if impact includes components such as continual/sustained privacy/anonymity, opportunities for withdrawing in case of unanticipated potential risks, and updates as separate phases of creation and engagement are achieved.

An example of how this worked in practice can be found in advocacy targets and impact-distribution strategy of Chaka Studio's *The Quipu Project* (2015).[47] Even as collective memory was used to initiate a call for justice, participants' anonymity was ensured by using a voice-based interactive platform. Another strategy could be a formal ethical review board comprising community members and/ or academics, fellow creative practitioners, and professionals like psychologists/ counselors may also be useful. As opposed to an Institutional Review Board, this could be structured as a Community Review Board.

## *Digital Communities*

The ethos of a community, namely, a space to share and talk, should be the real goal of an i-doc's design, but what is a digital community? It is a place where users can interact, build consensus, have conversations, share personal facts, and build trust with each other. For that purpose, a participative engagement strategy is key. Practices of participation and strategies to stimulate/build conversation foster long-term dialogues by promoting more in-depth interaction. This can generate and sustain interest/collectivization/empathy around specific social issues over a considerably longer timeframe than mainstream media. For example, user engagement strategies were deployed to build a base of 4.5 million plus direct and indirect users for *Question Bridge: Black Males* (2012).[48] The transmedia project comprises an i-doc, mobile app, multi- and single-channel installation, and a curriculum.

The question to answer when designing impact, however, is "whether such instances of solidarity or togetherness can eventually translate into more durable networks and communities that provide the basis for political contestation in the long run."[49] Only then would being part of an i-doc community help create more pockets of awareness, collectivization, and hopefully change. When an impact plan conceives of an i-doc as a "living archive," it expands the time frame by enabling multiple visits, across time zones and geographies, and can highlight how the issue might have evolved.[50] So, even if the average time spent on an i-doc may be a few minutes, the overall consumption figures and cumulative impact might be substantial. Dialogue can continue at any time and is as such, not hijacked by the perpetual-now dynamics of social networks or the acceleration of social life.[51]

## *Technological Inclusion, Preservation, and Foresight*

In *VozMob*, Amanda Garcés and Sasha Constanza-Chock worked with low-wage immigrant workers in the United States. While it was active (2008–2013), the project achieved both social impact and technological milestones.[52] As mentioned earlier, given that technology is rendered obsolete with increasing frequency, it is necessary that makers invest in forms of archiving that are not just online but also have real-world counterparts. As *Highrise* director Katerina Cizek asks:

> What kind of futures and challenges do creators see for their work? And how can we assure that these and other projects remain accessible in the forms that their makers intended?[53]

She argues that participation can be inbuilt in a creative process while also reflecting on questions of technology obsolescence when developing an impact plan. It is possible that archiving may be vital to ensuring future participation in some cases. Often, conceptualizing art interventions entails that makers train and help community members learn how to use digital tools and online platforms as well. Then, others use available, low-cost technologies. What mainstream media refuses to cover can thus be archived, shared, and celebrated.

This counterbalancing through collectively written history bodes well for impact. Creating strategies online or offline to preserve the outcomes of the conversations in its different formats is crucial and necessary. Often new technologies are designed "according to the logic of the matrix of domination, whereby designers, imagined users, values, affordances, ownership, governance, and other aspects of design are all set up to systematically reproduce white supremacist capitalist heteropatriarchy, both in process and outcome."[54] This is where low-cost mobile phones, push internet strategies to accommodate low-bandwidth, free open-source software, and an active resistance to power structures embedded in technology use can help direct impact design to facilitate inclusion, expression, and ownership. Long-term engagement and sustained crafting of alternate histories can be better ensured by meeting the communities where they are on the techno-social axis, especially when they are not digital natives.

## *Cross-Media Design*

It is relevant for i-doc makers to acknowledge that real-world events and transmedia avatars are what make i-docs more impactful. In some cases, i-docs may themselves represent impact for projects that have started offline (see the *Question Bridge* project). Cross-media approaches thus help consolidate audiences, diversify the range and appeal of the message, and help counter fragmentation of community attention and engagement. Transmediality also enables documentary projects to function as social enterprises,[55] wherein monetization benefits from commercial platforms can be redirected toward socioeconomic alleviation. Transmedia strategies are positive tools to provide catalysts for audience activism.[56]

Director Marissa Jahn offers a deliberative approach to audience engagement using cross-media.[57] Drawing upon her earlier cross-media work *Nanny Van* (2012) that sought to sensitize and collectivize domestic workers about their rights and legal remedies, her follow-up project *Careforce* (2018)[58] comprises a web series (travelogue), vehicles converted to mobile studios, dance workshops, a mobile app, and print media. An architectural intervention named *CareHaus* (2020)[59] that explores co-housing and caregiving for labor is also underway.

A cross-media story allows participants to choose the medium (web, social media, video platform, etc.) that they individually find more appealing and/or appropriate for contributing to the media event/experience/story. Focusing on the groups of people that want to participate by using suitable platforms enables the project to scale organically. Such community-centered participation is first ignited by establishing a participatory relationship between the platform creator and "local voices";[60] and second, by facilitating a gradual progression from awareness of the opportunity toward advocacy of participation, and eventually a call to action. In this regard, cross-media design can be used widely in impact plans to achieve plurality of forms of participation.[61] After all, "stories that are told together are stronger."[62]

## Outcomes of the Impact-as-a-Process Framework

I-docs have the potential to enable individuals and communities to reflect on events and share their memories. Witnessing and testifying about historical, environmental, and political reality can have a cathartic effect for those whose lives have been institutionally and systemically silenced. Since several documentaries work with the political and artistic intent of denying catharsis and therefore provoking action, we prefer the term *catharsis phenomenon*. This is in recognition of the fact that co-creation and collaboration allow space for dissent and disagreement in a manner that other sociocultural spaces may not. So, even if the artifact produces discontent, the methods are likely to provide an active engagement with events past that can suggest opportunities for justice and equity.

To ensure that an i-doc remains a site for "ideological-democratic struggle," involving communities through every stage of the project including refinement post-release is imperative (see Figure 4.2). In this manner, communities are also contributors to the trajectory and outcome of i-docs. By sharing the moderation and enabling communities to come together, i-docs can also acquire greater authenticity and longevity.

While the kind of impact model may vary depending on the nature and goals of an i-doc (or any other documentary), tracking impact by digital metrics is unlikely to be reversed. It is only by reinforcing the importance of being immersed in communities that i-docs can serve as tools that alleviate "voice poverty"[63] and

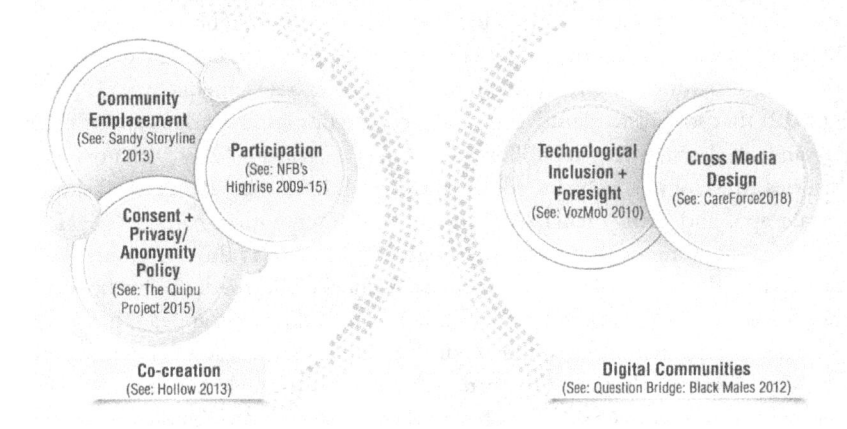

**FIGURE 4.2**    Outcomes of impact-as-a-phased-process. A framework for understanding and analyzing impact and engagement in i-docs.

*Source:* Figure by the authors

enable negotiation of identity and rights. We must encourage processes and outcomes embedded in listening carefully and empathetically because, in the words
of Shamira Raphaëla and Tessa Boerman, our creative choices impact "the representation of the world, affecting the perception of humanity, including the framing of Others, for generations to come."[64]

## Notes

1. See: Kate Nash, "Modes of Interactivity: Analysing the Webdoc," *Media, Culture &
Society* 34, no. 2 (2012): 195–210, https://doi.org/10.1177/0163443711430758;
Siobhan O'Flynn, "Documentary's Metamorphic Form: Webdoc, Interactive, Trans-
media, Participatory and Beyond," *Studies in Documentary Film* 6, no. 2 (2012):
141–57, https://doi.org/10.1386/sdf.6.2.141_1; Sandra Gaudenzi, "The Living
Documentary: From Representing Reality to Co-creating Reality in Digital Interactive Documentary," PhD diss (Goldsmiths, University of London, 2013); Adrian
Miles, "Interactive Documentary and Affective Ecologies," in *New Documentary
Ecologies*, eds. Kate Nash, Catherine Summerhayes, and Craig Hight (London: Palgrave Macmillan, 2014), 67–82, https://doi.org/10.1057/9781137310491_5; Judith
Aston, Sandra Gaudenzi, and Mandy Rose, eds., *i-Docs: The Evolving Practices of Interactive Documentary* (New York: Wildflower Press, 2017).
2. Nash, "Modes of Interactivity," 197.
3. See: Judith Aston and Stefano Odorico, "The Poetics and Politics of Polyphony:
Towards a Research Method for Interactive Documentary," *Alphaville: Journal of Film
and Screen Media* 15 (2018): 63–69, www.alphavillejournal.com/Issue15.html.
4. Sharon Lin Tay and Dale Hudson, "Undisclosed Recipients," *Studies in Documentary
Film* 2, no. 1 (2008): 80, https://doi.org/10.1386/sdf.2.1.79_1.
5. Nash, "Modes of Interactivity," 200.

6. See: Alessandro Gandini, "Digital Labour: An Empty Signifier?" *Media, Culture & Society* 43, no. 2 (2021): 369–80.
7. Jean Burgess, "Hearing Ordinary Voices: Cultural Studies, Vernacular Creativity and Digital Storytelling," *Continuum* 20, no. 2 (2006): 209, https://doi.org/10.1080/10304310600641737.
8. See: Linda Tuhiwai Smith, *Decolonizing Methodologies: Research and Indigenous Peoples* (New York: Zed Books, 1999), 125–26.
9. Smith, *Decolonizing Methodologies*, 126.
10. Daniel Marcus and Selmin Kara, *Contemporary Documentary* (London: Routledge, 2016), 82.
11. See: David Dufresne, "David Dufresne on Fort McMoney: Challenges, Narrative and Budget," interview by Sandra Gaudenzi, i-Docs, accessed June 18, 2021, http://i-docs.org/fort-mcmoney-today-david-dufresne-tells-us-whole-story.
12. See: Alpana Srivastava and Tanu Tiwari, "Rural–Urban Divide: Digital Inequality," in *The Routledge Handbook of Exclusion, Inequality and Stigma in India*, eds. Alapna Srivastava and N. M. P Verma (Abington and New York: Routledge, 2020), 113–15.
13. Eszter Hargittai, "Minding the Digital Gap: Why Understanding Digital Inequality Matters," in *Media Perspectives for the 21st Century*, ed. Stylianos Papathanassopoulos (New York: Routledge, 2011), 231, https://doi.org/10.4324/9780203834077.
14. See: Freya Schiwy, *Indianizing Film: Decolonization, the Andes, and the Question of Technology* (New Brunswick: Rutgers University Press, 2009).
15. See: Carles Sora, "Expanding Temporal and Participative Digital Horizons Through Web Documentaries for Social Change," in *Temps et Temporalités du Web*, ed. Valérie Schafer (Nanterre: Presses de Paris Nanterre, Paris, 2018), doi:10.4000/books.pupo.6193.
16. Thomas Poell and José van Dijck, "Social Media and Activist Communication," in *Routledge Companion to Alternative and Community Media*, ed. Chris Atton (London: Routledge, 2015), 534.
17. Frank Vanclay, *Social Impact Assessment: Contributing Paper Prepared for Thematic Review V.2: Environmental and Social Assessment for Large Dams* (1999), 3, accessed June 21, 2021, www.dams.org.
18. Helen Chiappini, *Social Impact Funds* (Cham: Springer International Publishing, 2017), 2.
19. See: Marissa Jahan, "Civic Art Series: Marissa Moran Jahn," MIT CMS/W; Anandana Kapur, "Co-Creation as Talkback: Using the Collaborative and Interactive Docu-Forms to (Re)imagine the 'Rape-City,'" in *i-Docs: The Evolving Practices of Interactive Documentary*, eds. Judith Aston, Sandra Gaudenzi, and Mandy Rose (New York: Wildflower Press, 2017), 26–37; Fabiola Hana, "Software and Its Structuring of Interactive Documentary," in *Activist Interactive: iDocs from the Global South. Poetics and Politics of Documentary Symposium* (Brighton: The Attenborough Centre for Creative Arts, University of Sussex, 2017); Katerina Cizek, "The Art, Ethics and Technology of Documentary Co-creation: Visiting Artist Katerina Cizek," *Arts at MIT* (April 10, 2015), YouTube, www.youtube.com/watch?v=owL2hQGsS7E.
20. Linda Candy and Ernest Edmonds, "Practice-Based Research in the Creative Arts: Foundations and Futures from the Front Line," *Leonardo* 51, no. 1 (2018): 63, https://doi.org/10.1162/LEON_a_01471.
21. Jean Rouch, "The Camera and Man," 11, accessed September 24, 2021, www.der.org/jean-rouch/pdf/CameraandMan-JRouch.pdf.
22. Ross Gibson, "The Known World," *TEXT* 9, no. 2 Special Issue, Symposium: Creative and Practice-led Research: Current Status, Future Plans (October 2005), 4, www.textjournal.com.au/speciss/issue8/Gibson.pdf.
23. Beth Karlin, Hyun Tae (Calvin) Kim, Ruth Kelly, Johanna Blakley, Corinne Brenner, and Patricia Riley, "Does Medium Matter? Exploring the Role of Virtual

Reality in Journalism," *The Media Impact Project,* USC Annenberg Norman Lear Center (2018), 23, accessed September 24, 2021, www.mediaimpactproject.org/uploads/5/1/2/7/5127770/frontlinevrreport_final.pdf.

24. Marcus and Kara, *Contemporary Documentary,* 73.
25. Marcus and Kara, *Contemporary Documentary.*
26. Sunetra Sen Narayan and Shalini Narayanan, *India Connected: Mapping the Impact of New Media* (New Delhi: SAGE Publications India Pvt. Ltd., 2016), 88–89.
27. Mary Joyce, "Impact Design: Stories of Surveillance Session," MIT Open Documentary Lab, YouTube video (September 27, 2018), www.youtube.com/watch?v=Bjl5Q-Xy4a0.
28. Harmony Labs, "Impact Design in VR: A Toolkit for Media Makers & Mission Driven Organizations," 14, accessed June 20, 2021, www.harmonylabs.org.
29. Harmony Labs, Impact Design in VR.
30. Doc Society, "The Impact Field Guide and Toolkit," accessed June 14, 2021, https://impactguide.org.
31. Doc Society, "The Impact Field Guide and Toolkit."
32. Sean Peter Flynn, "Evaluating Interactive Documentaries: Audience, Impact, and Innovation," M.S. Thesis (Massachusetts Institute of Technology, 2013), 152.
33. Diana Barrett and Sheila Leddy, "Assessing Creative Media's Social Impact," *The Fledgling Fund* (2008): 16, https://thefledglingfund.org/wp-content/uploads/2015/10/Impact-Paper.pdf.
34. Barrett and Leddy, "Assessing Creative Media's Social Impact," 16.
35. Barrett and Leddy, "Assessing Creative Media's Social Impact."
36. Will Douglas Heaven, "Our Weird Behaviour During the Pandemic is Messing with AI Models," *MIT Technology Review* (May 11, 2020), www.technologyreview.com/2020/05/11/1001563/covid-pandemic-broken-ai-machine-learning-amazon-retail-fraud-humans-in-the-loop/.
37. Flynn, *Evaluating Interactive Documentaries,* 18–19.
38. Eve Kalyva, *Image and Text in Conceptual Art. Image and Text in Conceptual Art: Critical Operations in Context* (Cham: Springer International Publishing, 2016), 171.
39. Mandy Rose in conversation with Katerina Cizek, "Documentary as Co-Creative Practice: From Challenge for Change to High Rise," interview edited by Anna Wiehl, in – Many. *i-Docs: The Evolving Practice of Interactive Documentary,* eds. Judith Aston, Sandra Gaudenzi, and Mandy Rose (New York and London: Wallflower Press, 2017), 38.
40. See: http://hollowdocumentary.com//.
41. See: Kapur, "Co-Creation as Talkback."
42. See: Michael Bauwens, "The Ladder of Participation: The Gradation of Control on Community/Corporate Polarity," *Fibreculture* 14 (2009), accessed September 24, 2021, https://fourteen.fibreculturejournal.org/fcj-097-co-creation-and-the-new-industrial-paradigm-of-peer-production/.
43. See: www.sandystoryline.com/.
44. See: Nick Couldry and Henry Jenkins, "Participations: Dialogues on the Participatory Promise of Contemporary Culture and Politics," *International Journal of Communication* 8, no. 3 (2014): 1129–51.
45. MIT Open Documentary Lab, "Collective Wisdom Symposium: Panel, Nothing About Us Without Us," *MIT Open Documentary Lab, YouTube video* (October 23, 2018), www.youtube.com/watch?v=xrflchWS_OE, 39:14–50:27.
46. See: Simon Lindgren, *Digital Media and Society* (London: Sage Publications Ltd, 2017); Adrian Miles, "Interactive Documentary and Affective Ecologies," in *New Documentary Ecologies,* eds. Kate Nash, Chris High, and Cathering Summerhayes (London: Palgrave Macmillan, 2014), 67–82.
47. See: https://interactive.quipu-project.com/#/en/quipu/intro.

48. See: http://questionbridge.com/.
49. Sora, "Expanding Temporal," 532.
50. Carles Sora, *Temporalidades Digitales: Análisis del Tempo en los New media y las Narrativas Interactivas* (Barcelona: UOC Press, 2016).
51. See: Hartmut Rosa, "Social Acceleration: Ethical and Political Consequences of a Desynchronized High-Speed Society," *Constellations* 10, no. 1 (2003): 3–33; Robert Hassan and Ronald E. Purser, *24/7: Time and Temporality in the Network Society* (Stanford, CA: Stanford Business Books, 2007).
52. Joel Pedro Espinosa, "Mobile Voices: A Mobile, Open Source, Popular Communication Platform for First-Generation Immigrants in Los Angeles," Citizen Media: A Global Innovation Competition, www.changemakers.com/citizenmedia/entries/new-entry-38.
53. MIT Open Documentary Lab, "Three Documentarians View the Future of the Digital Past," *YouTube video* (October 5, 2020), www.youtube.com/watch?v=hXXiThwG15A, 39:14–50:27.
54. See: Sasha Costanza-Chock, *Design Justice* (Cambridge: MIT Press, 2020), https://doi.org/10.7551/mitpress/12255.003.0007.
55. See L Matthew Freeman, "Transmedia Charity: Constructing the Ethos of the BBC's Red Nose Day Across Media," in *The Routledge Companion to Transmedia Studies*, eds. Matthew Freeman and Renira Rampazzo Gambarato (New York: Routledge, 2019), 306–13.
56. Lina Srivastava, "How Transmedia Can Lead to Social Change," *TEDx Transmedia Rome, YouTube Video,* 2011, accessed September 24, 2021, https://youtu.be/6GO_bXpckDM.
57. Marissa Jahn, "Audience Engagement Plan," MIT Comparative Media Studies/Writing, *YouTube video* (June 6, 2018), www.youtube.com/watch?v=GZBo67f3XSA&t=215s, 3:35–34:56.
58. See: www.careforce.co/.
59. See: www.carehaus.net/.
60. www.carehaus.net/.
61. www.carehaus.net/.
62. www.carehaus.net/.
63. See: Jo A. Tacchi, "Voice and Poverty," *Media Development* 1 (2008): 12–16.
64. See: Shamira Raphaëla and Tessa Boerman, "Call to Action," Framing of Us Initiative, accessed June 17, 2021, https://d25cyov38w4k50.cloudfront.net/downloads/Framing-of-Us-Call-To-Action.pdf.

# PART TWO

# Collaborations

# 5

# DEMOCRATIZING DOCUMENTARY AND INTERACTIVE SOCIAL MEDIA PRACTICES

*Gino Canella*

Sant Yàlla is a theater troupe from Yeumbeul, a neighborhood in Dakar's outer-city region. The troupe – whose name translates to "thanks to God" – is currently touring Senegal and thrilling local audiences with *Jaar Jaari Mame Cheikh Ibrahima Fall* (*The Life and Work of Mame Shaykh Ibra Fall*). The play recounts the life of Mame Shaykh Ibrahima Fall, the chief disciple of the Muridiyya, Senegal's homegrown Sufi order. Brian Valente-Quinn and I joined Sant Yàlla for 3 weeks in December 2016 to document the troupe's tour and explore how these artists navigate the tensions between representing and embodying religion on stage. This chapter focuses on the documentary practices we used in collaboration with Sant Yàlla to produce and distribute *Bamba, The Taste of Knowledge* (2018), a 22-minute documentary film.[1] Examining our filmmaking as co-creative research rooted in democratic participation, I discuss the ethical implications of using media to document, preserve, and disseminate local cultures.

Sant Yàlla's performance was inspired by Senegal's urban popular theater movement, where traditional performances mix with contemporary approaches to dance and music.[2] One characteristic of the urban popular theater movement is that performers do not train in programs run by conservatory-style schools; rather, they practice theater at intermittent workshops or on stages in cultural centers throughout Senegal's urban areas. Another characteristic of this movement is that community theater troupes typically apply a local focus to their material.

*Jaar Jaari Mame Cheikh Ibrahima Fall* exhibits a particular style within urban popular theater called *théâtre total*, or total theater.[3] Total theater blends drama, music, and dance, and it emphasizes participation and spontaneity. Thus, Sant Yàlla works in concert with audience members to showcase Senegal's religious traditions, particularly those of the Murid Sufi order. The performers encourage participation during the show by walking through the crowd and speaking

DOI: 10.4324/9781003174509-7

directly to the audience. Some audience members respond to these invitations with religious "fervor" – upon witnessing the show and hearing the songs of Murid folklore, they fly into a spiritual trance that includes yelling and uncontrolled movements. Audience members might also join the show and express their approval of the artists' performances by bringing fistfuls of bills to the stage. Although these interjections interrupt the show, they are part of the play's overall spectacle, and they augment the immersive nature of total theater.

Despite Sant Yàlla's considerable local success, its use of the stage to recount religious themes and re-create religious figures has been met with resistance from key figures within the Murid order who decry the mixing of theater and religion. In fact, Santa Yàlla was warned before launching this production that, without permission from Murid leadership, Murid devotees could show up at performances and prevent the show's opening. Although this has not happened so far, such a practice has been implemented before to censor Senegalese artists who were seen as taking liberties with Murid culture. In the 1980s, for instance, the stage production *Bamba Mos Xam* toured Senegal for years with great success but closed under mysterious circumstances (some believe under pressure from Murid leadership). Little evidence remains of *Bamba Mos Xam* – a few aged photographs and the stories of those who performed in the show or who witnessed it. Sant Yàlla seeks to build on the rich legacy of *Bamba Mos Xam* and bring Bamba's story to new audiences. Fearing that this history could soon be lost to future generations, Brian and I partnered with Sant Yàlla to preserve their stories in a documentary film. We hoped that the film could inform younger Senegalese audiences about Bamba and create spaces for people to debate and discuss performance, art, and religious expression.

Given the sensitivities with representing Bamba on stage, the stakes for Sant Yàlla and for Brian and me as researchers/filmmakers were considerably high. A rebuke from the Murid leadership could mar the young performers' careers and even put their physical safety at risk. Despite these risks, the young artists persist in defending the show and insist that it aims to spread awareness about the Murid order's culture, which they argue provides a moral compass for young people and serves as a national treasure to be celebrated by all. Most of the performers are not Murid devotees; instead, they view their role as artists who step in and out of character without betraying their religious identities. Some artists in the troupe use a "method" approach by immersing themselves in Murid culture and belief to the point of blurring the line between their stage role and their faith. This background informed how Brian and I navigated the ethics of collaborative cross-cultural research and developed our partnership with Sant Yàlla.

## Democratizing Documentary and the Making of *Bamba*

I entered this project as a relative outsider. In early 2016, I had a conversation with Brian about producing a documentary about Sant Yàlla, which is the focus of his research on West African performance culture. Prior to our meeting, Brian had traveled to Senegal numerous times and had several conversations with Sant Yàlla's performers and with community artists and Murid devotees who remembered *Bamba Mos Xam*. Brian and Mouhamadou Diol, the artistic director for theater company Kàddu Yaraax and a consultant for Sant Yàlla, discussed with Brian the possibility of making a documentary about Bamba, but neither had the technical experience needed to make a film. Sant Yàlla's stage production includes lively music, dancing, and vibrant colorful costumes, and Brian explained in our initial meeting that this spectacle lends itself perfectly to the visual medium. Sant Yàlla's story, he said, cannot be expressed fully through words.

Partnering with Brian to produce a documentary about Sant Yàlla was appealing to me for several reasons: the project challenged us to think through the limitations and creative potential that different mediums provide (e.g., text, audiovisual, social media); it offered opportunities to communicate with diverse audiences in various formats; and it created spaces in which to examine how documentary has the potential to promote interdisciplinary collaborations and democratize cross-cultural research.

Despite these possibilities and my initial excitement, I also had a few reservations. I do not speak French or Wolof, the primary languages spoken in Senegal, and I was unsure how I would incorporate my filmmaking into Brian's already-established partnership with Diol and Sant Yàlla. These concerns were eased, however, when I learned more about Brian's research. In his book *Senegalese Stagecraft*, he argues that a "sustained focus on theater as a sited expressive practice will underscore the political, social, and economic stakes involved in any form of innovative stagecraft."[4] This framework is helpful for examining the *sites* in which co-creative research occurs, and for investigating the social relationships embedded in documentary. By reviewing how we made *Bamba, The Taste of Knowledge* in collaboration with Sant Yàlla, I demonstrate the ways in which co-creative research expands the *sites* where cultures and knowledge are produced, contested, and disseminated.

Analyzing documentary as a series of social relationships that have the potential to democratize research requires defining a few key concepts. The first is *participation*. Media studies scholars have suggested that participatory video and community art projects have the potential to foster civic participation and promote social change.[5] I avoid media-centric analyses of participation by examining participation through democratic theory. Christian Fuchs defined participatory democracy as a "society in which all decisions are made by those who are concerned by them and all organizations (workplaces, schools, cities, politics, etc.) are controlled by those who are affected by them."[6] To apply these principles to our filmmaking with Sant Yàlla, Brian and I used co-creative Do-it-With-Others (DiWO) methods. In contrast to documentaries in which filmmakers remain detached neutral observers and view interviewees as "subjects," DiWO operates on a continuum of collaboration that demands additional ethical considerations from all participants. These considerations (for example, sharing editorial control and rethinking authorship) have the potential to level the filmmaking hierarchy and recognize participants as peers in the research process and as allies in civic life – as opposed to individual artists, directors, or performers. Thus, DiWO "provides a progressive re-working of documentary's historic role in the public sphere, as an open space for dialogue and a stage for the performance of citizenship."[7]

Similar to participation, *citizenship* is a somewhat ambiguous concept. Graham Murdock's definition brings clarity, though. He defined citizenship as "the right to participate fully in social life with dignity and without fear, and to help formulate the forms it might take in the future."[8] Regular and thoughtful attention to our roles as researchers/filmmakers – and to the power dynamics among all participants – encouraged Brian and me to co-produce media that visualized and exhibited powerful representations of Senegalese art and religion.

Our filmmaking and research recognized various approaches to video ethnography, and I aimed for what Luke E. Lassiter called "collaborative ethnography" – a method that encourages the organizations or groups being filmed and studied to be involved in the research through consultation and critique.[9] The interactive social media practices that Brian and I used throughout this project provided Sant Yàlla with numerous opportunities to consult with us and critique our practices and products. One instance is notable for revealing how interactive social media practices helped us democratize documentary. Following the filming of a rehearsal, I edited and uploaded a 50-second highlight video to Facebook. I tagged Brian and Diol, and the video spread quickly throughout Sant Yàlla's social networks, reaching more than one thousand views in the first 24 hours. This is not to suggest that participation can be quantified by social media metrics but rather how social media provides researchers with opportunities to invite participants into the research process. The following day, the artists excitedly asked me what they could do to facilitate the production. They joked that my edits to the beat of a drum had nice rhythm "for a *toubab*" (a somewhat derogatory term for a White person, but it can also be used affectionately). Despite my inability to communicate verbally with Sant Yàlla, I discovered that video and social media helped me speak with our partners. Through video, I communicated my professionalism as a filmmaker and the care with which I was handling Sant Yàlla's story. Further, I created an opportunity for Sant Yàlla to consult with me and critique my filmmaking.

This experience helped to establish trust between Sant Yàlla and me. After seeing the short highlight video, the artists subsequently felt comfortable offering feedback about my aesthetic choices, and they made suggestions for angles and shots during rehearsals and performances. The artists assumed the role of co-directors in these instances by adjusting their movements and ensuring that I was in position to document important moments. These interactions fostered a mutually beneficial project – I was able to produce compelling visuals for the film, and Sant Yàlla was able to promote its performance through video shared on social media. Publishing my research notes in real time via social media and taking direction from my partners about where to focus my literal or metaphorical lens may reduce, according to some scholars, the "ethnographicness" of this project.[10] Applying the principles of democracy, however, enhanced the collaborative nature of the project and allowed me to address important ethical questions: Who is the director of this project? How much editorial and creative control should I have? How should we distribute this film? Truly democratizing documentary required engaging our partners throughout all stages of the project, giving them a stake in the design decisions and outcomes of the research, and viewing Sant Yàlla's artists as colleagues.

Collaborative filmmaking also requires that filmmakers and researchers develop close and intimate relationships with their partners. Brian met Diol in 2013 and made multiple trips to Senegal over the next 4 years conducting research about Diol's theatrical work with Kàddu Yaraax. Prior to rolling our cameras, Brian spent considerable time meeting with Diol and community artists across Senegal. In 2015, Diol pitched the idea of producing a documentary film about *Bamba Mos Xam* to Brian, and they began considering the logistics and scope of the film. Although introducing cameras into a research project may change the relational dynamics among the participants and make it difficult to document candid moments, Diol and Sant Yàlla's artists welcomed me as a newcomer to the project. As performers, these artists were adept at switching into performance mode for the camera. While this provided us with dramatic footage for the documentary, it was also important to occasionally set the camera aside – or even leave our equipment at home – during conversations and planning meetings with Diol and Sant Yàlla. We wanted to move the production beyond superficial details or staged events and engage with the artists on a deeper human level.

Senegalese customs often required this deeper level of connection. Before filming most interviews, for example, Brian and I sat for hours with interviewees, enjoying lunch, discussing the documentary's focus, and learning about the sensitivities required to communicate Bamba's story through theater and film. These conversations required a lot of patience and forced us to slow down the filmmaking and research processes. We benefited greatly in these instances from the assistance of Ousmane Guèye of Touba, who provided us with his local expertise, made important introductions with key figures, and helped us navigate Senegal.

## Interactive Social Media Practices as Cross-Cultural Research

Technology and digital media are raising provocative questions for researchers about the ethics of participation, but these questions reflect an old divide within the field of video ethnography. The classical Chicago School model of the early twentieth century promoted a positivist approach to video ethnography that included recording public behaviors and rating or coding the footage.[11] In contrast, new ethnography encouraged researchers to be much more involved with their research subjects and to "possess an extensive knowledge and expertise of the culture."[12] These approaches are often called "presentation" (objective social science) and "research practice" (subjective interpretation). *Presentation* typically uses a *cinema-vérité* style that favors wide and medium shots, minimal editing, and ambient sound as opposed to music (notably Robert Flaherty's *Nanook of the North*, 1922). This gives viewers the impression that events are depicted "as they happened," without any outside interference from the filmmakers. *Research practice*, on the other hand, views the camera not as a "fourth wall" that divides filmmakers from participants, but rather as a "fluid wall . . . [that] recognizes the mutual benefits of open communication and adaptable interactions."[13]

Our filmmaking with Sant Yàlla reveals how the distinctions between old and new ethnography are becoming more pronounced with digital media. Sharing video in real time on social media changes who has access to the data, how analysis and interpretation occur, and what forms research takes. Inexpensive video cameras and free editing software have made media production more accessible for hobbyists and researchers, which has increased the demand for creative research within the academy. Video ethnographers and anthropological filmmakers have previously discussed returning to research sites to "give back" to the communities with which they worked. These trips might include offering art and photo books to their collaborators as gifts or hosting a film screening in the community where the research was conducted. Today, communities do not need to wait months or years to view, edit, and co-create media with researchers.

Interactive social media practices alter the speed of data collection and analysis, create new spaces for collaboration, and challenge researchers to reconsider the ethics of subjective interpretation. Anthropologist and filmmaker Paul Henley argued that "active engagement on the part of the filmmaker . . . is bound to involve some measure of subjectivity."[14] He also believed the camera provides researchers with opportunities to become intimately engaged in people's lives and achieve a level of understanding that is inaccessible to filmmakers/researchers who insist on remaining neutral or distant. "The implicit theory of knowledge underlying this approach," Henley wrote, "is that true social reality is not to be found in the superficial observable details of everyday life but rather in the underlying relationships, sentiments, and attitudes which sustain them."[15] The relationships and sentiments that Brian and I developed with Sant Yàlla and other community artists in Senegal are not explicit in the film's images. They did, however, motivate how the images were produced, what questions were asked, and whose expertise was relied upon in the film. Our relationships with Ousmane and Diol, for example, influenced who we interviewed and how these interviews were conducted. During interviews, Ousmane and Diol would sometimes interject with clarifications or suggest follow-up questions. Democratizing documentary, therefore, asks filmmakers and researchers to reconceive participants' roles and rethink what it means to observe.

In addition to using my personal Facebook page to share the 50-second highlight video with Sant Yàlla, we also created a dedicated Facebook page for the film.[16] We learned during our time in Senegal that Facebook is the dominant social media platform there, so we decided it was the best venue on which to promote the film and engage with local audiences. Brian and I provided Diol with administrative access to the page, and we spent about $30 on targeted ads to promote the page. One of the first posts we shared after creating the page included the highlight video discussed earlier. Diol and the troupe continue to upload videos and photos of performances to this page to promote upcoming shows and grow Sant Yàlla's audience. The page, which has about 700 followers, increased the troupe's visibility and provided Senegalese audiences opportunities to critique Sant Yàlla's performance and the documentary.

Despite the myriad concerns that scholars and activists have rightly expressed about Facebook regarding surveillance, personal privacy, and the spread of misinformation, the site offered us a venue in which to identify audiences for the project and collaborate across geographic distances with our community partners. Because so much scholarship is behind paywalls and written in English (with dense academic jargon), sharing excerpts of the documentary on Facebook helped us engage with audiences who otherwise would not be able to access this story and our research. When I shared an image of my edit suite months after I left Senegal, for example, I let our collaborators know that we were making progress and moving into post-production, which generated excitement about the film's release.

Reading and responding to comments on our posts as we moved into script writing and editing also provided us with instant feedback about how the project was being received by local audiences. Because most of these comments were written in Wolof, Brian regularly consulted with Diol and Wolof experts to ensure that we were understanding all of the nuances. In a notable example, several comments about the highlight video disparaged Sant Yàlla's women artists, arguing that their clothing is inappropriate and that women should not speak publicly about religion. Brian discussed these comments with Diol as we considered how to portray gender in the documentary, remaining mindful of how the documentary could affect Sant Yàlla. Although we did not directly address this controversy in the film because we felt it was outside the scope of the story, we did include interviews in the film with several female artists who shared their views on performing religious themes as non-Murids.

Prior to sharing the documentary publicly, we uploaded a first draft of the film to a password-protected Vimeo page and invited Diol to provide feedback. After a few minor revisions, we shared the finished documentary to the film's Facebook page. Brian and I discussed some reservations he had about posting the documentary online. He was concerned that the film would be downloaded and shared without our or Sant Yàlla's permission. We ultimately agreed that if we wanted to truly apply the principles of democracy, we cannot simply espouse those principles – they must guide our work. The documentary has indeed been downloaded and republished on YouTube, partly because YouTube is more accessible in Senegal than Vimeo. These experiences forced us to think critically about audience, authorship, and peer-review. Democratizing documentary through interactive social media practices meant encouraging Diol and Senegalese artists and audiences to participate in the writing, editing, and distribution of Bamba. Social media allowed us to give those most affected by our research a stake in shaping it.

## Visualizing Bamba and Religious Imagery

Throughout urban and rural Senegal, one finds reproductions of the only known image of Amadu Bamba – a 1913 colonial photograph that has become the centerpiece of a rich and interactive culture of religious iconography among Murid devotees. Bamba's image performs a crucial spiritual function through its multiple reproductions on the cityscape (see Figure 5.1). The visual manifestation of Bamba transmits the saint's *baraka*, often translated as "charisma" but what others have translated as "aura" to those who see it.[17] This passes on spiritual blessings to onlookers and to those who facilitate the image's circulation, specifically artists or devotees who place it in open view. The image functions beyond the realm of metaphor. It does not "stand in" for another implied meaning, but rather it facilitates an engaged relationship that brings the viewer into contact with Bamba's spiritual essence. Within the framework of these representational practices, any theater troupe or filmmaker eager to present an adaptation of Bamba's life must

**FIGURE 5.1**  Bamba's image (right) is painted on walls throughout Senegal.

*Source:* Photograph by the author

carefully consider how stagecraft and visual media give voice and movement to the saint's sacred image.

As White, Western researchers and filmmakers, Brian and I had to remain attuned to these nuances and recognize that some religious authorities believe theater and other visual representations of Bamba go too far. When a theater troupe takes the stage to tell Mame Shaykh Ibrahima Fall's story, this typically involves an actor embodying a religious figure and speaking as if from the voice of him. This differs greatly from visual reproductions of the saint or references to him through music where the religious figure retains his otherworldliness or his relation to the unseen world, so closely examined in the Sufi tradition.

Instead of speaking *as* Mame Shaykh Ibra, Sant Yàlla used a creative stage narrative technique in which the lead actor speaks as an unnamed narrator and recounts the biography of the religious figure. He occasionally introduces a scene by declaring "Mame Shaykh Ibra once said . . ." and then performs an episode of the disciple's life as an intermediary recounting the tale for the supporting actors, rather than as the embodiment of the disciple himself (see Figure 5.2). Through roleplay, Sant Yàlla makes its play acceptable to audience members who would have otherwise opposed actors speaking as Mame Shaykh Ibra or as his master Shaykh Amadu Bamba. We also utilized this technique in our film by avoiding voice-over narration and letting the community artists and local experts we interviewed tell Bamba's story.

These editorial decisions were informed by a series of meetings between Sant Yàlla and Cheikh Fall, the director of *Bamba Mos Xam* (see Figure 5.3). We organized these meetings for the documentary and filmed them to document how art

**FIGURE 5.2**  Film still of Xadim Beye, lead performer of Sant Yàlla, discussing Bamba's story during a show in Yeumbeul.

*Source:* Photograph by the author

**FIGURE 5.3** Cheikh Fall discusses *Bamba Mos Xam* with Sant Yàlla.

*Source:* Photograph by the author

and theater have the potential to bridge generational understandings of Bamba. These meetings represent what Faye Ginsburg called "ethnographic media," which are video and film that mediate social relations. Indigenous media, she wrote, "communicate something about that social or collective identity we call 'culture,' in order to mediate (one hopes) across gaps of space, time, knowledge, and prejudice."[18] Sant Yàlla's members were eager to consult with Fall on their pressing concerns regarding the hidden social and religious taboos associated with representing holy figures on stage. Fall understood their concerns and, in fact, had experienced some harrowing encounters in the course of *Bamba Mos Xam*'s 15-year run. By organizing these meetings between Sant Yàlla and Fall, the documentary intervened in Bamba's cultural and religious heritage by documenting Fall's experiences as an actor and director – which provided context, background, and visuals for the film – and created space for Sant Yàlla to discuss their art and spiritual leanings. Fall encouraged the young artists to continue their work but asked them to rely upon the authorization of prominent Murid leaders.

Filming Sant Yàlla's stage production and these encounters with Fall produced layers of media and visual storytelling that required considerable care from us as filmmakers/researchers. Collaborative documentary, as opposed to extractive storytelling or investigative journalism, demanded that we slow down, earn the trust of our community partners, and share producing and directing responsibilities with them. Although Brian and I earned a significant amount of trust throughout our time in Senegal, we needed to rely often on Diol to facilitate our work. In addition to distributing our documentary online, Brian has returned to Dakar several times to organize screenings of the film with Diol. Much like Sant Yàlla's "total theater" method – where the artists march into a public square, begin performing, and attract an audience of curious onlookers – these screenings have been pop-up showings in busy public spaces. The sounds and images of the film draw passersby to the screen and encourage dialogue among community members who often recount their personal experiences with Bamba, Muridism, and the saint's visual image.

Indeed, a key strength of the documentary has been its ability to spur conversations about the religious themes depicted in the film. Following a screening at the West African Research Center in Senegal, for example, attendees had a spirited debate about whether Sant Yàlla's performance was an appropriate act of religious devotion. Conservative Muslims argued that the young artists were being disrespectful with iconic religious imagery and making a mockery of Muridism. Others argued that religious expression should not be dictated by a select few, and that Sant Yàlla's performances spread Bamba's message to new and diverse audiences. The documentary has also screened at several U.S. research centers focused on media, religion, and African studies; at international film festivals, including the African World Documentary Film Festival and the Ethnografilm Festival in Paris, France; and it has been reviewed by academic journals. Using a multifaceted distribution strategy was one way we attempted to reach academic and non-academic audiences, revealing how co-creative research creates additional sites for culture and knowledge to be produced and shared.

## Conclusion

Nicholas Mirzoeff and Jack Halberstam challenged media studies researchers to re-examine their research practices in a *Cinema Journal* dossier titled "Decolonize Media: Tactics, Manifestos, Histories."[19] The authors engaged critically with race, gender, class, and power, and they offered seven suggestions for decolonizing media studies, all of which relate to the collaborative documentary practices discussed in this chapter:

> (1) Listen. To the colonized, to the historically underrepresented, to your own body; (2) Use and create open-source materials; (3) Study or learn in languages beyond English (and other colonial languages); (4) "Text is not enough." Produce in many forms; (5) Collaborate in your research: faculty with students, academics with the communities they serve; (6) Be "producers not only consumers" from the outset of learning; (7) And try to live up to the injunction "ethics above all."[20]

We created open-source scholarship in multiple forms by producing films and distributing them online. We studied and learned in languages beyond English when we worked with Wolof translators to produce a bilingual documentary. We collaborated with our community partners by involving them in our editorial decisions and by soliciting and responding to their real-time feedback on social media. As the boundaries between academic disciplines continue to blur, researchers are inventing new ways of studying media, religion, and art. Centering the social within documentary decolonizes media studies by forcing scholars to re-evaluate, revise, and update dominant theoretical frameworks and accepted methodologies. Co-creative research compels scholars to consider who research is for.

The *form* of scholarship also helps us realize how co-creation upends notions of participation and citizenship, and it provides communities with opportunities to curate alternative archives. Jacques Rancière wrote that the *form* of politics represents the "distribution of the sensible."[21] Documentary, as a visual medium, asks viewers to witness and make sense of the world. Documenting social life and distributing it to publics, Rancière argued, encourages viewers to reimagine the terrain of politics. "The politics of works of art . . . plays itself out in the way in which modes of narration or new forms of visibility established by artistic practices enter into politics' own field of aesthetic possibilities."[22]

Co-producing *Bamba, The Taste of Knowledge* with Senegalese artists challenged us to formulate our research questions in partnership with the community. Artists and activists who wish to produce multimedia with community groups should recognize the power dynamics between themselves and the participants, rely on local expertise to guide the direction of their projects, and enter communities with humble curiosity.

This documentary gave Brian and I opportunities to share Bamba's story, consider the tensions between religious expression and art, and understand how creative research practices affect culture. Sant Yàlla's practices (e.g., music, theater, and dance) and the practices Brian and I used to share Bamba's story (e.g., film, public screenings, social media, and research articles), expand our ideas about religion, art, and culture. Through co-creative research that embraced tension and visualized alternative modes of expression, we centered grassroots perspectives and situated Bamba's story in broader sociopolitical and historical contexts. Co-creation democratizes filmmaking and fieldwork, and challenges researchers and audiences alike to reconsider the taken-for-granted and rethink what we know.

## Notes

1. *Bamba, The Taste of Knowledge,* directed by Brian Valente-Quinn and Gino Canella (2018, United States), https://vimeo.com/264755999.
2. See: Brian Valente-Quinn, "Trance States and Sufi Stages: The Poetics and Politics of Murid Theatre in Senegal," *Theatre Journal* 72, no. 4 (2020): 425–42.
3. See: Brian Quinn, "De-centering Theatrical Heritage: Forum Theater in Contemporary Senegal," *African Studies Quarterly* 14, no. 3 (2020): 75–88. https://asq.africa.ufl.edu/quinn_march14/.
4. Brian Valente-Quinn, *Senegalese Stagecraft: Decolonizing Theater-Making in Francophone Africa* (Evanston, IL: Northwestern University Press, 2021), 6.
5. See: Shirley A. White, ed., *Participatory Video: Images that Transform and Empower.* (Thousand Oaks, CA: Sage, 2003); Henry Jenkins. *Convergence Culture: Where Old*

*and New Media Collide* (New York: New York University Press, 2006); Clement Chau, "YouTube as a Participatory Culture," *New Directions for Student Leadership* 128 (2010): 65–74, https://doi.org/10.1002/yd.376.

6. Christian Fuchs, *Social Media: A Critical Introduction* (Thousand Oaks, CA: Sage, 2014), 14.

7. Mandy Rose, "Making Publics: Documentary as Do-it-With-Others Citizenship," in *DIY Citizenship: Critical Making and Social Media*, eds. Megan Boler and Matt Ratto (Boston, MA: MIT Press, 2014), 203.

8. Graham Murdock, "Rights and Representations: Public Discourse and Cultural Citizenship," in *Television and Common Knowledge*, ed. Jostein Gripsrud, 7–17 (New York, NY: Routledge, 1999), 8.

9. Luke E. Lassiter, *The Chicago Guide to Collaborative Ethnography* (Chicago, IL: University of Chicago Press, 2005), 15.

10. Marcus Banks, "Which Films are the Ethnographic Films?" in *Film as Ethnography*, eds. Peter Ian Crawford and David Turton in association with the Granada Centre for Visual Anthropology (Manchester: Manchester University Press, 1992), 12.

11. Anne-Marie Ambert et al., "Understanding and Evaluating Qualitative Research," *Journal of Marriage and Family* 57 (1995): 885, https://doi.org/10.2307/353409.

12. Wesley Schrum, Ricardo Duque, and Timothy Brown, "Digital Video as Research Practice: Methodology for the Millennium," *Journal of Research Practice* 1, no. 1 (2005): 3, http://jrp.icaap.org/index.php/jrp/article/view/6/11.

13. Schrum, Duque, and Brown, "Digital Video," 5.

14. Paul Henley, "Filmmaking and Ethnographic Research," in *Image-based Research: A Sourcebook for Qualitative Researchers*, ed. Jon Prosser (Philadelphia: Falmer Press, 1998), 6.

15. Henley, "Filmmaking and Ethnographic Research," 6.

16. www.facebook.com/BambaFilm.

17. See: Allen F. Roberts and Mary Nooter Roberts, *A Saint in the City: Sufi Arts of Urban Senegal* (Los Angeles: Fowler Museum of Cultural History, 2003).

18. Faye Ginsburg, "Indigenous Media: Faustian Contract or Global Village?" *Cultural Anthropology* 6 no. 1 (1991): 104.

19. Nicholas Mirzoeff and Jack Halberstam, "Decolonize Media: Tactics, Manifestoes, Histories," *Cinema Journal* 57, no. 4 (2008): 123, https://cdn.ymaws.com/www.cmstudies.org/resource/resmgr/in_focus_archive/InFocus_57-4.pdf.

20. Mirzoeff and Halberstam, "Decolonize Media," 123.

21. Jacques Rancière, *The Politics of Aesthetics: The Distribution of the Sensible*, trans. G. Rockhill (New York, NY: Continuum International, 2000).

22. Rancière, *The Politics of Aesthetics*, 65.

# 6

# AN OUTSIDER APPROACH TO CINEMATOGRAPHY

Native Representation, Breaking the Norms, and Finding New Ways to Explore Indigenous Spaces

*Malek Rasamny and Matt Peterson in conversation with Rania Al Namara. Edited by Rania Al Namara*

When Malek Rasamny and Matt Peterson met in New York in 2009, they already shared a common interest in experimental film, art, radical politics, and the connections between them. Years later they went on to cofound *The Native and the Refugee* project, a multimedia project profiling Native American reservations in the United States alongside Palestinian refugee camps in the Middle East. Through short films such as *Indian Winter* (2017) or *History of the Camp* (2015), both part of the larger aforementioned project, Matt and Malek document community struggles and everyday life in both spaces not only investigating the places themselves but, within the larger *The Native and the Refugee* project, juxtaposing them to create a platform of solidarity between communities in North America and the Middle East.

More recently, based on their previous experience in the Native territory of Akwesasne, they have collaborated with Kahentinetha Rotiskareh wake and Philippe Boudin on the co-edited book *The Mohawk Warrior Society*.[1]

In this interview, Malek and Matt reflect on their experiences and immersion inside American Indian reservations and Palestinian refugee camps. Through visits to these spaces, they collected firsthand accounts from Native residents, consulted local audiences and activists throughout the process of production and eschewed the use of voice-over in all their films thus blurring the lines between conventional structures surrounding author, subject, and audience and the patterns of reception that lie between them. The narratives documented in their short films, which forsook personal narratives for communal ones, were intended to be empowering both to the communities depicted as well as other communities engaged in similar struggle. By highlighting the careful analysis of those within these places the project strived to understand the macro-structural processes at

DOI: 10.4324/9781003174509-8

work in creating and defining these spaces while on a more philosophical level attempting to put forward a conception of reservations and refugee camps as unique spaces that bring forth distinct political realities and philosophies.

RA: How did you meet each other and how did you start working on experimental films?

MR: My family is from Lebanon but I grew up between New York and Lebanon eventually moving to New York City after college. It was there that Matt and I both found ourselves within certain very specific milieus located at the intersection of experimental film and radical politics and, as a result, we kept coming across each other at different events or gatherings. Matt was curating this radical political film series called Red Channels (2011), and he was opening it up into a collective project, so I started participating in that process with him. This was right before the time of Occupy Wall Street, when the Palestinian solidarity movement was beginning to come into full force. It was a dynamic time for independent, politically engaged film screenings, with a lot of new microcinemas operating around the city, so it's within that environment that we came together. What drew us to the idea of the *The Native and the Refugee* project in particular was a similarity I noticed having lived between New York and Lebanon: a similarity between Palestinian refugee camps and Native reservations, how they were located and positioned within the nation states they were in.

MP: Because of our citizenships, we have the ability to move between these spaces so we decided if we want to enter these places to do some kind of film project, it would have to be toward the goal of building something shared together and not just simply as a personal experience for ourselves. This is something we had been thinking about within our work in Red Channels and in conversations we were having about media and radical politics back in 2010. From there arose this idea of an explicitly multimedia project juxtaposing the reservation and refugee camps, a project which we started in 2014.

RA: So, in your approach to interactive documentary, what kind of skills or practices do you apply in your production that differs from traditional documentary production?

MP: The primary component of our visual and research practice was to visit and exclusively focus on the places themselves. We wanted to focus solely on the voices, experiences, and visual images of those living in a reservation or camp rather than talk to journalists, academics, scholars, or experts in major cities about what they thought about these realities. In none of our films do we ever present ourselves as narrators; there is no voice-over in any of the films; we ourselves do not really say anything directly. Our approach was to collect these testimonies and to edit them together in a way that we felt was faithful to our experiences within the spaces. This produced something different from normal documentaries which focus on individual characters or narratives or human-interest stories: a young girl learning to play soccer or something like that.

We tried to position ourselves as facilitators, to use audiovisual media to document and disseminate an analysis of the reservation and refugee camp, so both us and our audiences could think about these questions together as we produced and screened our short films in each place. We wanted to document these spaces that American or for example Lebanese citizens don't normally see, that are kept a bit hidden, by visiting and allowing the description, analysis, and narrative to come directly from the inhabitants. Immersing ourselves was our way to think about our own realities as citizens of these countries and about what it means that the United States or Lebanon have these exceptional spaces within them.

MR: I'd like to emphasize what Matt said about focusing on the analysis as opposed to the personal story but it's not only that. We are not using the characters to simply provide contextual details or information that could be found elsewhere. We tried to focus on the actual analyses of the subjects featured in the films; what they genuinely thought of the present moment, the challenges and potential paths forward. We wanted these moments of reflection to emerge spontaneously in a way that's different from using characters as a kind of empty cipher to deliver a message that you, as a director, want the audience to know. We had to be open to hear what people had to say and then try to create a montage of the most compelling, articulate, interesting, or effective analyses that we ourselves heard and learned from.

RA: So, I want to ask you more about how you see the relation between the producer, the subject, and the audience, how would you define that relationship?

MP: Most of the people we worked with were thought of as collaborators and not just subjects. Because we were not really familiar with these places, part of our research and methodology was to find people that were engaged in some form of visible political or social activity in these spaces and then work with them to make the film that, in part, they wanted to make. So, in a way they were all also producers in addition to being subjects. They would show us what they wanted to show us; they would talk about what they wanted to talk about; they would take us to the particular parts of the refugee camps or the reservation that they wanted us to document.

So we weren't like objective, neutral outsiders, just some random people coming in and making our own portrait of the places; it was always very partisan, made in accordance with the people we choose to work with as well as guide us. When we would take the footage back to New York to edit, we would send them back rough cuts and ask for feedback and suggestions. Then we would revisit the places to show them the films and have a discussion about both the films that we shot in that particular place but also about the films we made elsewhere. So, the discussions were not just about the films we made about you, but also asking, "what do you think about this film we shot at the Aida Refugee Camp in Bethlehem, or in Akwesasne?" We tried to get this broader perspective on the project from the "subjects," the participants, and the collaborators, in order to think through this juxtaposition between the reservations and refugee camps, to spell out this or that concept, to elaborate on what we had, and to gather all the material we needed.

And a number of the cinematographers and editors that we worked with were Indigenous, or Palestinian, or Arab, so we would obviously discuss with them; what do you guys think, how should we shoot this, how should we edit that, or how should we tell the story? Everything was collaborative, both with our technical partners, our various collaborators, and our "subjects." This is especially true in regard to our two short films[2] produced about Standing Rock, all of the participants there were definitely co-producers.

MR: We blurred the lines between subjects, producers, and audience, so that the watching of the film became a part of its construction. In that way the project became a kind of circular process, one which collapsed those boundaries. For us, the idea of the audience is something that we tried to keep very much in mind because often people focus on it only at the end of the production. They do not really think of the question of audience as political; the question of who is the intended audience for this? And when you don't purposefully politicize your idea of the audience, oftentimes the audience then automatically and subconsciously becomes this white, male, middle-class, Americanized "anonymous figure" or consumer that already exists in the back of your head. For example, with our first two short films from 2015, *We Love Being Lakota* and *The Way of the Longhouse* both made in Native reservations, the audience in mind was specifically Palestinian refugees. That doesn't mean that only Palestinian refugees can watch it or that it's only for them, but that was the audience that we had in mind when we made those films. We were documenting people at the Pine Ridge and Akwesasne reservations for Palestinians in refugee camps, and so that was something that was always in the back of our heads. That goes back to the question of what is the purpose of this film and who is the intended audience?

Part of the reason we were given access to represent these spaces in the first place was that the project in general was always intended to be this act of ongoing transmission, this two-way street, both sides learning and receiving from the other. As we were bringing documentation from the reservations to the camps, and from the camps to the reservations, it was never merely about coming in and taking information, analysis, or images from these places *to* somewhere else but about attempting to facilitate modes of exchange. In this collapsing of the audience, the producer and the subject there is a change in the form and nature of documentary wherein documentary goes from being this static unidirectional object to becoming a participatory platform of communication between communities who, for political, geographic, and economic reasons, are unable to communicate with each other otherwise.

RA: I'm also curious about the kinds of technology you use for shooting your stories; do you use very sophisticated equipment?

MP: This has mostly been up to the cinematographers who we worked with, many of whom work as independent artists and filmmakers. They all had their own equipment, but aside from that we didn't really rent any flashy gear. We never really had a budget for normal, industry standard rates of how much a cinematographer makes per day on a commercial shoot. Most of the people, like Adam Khalil[3] and Vanessa Teran, had a personal and political connection to the project so people were collaborating for different reasons outside of a normal work-for-hire approach. Editing software nowadays is pretty accessible and cheap, so most of that happened on normal, standard laptop computers anyone might have at home. This was never approached as a commercial documentary project, we always saw it as an independent, artistic, political project.

MR: Those technical decisions were always a product of discussions we would have with each individual cinematographer, and what they thought would be appropriate in the different spaces. So in the camps having a steady cam might be the appropriate way to shoot the space as you're walking around or in some of the reservations you might need a certain lens to shoot from a distance to project a sense of space. It all came out of conversations we would have with our cinematographers but in general Matt's right: it was pretty sparse.

RA: How can this kind of interactive documentary production help change understandings surrounding the general narrative of Native Americans?

MR: The question of representation within Native communities in particular is very loaded because of the violent history of American colonialism and forced assimilation. The idea of Natives presenting themselves or being represented before a white gaze is something pretty deeply embedded in this history. Our way to work against that legacy was in seeing our project and work as being about natives representing themselves directly to Palestinian refugees, or to other colonized, oppressed communities, as opposed to an anonymous, generalized imaginary of an American audience. From the beginning, our aim was for everyone in our films to represent themselves in the way they wanted to be seen. In doing this, we tried to challenge or politicize certain notions of objectivity in our work. What truth are we documenting? Which reality are we choosing to focus on? For example, if you are looking at mainstream media depictions of Native reservations, and Pine Ridge Indian Reservation in particular, there's this concept in American media called poverty porn. To engage in poverty porn is to portray people in a way that emphasizes their poverty, instances of abuse, drug addiction, etc., emphasizing such things in order to elicit pity and sympathy, oftentimes at the expense of the subject's dignity. Now, of course, there is drug addiction, there is abuse, alcoholism; there is poverty on Pine Ridge but there's also dignity, there's a spirit of resistance, there's a sense of defiance. There's also a spirituality, a connection to the land, a sense of intense kinship. All these things exist, they're all real but what you choose to focus on and why can be, in some ways, a political question.

We wanted to represent the people in Pine Ridge as they would like to be represented, as militants, as having a proud history of resistance, defiance, strength, rootedness, connectedness, a love for each other, and a love for the land that they're on. Pine Ridge was the first place we visited, *We Love Being Lakota* (2015) was the first film of *The Native and the Refugee* and so that was our introduction into the project. We wanted, then and now, to circumvent certain notions of objectivity not by falsifying the reality of the camps or reservations, not by engaging in fiction but by making documentaries that were quite purposeful in the decisions they made and what realities they chose to emphasize.

Honestly and unfortunately the mere fact of us depicting Native communities struggling in the present day can, to some degree, be read as a political decision. Generally, in American popular culture there is an over-historization and odd preservation of a certain image of Native people as being just part of the historical landscape of the country as opposed to a contemporary community that is actually growing in population. People should realise that Native communities are very much here and alive and part of the present day fabric of this country.

MP:  One of the things we often spoke about within this project is that in New York City, and a lot of American cities, and a lot of college campuses, the Palestinian movement might be better known than the Native reality in America. Even politically engaged people might know more about the political intricacies of the West Bank or Gaza than they know about the closest reservation to where they're living, or what Native territories and tribes are local to where they live or grew up. So in that way the Native experience was more foreign than the Palestinian experience for a lot of our audiences, especially before Standing Rock, which started in the spring of 2016, and brought a lot of international coverage to Native struggles.

But, before that, Native life was very much invisible in American culture. There's not a lot of media representation, there's not a lot of reportage, they're often framed as a historical phenomenon rather than a contemporary movement or community. So, our project, in juxtaposing them, was to put these two experiences of settler colonialism, that began in different centuries, in dialogue together. To think about the different temporalities of settler colonialism that are both ongoing. All of our footage in both the refugee camps and the reservations was contemporary; we didn't use any archival or historical footage, and in the films, we didn't explain any of these histories ourselves; we let the people explain their own histories as they wanted to explain them. We never said, "in 1750 this happened," or, "in 1948, that

happened," etc. It's all contemporary dialogue, interviews, narrative, and testimony. Everything is completely grounded in the present. If and when the
past is discussed, it is from the vantage point of the here and now. The larger
historical and political struggles of both Natives and Palestinians are distilled
temporally and geographically through an understanding of the realities they
produce in these particular spaces at this particular moment.

RA:  What inspires you to continue producing these types of interactive films
allowing you to, as you said, give a certain license to the subject to present
their own narrative? What other practices would you like to emphasize?

MP:  Refugeehood is increasing on a global scale, stateless peoples will continue
migrating across borders because of war and poverty and disease and cor-
ruption and genocide. The figure of the refugee is only going to grow,
and continue to problematize nation-state realities, troubling how states deal
with the uncertain and unstable dynamics between citizenship and refugeehood. Likewise, we feel that concepts surrounding indigeneity, land and
ecology are in fact related to this same question. As we try to confront climate change, we will have to think deeply about how and why it is that we
arrived at the ecological situation we're in, how modern industrialization
and development have led to the unsustainable path that we are now on.

MR:  Yes both the figure of the Native and that of the refugee point to a profound
reckoning that has to take place concerning how we organize ourselves as
people and how we envision our relationship to the land we are on. The
conceptual challenge that the figure of the Native and the refugee pose
is double-sided. On the one hand, people are looking toward Indigenous
conceptions of land, ways of life and ecology as methods of rooting ourselves further into the territory upon which we exist but in a manner that
is altogether different than the exploitative relationship provided for by the
modern nation-state. Simultaneously, and from the opposite direction, is
this undercurrent of the refugee, the people whose very existence places
them outside the nation-state model, whose very existence forces them and
us to question the purpose and value of what it means to be a citizen. Where
do they go, how do they survive, how may their humanity be realized and
recognized? That general dynamic, even aside from the specific question of
Palestinian refugee camps or Native reservations, represents a global phenomenon that will continue to yield more challenges, questions, planes of
struggles, and horizons of potential as time goes on.

## Notes

1. Louis Karoniaktejah Hall et al., eds., *The Mohawk Warrior Society: A Handbook on Sovereignty and Survival* (Oakland, CA: PM Press, 2022).
2. The two short films in question *All My Relations* (2016) and *Indian Winter* (2017)
are a part of the larger multimedia documentary project *The Native and the Refugee*
(ongoing).
3. When we approached Khalil about doing an interview for this book, he introduced us
to Peterson and Rasamny to discuss their collaborative practices.

# 7

# REFRAMING CREATIVE PRACTICE FOR TELLING FACTUAL STORIES OF WAR AND TRAUMA THROUGH ORAL HISTORY INTERACTIVE DOCUMENTARY (OHID)

*Leonie Jones*

On Remembrance Day, November 11, 2016, *The Battle of Fire Base Coral*[1] feature documentary premiered in Australia on Fox's History Channel. This screening represented the culmination of many years working with returned Australian Vietnam War soldiers who experienced the Battle of Coral Balmoral in 1968. The purpose of the documentary was to bring a sense of justice and social recognition to the Coral Balmoral veteran community by informing a general audience of the veterans' experience. The veterans maintain their stories are yet to be fully told and as returned soldiers they have suffered an enforced sociopolitical silence compared to soldiers returning from previous wars. In telling their stories to a wide Australian audience, they seek agency and voice.

The documentary that aired on the History Channel was a general story based on 150 audiovisual oral interviews conducted with veterans of the Battle of Coral Balmoral. However, criticism from some veterans suggested that I had not told difficult storylines. It suggested what I already knew: that representation of this story in a traditional linear form with its necessary editorializing and time constraints did not and perhaps *cannot* enable expansive authentic representation of multiple voices and events in complex stories such as the Battle of Coral Balmoral. The implication for silenced voices is the inability to have a meaningful effect on the events of the experience being told, resulting in potential misrepresentation of the reality experienced and continued feelings of disempowerment.

While I was happy with the outcome of the linear documentary in its purpose to raise awareness, I was not happy with the limitations that restricted voice. This representational problem caused me to seek new ways many and varied voices can be heard. My challenge was to develop a method of telling stories of trauma and war designed to meet participants' needs to speak and be heard on their own terms and in their own words rather than through "hierarchical media as a forum

DOI: 10.4324/9781003174509-9

for privileged voices."[2] To meet this challenge, I embarked on a creative practice exploration that combined my established oral history-based documentary film practice with interactive documentary.

The result is a three-tiered storytelling strategy I have termed Oral History Interactive Documentary. OHID relies on the synergy between oral history, documentary film, and interactive documentary as methods and forms of storytelling. Drawn together by their teleological interests in negotiating stories of conflict and trauma, oral history, documentary film, and interactive documentary, each could record and tell alternative versions of contemporary history, especially stories of marginalized communities. Acting together, their immediacy, polyvocality, and accessibility provide a new form of speaking and coherence that is particularly suited to communities who seek agency and voice. This chapter maps my creative practice journey toward developing an Oral History Interactive Documentary, *26 Days: The Battle of Coral Balmoral.*[3]

## Background to the Battle of Coral Balmoral

In 1968, a mix of national servicemen, "nashos"[4] and regular soldiers, fought Australia's largest, longest, and most costly battle of the Vietnam War. More "Diggers"[5] were killed and wounded during this prolonged engagement than at any other time during Australia's 10-year involvement in the Vietnam War. The Battle of Coral Balmoral took place in Vietnam from May 12 to June 6, 1968. It was a series of battles in which an Australian Task Force operating in an area away from its base in Phouc Tuy Province was pitted against a Division of North Vietnamese Regular forces. On four occasions, the 7th North Vietnamese Army (NVA) Division attacked the Australian Bases Coral and Balmoral in human wave assaults with the support of mortars, rockets, and heavy weapons. On three occasions, Australian forces fought prolonged encounters with enemies who were well entrenched in heavily defended bunker systems. During this period of 26 days, there were 56 other contacts and firefights with enemy forces.

This battle was a major political and strategic victory for the Australian Task Force in South Vietnam and for the Australian Government. However, unlike other wars of Australian involvement, the Vietnam War was a war that affected not only a generation of Australian people but was also the subject of intense scrutiny from a divided society. Central to the division within Australian society was the polarizing effect of the *National Services Act 1964*. By 1969, conscription had divided the nation. There seemed to be no middle ground with those in favor on one side and those against it firmly on the other. It was an unpopular "dirty" war, lacking the sense of national duty and righteousness of the Great War and World War II. It was also a war that did not generate a "winner's history,"[6] leaving social ramifications that had a continuing impact and effect on Australian society. As a result, the Anzac Legend came under fire, and by 1969, the Digger was "no longer a culturally secure symbol in Australian society" (Cochrane 1990, 180). Bearing the brunt of social resentment, Vietnam veterans recall being spat upon and branded "murderers, rapists, and at best fools."[7] By 1971, Vietnam and its veterans were no longer a priority.[8] The Vietnam era soldier, having previously assumed he would be secure in the nation's military tradition, moved into a cultural abyss that would last nearly 50 years.

The veterans of the Battle of Coral Balmoral see themselves as having been unfairly caught in a time of political and social upheaval. They went to the war in Vietnam in 1968 with the nation's blessing but came home in 1969 recast as representatives of an unpopular war. As a result, they have been shunned and forgotten, which has caused this community an enduring sense of injustice and grief. They feel dispossessed of their own history and their place in Australian history. It is within these warfare and post-war sociocultural experiences that, as an oral history documentary filmmaker, I sought to record the veterans' memories in order to help raise their voices.

## Rethinking Documentary Creative Practice in Terms of Interactive Documentary

Like many filmmakers seeking new ways to express, I brought with me linear film production praxis but no experience in interactive documentary. Research soon revealed that interactive documentary exists within the tradition of documentary yet expands documentary's voice and advocacy potential by merging with technologies and tools offered by Web 2.0. Significantly, interactive documentaries are founded on massive databases, one of which I had in the form of 150 audiovisual oral history interviews. By rethinking how the oral histories could be employed to tell the veterans' story, I directed my practice from a linear broadcast television format to an interactive web-based system where temporal restrictions are removed and causal linkages are enhanced.

The shift to interactivity documentary re-conceptualizes the notion of author from the previously preferred documentary film author/viewer dichotomy to a tripartite co-creation relationship between media producer, content, and user. At a basic level, for meaning to occur, the user makes choices by interacting in the virtual world.[9] This means the concept of voice in interactive documentary occurs through a negotiated and performed relationship between author(s), content, and user. The user is able to choose how to move through the i-doc in a negotiated space according to, and within the parameters of the database and navigational functions. The database material is arranged according to pre-existing rhetorical intentions consistent with the documentary's social purpose. As Screen Australia[10] reminds us, the difference between a database and an i-doc is the *intention* of documentary: to present a point of view or perspective(s) through storytelling. The question as to how content might be arranged in a project and how it is situated in relation to other content or linked points to the significance of the database within an interactive environment, as its very existence within interactivity challenges the concept of authorship by opening pluralistic and unpredictable readings.[11]

This raises further questions as to how speakers and potentially vast array of content might be arranged and situated in relation to other content. The arrangement of content is further complicated by navigational functions; what pathways does the user need to take in order to access specific content? Access also includes the way in which the user engages with the argument that sits in the content, referring to the sensory and cognitive process in which the user watches, reads, hears, or engages in debate with the content.

## Reviewing Exemplar I-docs

I commenced my creative practice by reviewing and testing i-docs that dealt with telling stories of trauma and conflict. I wanted examples of design, authorship, style, navigation, and interactivity to help scaffold my creative practice choices. Unfortunately, I did not find a single, battle-specific interactive documentary, which opened an opportunity for this research to help fill that gap.

The most notable exemplar i-docs were *The Prisons Memory Archive* (2007), *Sandy Storyline* (2012), and *First World War: The Story of a Global Conflict* (2014). These exemplars share stories consistent with post-conflict themes of trauma, survival, and resilience. In these i-docs, no one narrative is privileged over another with the i-docs encouraging the user to seek, explore, and experience multiple, contrasting points of view according to time and place. *The Prisons Memory Archive* engages in a co-ownership, participatory production style that encourages interviewees to be involved in the edit phase and how they are represented on screen. The database for *The Prisons Memory Archive*, a hypertext mode i-doc, is founded on edited excerpts from oral history interviews. *Sandy Storyline* employs a participatory mode of interactivity employing mobile technologies to build its database. Short "snap-shot" recordings, captured and uploaded using webcam, personal camera or smartphone by witnesses form an ever-expanding database offering freedom to the user to engage with not only producer included content but also inclusions from other user/participants.

In contrast to *The Prisons Memory Archive* and *Sandy Storyline*, *First World War: The Story of a Global Conflict* is not centralized around eyewitness stories of a single or contained event or experience; rather it approaches storytelling from a global perspective. The treatment of narrative is marked by its similarity to both linear and interactive documentary production processes by interweaving content around seven core-themed "video chapters" designed for a learning experience. The "chapters" feature archival footage combined with audio interviews of seven historians whose voices determine the narrative. The benefit of this omniscient narrator style of discourse is reminiscent of expository documentary form[12] as it creates trust, authority, and a compelling narrative. However, in interactive documentary form, the reliance on one authority on each topic lessens opportunity for alternative points of view.

Drawing from these i-docs, I recognized oral history rather than a social media-based ad hoc approach could lessen the information overload by providing an organizing methodology, which could be usefully linked using a hypertext mode of interactivity. I had found *Sandy Storyline* so vast and so extensively organized into lists of categories that I often lost the thread of the many narratives. As a consequence, themes of place, time, and survival became lost in the options. The idea of community diminished and my enthusiasm for ongoing engagement lessened. *Sandy Storyline* demonstrated the employment of participatory mode could open pathways for those veterans who have not contributed an oral history interview. *First World War: The Story of a Global Conflict* delivered an overarching narrative that could help frame individual stories, which counters the lack of back-story I experienced in *The Prisons Memory Archive* and *Sandy Storyline*. When stories are deeply linked to and framed by national narratives such as the Coral Balmoral story, a storytelling mechanism that makes obvious this relationship is useful, so the storytelling is grounded in context.

## Setting Up a Collaborative Group

Storytelling for survivors of war and conflict is an occasion where they have relative control over their narrative and where their perspectives, silenced elsewhere, become prominent.[13] Forming an ethos of inclusivity is intended to form part of the healing processes because public acknowledgment of a participant's story is a process through which people can feel validated. Having already developed and maintained a strong working relationship with veterans through the documentary project, there was no shortage of collaborators. These collaborators represented a cross section of military units and ranks present during the battle.

Prioritizing co-creation and collaboration with the Coral Balmoral veterans was a "positive designation for this type of media production arrangement"[14] as it encourages interviewees to be involved in how they are represented. As co-creators, the Coral Balmoral veteran community is positioned as both subject and user.[15] In this sense, the veterans are both collaborators and target audience as throughout the oral history interview process, and anecdotal evidence gleaned at various unit reunions, the veterans indicated an incomplete understanding of the battle. Unsurprising, given the size, complexity, and length of the engagement, therefore committing to opening up these storylines serves to establish the various narratives, create avenues to new knowledge, dispel myths, and act as a form of expression.

As the i-doc evolved to prototype, I engaged in a review/response cycle through a Coral Balmoral veteran-only Facebook page. The aim was to test, debug, and gain feedback. From this process, I was able to ascertain how the veterans wanted their stories presented in this new form. The feedback loop was invaluable as I was able to pinpoint the pivotal story moments as the veterans saw them, which helped build the narratives through structural re-alignments.

Toward the end stages of development, I realized that despite my commitment to co-creative practice, I wanted a greater degree of control over final decision-making. This became evident as I worked through the data entry and design stages when I needed to make decisions so the project could be finalized. These decisions were mostly editorial but technically influenced. That's not to say the process became directorial, as negotiations still occurred prior to most decisions, and the veterans' eventual approval of the final OHID.

## Designing the OHID

Drawing from the oral histories and collaborating with the veteran community determined the aims of the OHID. Historical accuracy is paramount to this community as it underpins the tension between memory and recorded history that has frequently been part of their post-war legacy. There was also a need for the individual soldier to be heard within the larger military and sociopolitical story of Coral Balmoral. These needs meant devising a narrative strategy that placed the individual within the battle experience, and given the extent of cultural factors influencing the Coral Balmoral story, the narrative strategy also needed to contextualize the veterans' stories beyond the battle itself. This included their treatment upon return to Australia in 1969 leading to their present-day discontent.

The i-doc also needed to encourage a progressive interactive environment that avoids overpowering users with a seemingly impenetrable amount of material, which could obscure the nuance of the story and thus the purpose. I was also mindful of Screen Australia's definition that an overarching narrative point of view distinguishes an i-doc from a database and that story is key. It must also be entertaining and informative and, as Sue Maslin points out, the story should be organized, efficient, and educational.[16] Therefore, the ability to explore critical information and stimulate user engagement was key for this i-doc. Critical analysis of the exemplar i-docs suggests these are made possible through the different modes of browsing and interaction. I quickly concluded that the complex and complicated story of the Battle of Coral Balmoral was best served with three tiers of storytelling: contextual, individual, and participatory.

Fortunately, my oral history documentary practice includes a hybrid military/ guided life interview method that allows for deep, rich accounts of this event and its people. The method gathers individual recollections that allow for comparison, contrast, themes, and topics to emerge, all of which potentially provide the basis for story structure in the i-doc. This hybrid method is informed by Stephen Everett's *Oral History Techniques and Procedures* for its military focus and a guided life oral history interview approach drawn from the work of Alessandro Portelli and Alistair Thomson.

The military oral history technique developed by Everett's method allows a non-military interviewer to structure a set of questions that enable a military history interview with some authority.[17] Developed during the mid-1980s, this methodology is used by the U.S. Army Center of Military History for oral history interviews with returned service personnel. This approach provides for a subject-related, comparable collection of each individual soldier's experience. Everett's military techniques and method fulfill an evidentiary need by providing causal and strategic details of the historical event while encouraging polyvocality.

Acting jointly with Everett's method is the second part of my interview methodology, a life history interview technique. According to Thomson, a life history approach follows "the contours of a person's life and the priorities of the narrator, with the interviewer gently probing and stretching the account for added detail, depth, and complexity."[18] In this way, the focus is not confined to a particular topic, instead embracing the sometimes smaller, intimate stories. For this reason, a life history approach is a qualitative research method for gathering information on the subjective essence of one person's entire life that is transferable across disciplines. It has been used to explore tensions between individual and collective forms of memory. Together, these methods record the impact of the experience over time providing a framework in which to contextualize the veterans' experience in a broader social, political, and cultural sense, while themes and topics originating from the collection provide a further source for storytelling.

My interview technique is conversational, guided by a list of questions informed by research and based on Everett's and the life story interview approach. Questions pertained to both autobiographical and military inquiry. I began each interview with an easy chat introducing myself, the project aims and how the interview would progress. I did this in an area away from the camera setup so the interviewee would begin to know me and feel confident in the process. At this point, I asked the interviewee about the music he could recall from the sixties. This sensory trigger enabled me not only to distract the interviewee from the technical considerations of the interview as the camera, lighting, and sound setup can be intimidating but also to commence the process of remembering. The interview format was long form, with an average length of 40–50 minutes.

On a few occasions, veterans would recall incidents or events that upset them and they would become emotional and, at times, weep and request the camera be turned off while they recomposed themselves. I respected their rights for privacy, confidentiality, and emotional composure, and in every case, I obliged and stopped the camera recording. In these circumstances, the requirements of the interviewer can be more acute at an interpersonal level, and this became a significant part of my own experience. Some of the interviews became emotional, and my challenge as interviewer was to share the emotions, show empathy, and gently guide the veteran back to a place where he was comfortable continuing his story.

Dealing with their stories of trauma became a significant part of my own experience. Oral historians working with individuals and communities who have experienced trauma can take on "secondary trauma," as observed by Mary Marshall Clark with interviewers working with survivors of the September 11 attacks in New York. Clark says interviewers "needed more of an outlet for the trauma they were accumulating" and that symptoms such as lack of sleep and taking on the physical symptoms of the victims indicated acute stress.[19] She then engaged a psychologist working in trauma to speak with not only the interviewers but also the narrators, an action she attests to, which was successful.

On occasion, I too became emotional. Interviewing Battalion Chaplain Father John Tinkler, a well-respected and loved Battalion priest, I discovered that one of his duties was to write to the parents of the young men who had been killed at Fire Support Base Coral. How he penned those letters struck a particularly emotional chord within me, and I broke down into tears. Perhaps as a mother of two sons my empathy was too close. I still find it very difficult to watch this interview.

Disagreement and discrepancy around individual recollections and the historical record was a prime motivator for some veterans to tell their stories. Guided life history interview method enables comparison between veterans' accounts, the importance of which Portelli attests in his examination of the death of union worker Luigi Trastulli.[20] Portelli draws attention to the value of not only verifiable comparable evidence but also the "falsity" in oral narratives. Accordingly, the oral history interviews underwent scrutiny against each other and against other primary historical sources such as commanders' logs, diaries, and radio logs. Further comparison of this project's oral histories was tried against the Australian War Memorial's (AWM) official history publication *On the Offensive, The Official History of Australia's Involvement in Southeast Asian Conflicts 1948–1975.*[21]

The comparison revealed inaccuracy in how the battle has been recorded. According to veterans, the incorrect reporting of vital parts of their stories includes accounts of the geographical location of the fire support base which placed the base closer to a known NVA stronghold, and the placement of the 1 RAR Mortar platoon on the perimeter of the fire support base, on the night of the first attack. The influence of the AWM's official history is profound and continues to be referenced in other academic publications.[22] As a result, an ongoing concern for the Coral Balmoral veteran community is that the official history, while it remains incorrect, has a continued flow-on effect that until the inaccuracies are corrected, potentially prohibits an end to their stories.

## The OHID

The structure of the OHID became more obvious as I experimented with the three tiers in Klynt media-authoring software. Klynt has a graphical user interface that isn't reliant on high levels of technical expertise. Klynt moves away from linear editing strategies used in film production to a nonlinear storyboard-style interface, which is populated by nodes. A node is a basic unit within a structure that contains data and may be linked to other nodes. Different types of media can be imported, allowing for the inclusion of assets such as photographs, letters, video clips, audio clips, and maps. Nodes can be arranged and grouped into ecosystems according to requirements, which allows for multiple points of view and additional information that could not be included in the television documentary. Nodes build into a mind map of the project's narrative scheme, providing the navigational choices available to the user. Nodes become pages when published on web. I experimented with combinations of nodes creating ecosystems and linkages anchored to the database node holding the oral history interviews.

### First Tier – Contextual Storytelling

The aim of the first tier was to create an authorial narrative that situated the broader military story in context to the sociopolitical climate of the era. Drawing from exemplar i-docs provided me with ideas as to how to situate the individual Coral Balmoral veteran stories within a national narrative while keeping individual oral histories intact. The center of the narrative needed to remain with the individual veterans so that the complexity and variation of their experiences over time remain in focus, yet they also need to sit within a context that gives them meaning. In this project, the veterans' story is bookended by public opinion "mashed together" with changing constructions of the Australian soldier prior to and upon return from Vietnam.

In *26 Days: The Battle of Coral Balmoral* contextual storytelling occurs through a series of ten short narrative video clips. Each story was formulated according to the significance placed on them by the veteran advisory group and the oral history interviews. The ten story parts are organized temporally according to action over time, a period spanning 26 days and bookended by cultural influences prior to and post-battle. This includes a brief contextualization of the sociopolitical climate in Australia in 1967–68 in part one, and the veterans' reflective thoughts about the battle and their treatment upon return in part ten. Part one, *Loyalty*, aims to show general public and veteran attitude toward the Vietnam War and national service in order to set the political, social, and personal scene prior to the Coral Balmoral soldiers disembarking to Vietnam in 1968. This situates the veterans' personal and sociopolitical situation before going to Vietnam in 1968 and then, through comparison in part ten, provides a fuller, richer understanding of their experience.

The length of each clip is kept short so as to maintain the user's interest, while conveying information and emotional intent about the Coral Balmoral story. Users are able to watch the clips or skip to other options. Each story part is produced from the veteran oral history interviews and complimented with assets including archival film, documents, and maps usually found in traditional documentary.

## Second Tier – Individual Storytelling

The 150 audiovisual oral history interviews recorded with the Coral Balmoral veterans provide the foundation for the OHID. The oral histories are housed in a parent node, which forms the database. The function of the oral history parent node is to provide individual, unedited storytelling and the evidential and organizational base.

The process of organizing the interviews into accessible, user-friendly searchable fields began with the more obvious and logical starting point of organizing through military unit and sub-unit. Veterans are organized into these groups militarily through their service, then socially through various associations and organizations so this was an obvious choice. Another obvious organizing method was to search veterans by name. Borrowing from exemplar i-docs, I also included the capacity to search the oral histories by conceptual categories as focus on specific topics mattered to the veterans. Some of these themes related to national narratives and were part of the broader story of Coral Balmoral, while others related to battlefield themes such as mateship and loss. Klynt also includes the ability to annotate timelines, so each individual oral history could be annotated according to chosen key words or phrases, allowing for focus on themes. I was then able to group these key words into a search category, similar to *Sandy Storyline*, which linked back with the broad-based story or the individual oral history. The benefit of the annotation capability is that it allowed shortcuts to specific topics, rather than the user having to watch a whole oral history interview.

The oral history interviews demonstrated that the veterans frame their stories based on events or actions in time. Veterans rarely commence the story in the middle of their 26 days at Fire Support Patrol Base Coral. Instead, they commence their stories with the fly-in on day one, May 12, 1968, because the insertion into the area, fraught with "stuff-ups"[23] began their experience. This is not to say that all veterans remember all the same events, nor do they recall all events as significant. They tend to remember events based on experience gained in their military units and how it affected them. For example, most artillery veterans I interviewed from 102 Battery, who bore the brunt of the North Vietnamese Army frontal attack on the first night, recall this event in great detail. However, most "gunners" do not recall the second attack and place little significance on the event if they do. In contrast, the infantrymen from 1 RAR, most notably A Company who were on the perimeter of the base and thus on the frontline during the second attack, emphasize this as a major event. Analyzing the oral history interviews allowed for major timeline events and thematic topics to surface and are the basis for each of the story parts that form the broad-based story tier.

## Third Tier – Participatory Storytelling

The issue as to how a veteran who was not interviewed could contribute was solved with the inclusion of a participatory mode of interactivity. Veterans are able to write their stories on Facebook, upload a video clip filmed with mobile phone, or add photographs and other documents. The Facebook icon is featured throughout the OHID and acts as a live button that links users to the *26 Days: Battle of Coral Balmoral* Facebook page. The user is invited to join the conversation through questions or comments designed to engage the user. For example, in part one, *Loyalty*, questions include "What do you think of National Service?" and "Do you have a National Service story to share?" This function facilitates debate generating discussion and insight into cultural memory and how it is transmitted over time and through history. It is designed to empower veterans by enabling them to put on record their experiences and reflections or not. In so doing, it becomes a living discussion that potentially generates and uncovers new knowledge leading to new ways of thinking.

During this design phase, I struggled in Klynt as the potential was enormous and my technical ability was limited. I felt at times the idea of the project was moving away from storytelling through oral history and documentary into a mass of choices. I was concerned users could easily become lost in the overwhelming amount of information, as was my experience with *Sandy Storyline*. I questioned whether the i-doc was becoming something of a didactic educational tool and no longer the voice of the veterans. When doubt crept in, I consulted my co-creators who helped strategize complexity into designing meaningful narratives. This meant going back into Klynt and regrouping according to the ten story parts, themes that were important to veterans, and making obvious the individual oral histories through linking patterns.

The OHID went live in May 2020 to coincide with the anniversary of the Battle of Coral Balmoral. It forms the nation's largest database of oral history interviews for this engagement. So, what was the feedback? Did it meet the needs and aims of the Coral Balmoral veteran community?

The veteran's feedback tells me they are pleased and appreciative of how their stories are finally being told. Both general and specific feedbacks were received from veterans or family members via the Battle of Coral Balmoral Facebook page, personal email, or telephone. Overwhelmingly, the comments were positive and supportive of the project. Some responses corrected spelling of surnames. Most complimented the depth and scope of material that was available in the OHID. They were intrigued with the additional information provided in the conceptual category, remarking how significant these themes are to their stories. Others reported that they were brought to tears when listening to some of the experiences of other veterans.

In terms of accuracy and presentation, the responses from individuals affirmed the representation of their unit's story. Veteran Brian Cleaver commented on the OHID's educational value. Cleaver advised that he employed the prototype in his educational activities associated with the Western Australia Premier's Office ANZAC Student Tour program. Cleaver commented that the prototype was so informative and engaging for the secondary school students that it is now an educational supplement attached to that program.

## Conclusion

This project undertook to restore the voice and pride of the Coral Balmoral veterans' exploits, and to tell their stories to the wider community. Many challenges and questions were encountered throughout this creative journey. These included how to build a framework that embraces collaboration and how to integrate the strengths of three different yet overlapping fields of post-conflict storytelling. I was also challenged by how to apply this framework creatively and technologically. These questions were addressed through research, critical analysis, experimentation, and collaborative conversation with the veteran community. This research has, importantly, developed a strategy for communities who are keen to mobilize themselves, and audiences, in a demand for justice.

It is hoped that contemporary history documentary makers faced with similar problems, or communities who seek to raise their voice in an analogous way to the Coral Balmoral veterans will consider OHID as a creative practice strategy. By providing an understanding of processes involved in this research, it is anticipated that this creative practice strategy will be replicable, particularly in application to other fields of post-conflict storytelling. Intriguing is how other areas in factual storytelling, not concerned with post-conflict storytelling, benefit from this research; can the OHID strategy be applied across other types of factual storytelling?

## Notes

1. *The Battle of Coral Balmoral,* directed by Leonie Jones (Sydney, Australia: Fox Studios, Meanjin Entertainment, 2016) DVD.
2. Mary Mitchell, "Where Voice and Listening Meet: Participation in and Through Interactive Documentary in Peru," *Glocal Times* 22, no. 23 (2015): 11.
3. The Interactive Oral History Documentary *26 Days: The Battle of Coral Balmoral* can be accessed at www.fsbcoral.org.
4. National Serviceman known colloquially as "nasho" is a chiefly Australian colloquial term used to describe a person doing military national service. National Service was compulsory military service for young Australian men under the National Service Scheme between 1964 and 1972 (Australian War Memorial 2017).
5. The term "Digger" is a colloquial term used to describe Australian and New Zealand soldiers. Its origins date from World War I.
6. Jeffrey Grey and Jeff Doyle, *Vietnam: War, Myth & Memory* (Sydney: Allen & Unwin, 1992), ix.
7. Robert Costello in oral history interview with the author, 2006.
8. Jane Ross, "Veterans in Australia: The Search for Integration," *Vietnam Generation* 3, no. 2 (1991): 67.
9. See: Judith Aston and Sandra Gaudenzi, "Interactive Documentary: Setting the Field," *Studies in Documentary Film* 6, no. 2 (2012): 125–39, http://dx.doi.org/10.1386/sdf.6.2.125_1.
10. Screen Australia is the Australian Federal Government's key funding body for the Australian screen production industry, created under the Screen Australia Act 2008. It provides industry information and represents Australia's screen industry internationally.

11. See: Hart Cohen, "Database Documentary: From Authorship to Authoring in Remediated/Remixed Documentary," in *Culture Unbound Journal of Current Cultural Research* 4 (2012): 327–46.
12. See: Bill Nichols, *Introduction to Documentary*, 2nd ed. (Bloomington: Indiana University Press, 2001).
13. See: bell hooks, *Yearning: Race, Gender, and Cultural Politics* (Boston: South End Press, 1990).
14. Mandy Rose, "Preface," in *i-docs The Evolving Practices of Interactive Documentary*, eds. Judith Aston, Sandra Gaudenzi, and Mandy Rose (London: Wallflower Press, 2017), 6.
15. Sandra Gaudenzi, "User Experience Versus Author Experience: Lessons Learned from the UX Series," in *i-docs The Evolving Practices of Interactive Documentary*, eds. Judith Aston, Sandra Gaudenzi, and Mandy Rose (London: Wallflower Press, 2017), 120.
16. Sue Maslin, *The Journey of Documentary* (Film Art Media: Webisode April 1, 2012), www.youtube.com/watch?v=ZB8CIWuf4.
17. See: Stephen Everett, *Oral History Technique and Procedures* (Washington, DC: United States Center of Military History, United States Army, 1992).
18. Alistair Thomson, *ANZAC Memories: Living with the Legend* (Melbourne: Monash University Publishing, 2013), 268.
19. Mary Marshall Clark, "Case Study: Field Notes on Catastrophe: Reflections on the September 11, 2001, Oral History and Memory Narrative Project," in *The Oxford Handbook of Oral History*, ed. Donald Ritchie (London: Oxford University Press, 2011), 256–63.
20. See: Alessandro Portelli, *The Death of Luigi Trastulli and Other Stories: Form and Meaning in Oral History* (New York: State University of New York Press, 1991).
21. See: Ian McNeill and Ashley Ekins, *On the Offensive, The Official History of Australia's Involvement in Southeast Asian Conflicts 1948–1975* (Australia: Allen & Unwin, 2003).
22. See: Paul Ham, *Vietnam the Australian War* (Sydney: Harper Collins, 2007).
23. A "stuff-up" is Australian colloquial language that means error.

# PART THREE

# Poetics

# 8

# INTERACTIVE MULTISPECIES DOCUMENTARY METHODS IN WRETCHED WATERS

## The Slow Violence of the Rio Doce Disaster

*Isabelle Carbonell*

On November 5, 2015, a dam from an iron mining operation in Bento Rodrigues, Brazil, suddenly cracked and released 60 million cubic meters of toxic sludge down the Rio Doce, "The Sweet River." This tidal wave of mud then made a 17-day, 800-km downstream journey, rushing toward the Atlantic Ocean, submerging two towns, drowning 19 people, deeply poisoning the water, and asphyxiating fish and other living beings: effectively wiping out an entire ecosystem. Variously called in the media as the "Bento Rodrigues dam disaster" or the "Mariana dam disaster" from the two towns close to its epicenter, the mud tailings destroyed and remapped the entire Rio Doce watershed, and it is not only Brazil's but also the world's most extensive tailings[1] disaster on record. Less than a year after we finished making *The River Runs Red* (2018)[2] in response to this catastrophe, unbelievably, the same mining company[3] had a second catastrophic dam failure on January 25, 2019, less than 60 km away from the Rio Doce, in a town called Brumadinho on the river Paraopeba. This new disaster, while "only" releasing 12 million cubic meters of tailings, drowned nearly 300 people in the mud tidal wave, making it the world's worst tailings tragedy in terms of human loss. These are two grim world records, both of which irreversibly poisoned two entire watersheds. Though seemingly spectacular and sudden in scope, these disasters draw on a long history of slow violence that dates back to the region's colonial mining roots.

*The River Runs Red* is an interactive documentary that seeks to explore how to perceive slow violence in the river for both humans and more-than-humans through a poetic dialectic of new attunements. This project combines two core ideas. First, the site of the Rio Doce is crucial for investigating the long and multifaceted history of slow violence that spans the centuries before and after the disaster. Second, the project proposes experimental documentary film, combined

DOI: 10.4324/9781003174509-11

with an experimental interactive interface, as an embodied, sensorial, emplaced approach for capturing the long now of slow violence. How can interactive documentary rethink narratives of slow violence, for both humans and more-than-humans (defined in the next section), through the form of water? This chapter will span the importance of thinking with water, of defining multispecies cinema, of several water-based interactive sound, web, and VR projects, and end with a thorough review of the Rio Doce disaster and the methods behind the interactive film project *The River Runs Red*.

## More-than-Humans, Slow Violence, and the Anthropocene

The category of "human" is fraught, representing a complex, differentiated sociopolitical and economic construction, not to mention the term does not acknowledge the pluriverse within each of our bodies – more accurately described as "holobionts,"[4] or an assemblage of a host and the many organisms living in or around it. To take stock of the violence of colonial destruction that has resulted in oppressed, subaltern, less-than-human, and otherized perspectives and persons, various terms have been used, such as "sacrificial people"[5] or the "nobodies,"[6] or even the sci-fi "Terrans."[7] In turn, "more-than-human" is defined to include not only humans and Aquans but also whole ecosystems, landscapes, mammals, amphibians, plants, water, viruses, stone-like quartz, and even quarks.

So many bodies of water around the world have become wretched waters: sites of contamination with extensive mining waste, oil refineries, pulp mills, hydroelectric dams, nuclear power plants, radioactive decay, pesticides, fertilizers, flame-retardants, plasticizers, and other environmental devastation that is the result of centuries of "watershed colonialism"[8] and other anthropogenic activities. The phrase "wretched waters" echoes Franz Fanon's groundbreaking book *The Wretched of the Earth*. Fanon provides a psychological analysis of the dehumanizing effects of colonization on both an individual and a nation, advocating for the need for decolonization that called upon the oppressed – the wretched of the Earth – to collectively revolt against imperialism and colonialism and create a new world.[9] I follow Jennifer Wenzel, Ros Gray, and Shela Sheikh's pivot to reread and extend Fanon's ideas to the more-than-human: the Earth, too, is wretched, and "in order to fully grasp the violence of colonialism upon its subjects . . . it is necessary to also address the violence carried out upon the landscape and environment."[10] In these times of deep ecological crisis and wretched waters, nonfiction filmmaking allows a nonlinguistic attunement[11] to the world that opens new speculative possibilities for creating multiple future worlds; and multiple futures *must* be attended to in the dangerous exterminism of the singular universe of the so-called Anthropocene – a term I disambiguate further on. Interactive documentary methods that engage with multispecies cinema (defined in the next section), especially projects attentive to slow violence, require a new approach: one that is plural, multilinear, world-making, future-making. These new methods call for acts of speculation that open the imagination to relearn different ways to see, hear, know, feel, and understand the long now of our ecological crises.

The word "disaster" mentioned earlier is used to denote not only a sudden event, like the dam failures on the Rio Doce and the Paraopeba, but also the slower, invisible harm which both precedes and follows the moment of the dam ruptures. Rob Nixon describes this type of long-term, non-spectacular, far-reaching ecological harm as "slow violence."[12]

*The River Runs Red* traces more-than-human histories following this disaster in the so-called Anthropocene. Though "Anthropocene" or the "Age of Man" has been proposed as a new epoch to describe today's various global environmental crises, other scholars have proposed alternative names, including "Capitalocene"[13] and "Chthulucene"[14] as correctives. The shift avoids the simplistic, universalizing discourse of "Anthropocene," which assigns the culpability for global environmental crisis equally to all humans as an undifferentiated whole. Instead, "Capitalocene" allocates responsibility to capitalism, which is a complex socioeconomic, political system of power and profit that continues to affect global environmental change. "Chthulucene" pivots by acknowledging that the world is as yet unfinished and "made up of ongoing multispecies stories and practices of becoming-with in times that remain at stake."[15] Multispecies cinema takes up this call to ongoingness, where "chthonic ones are not confined to a vanished past."[16] Bodies of water – like those featured in the projects discussed in the following: the Rio Doce, the Guadalquivir river, Chad Lake, and the Everglade swamps – tie together entire continents, civilizations past and present, human with non-human, and sediments with atoms. Waterscapes such as these launch us into a different type of world-making practice, where the assemblage of a lotic ecosystem "generates not a singular knowledge of the world but a world multiple,"[17] and as such, these bodies of water are prime sites to investigate representations of slow violence in the Chthulucene.

## Multispecies Cinema

If we take seriously that a landscape, or a waterscape, is an assemblage of more-than-human relations, an embodied historical accretion, then Heather Swanson argues that landscapes themselves are *multiple* because they emerge from multiple projects. Indeed, can nonhumans make worlds?[18] If so, can we think "with" and not "about" rivers or lakes or swamps, as water leads us to multiple ways of knowing? Indeed, what if interactive or VR documentary methods attempted to "think with, not about" more-than-humans through new investments of sensorial, embodied, and speculative practices?

As suggested earlier, multispecies cinema is a nonlinguistic attunement with more-than-human worlds which explores the interrelationships and entanglements of an ecosystem.[19] Nonlinguistic is defined as not consisting of human speech and language. Multispecies cinema is part of sensorial and embodied cinema, though a longer discussion of its cinematic roots is beyond the scope of this chapter.

Embodied cinema – where bodies are both humans and more-than-human – arrived with advancements in photographic technology in the form of small, inexpensive, and portable cameras, often custom-made. Sam Easterson's *Animal Cams* (1998–2008) is one such example, where he attempted to gather the "point of view" of many different more-than-humans: a bison, a duck, an alligator, a pitcher plant, and a tumbleweed, to name a few. Pooja Rangan calls his cinema a "practice of surrender,"[20] as Easterson lets go of controlling the camera, the animal, or the frame. Though giving more-than-humans a "point of view" is anthropocentric in aim, the filmic results are not always immediately legible to a human subject, and this disorientation produces what Rangan argues is a Marksian haptic – or visually tactile – image. Haptic images play upon a type of synesthesia, and they are an "immanent way of being in the world, whereby the subject comes into being not through abstraction from the world but compassionate involvement in it."[21]

Multispecies cinema builds on these prior sensorial, embodied techniques, yet also asks if the senses are *emplaced*[22] in a larger ecology interrelated with intersecting worlds of humans and more-than-humans. One such example is Barbara Fluxa's *Testimonios Futuros* (2007), a sensorial and emplaced exploration of the waste of the river Nalón in Northern Spain, once deeply contaminated by coal mining. Fluxa refocuses agency within the river's currents by launching a camera and hydrophone in a waterproof container, suspended by two plastic bottles and a flotation device, to float down the Nalón river for eight kilometers over 3 days until it reaches the ocean.

Interactive projects such as *Guadalquivir* (2013)[23] look at the entire length of a river through a series of 360° soundscapes, focusing on certain species and their habitats. The user is invited to pan different landscapes in linear progression down the river and tune in to different more-than-human sounds. The Guadalquivir, whose name derives from the Arabic word for "the great river," crisscrosses Spain and is its only navigable river with a legendary history dating back to the Phoenicians. In 1998, a holding dam burst, releasing five million cubic meters of mine tailings, deeply polluting the waterway – a poignant parallel to my own project in Brazil. Though the i-doc *Guadalquivir* unfortunately does not touch on its own environmental disaster, it does decenter the human in its observation of the natural world through both image and sound, recreating both land- and soundscapes that attempt to draw attention to the diversity of ecosystems that the Guadalquivir unites.[24]

Virtual reality projects like *Swampscapes* (2018) and *Le Lac* (2019)[25] try to use 360° sensorial immersion in a swamp and a lake, respectively, to explore issues of long-term slow violence and environmental devastation. *Swampscapes* delves into Florida's Everglades, one of the largest swamps in the world. In 1848, it was proposed to develop plantations in the Everglades in the quest for more profitable land to exploit with slave labor. Today, over 50 percent of the original Everglades has been drained to increase farmland to harvest sugarcane or develop urban areas which started a devastating ecological disequilibrium.[26] *Swampscapes* seeks to both explore this history and also find ways to negotiate the future of this ecosystem and the web of both humans and more-than-humans which live within it. The VR piece comprises seven local "guides" that lead us through different sites and themes such as extinction, health, and Indigenous world views. Concerned with the accessibility of the 3D VR piece,[27] director Elizabeth Miller and her team also produced a website which features 2D films, a photo gallery, an interactive "swamp symphony," and a host of pedagogical materials to help integrate the project in classrooms. The polyphony[28] of voices in the VR piece (replicated in the films) is essential in creating a mosaic of viewpoints, though the "voices" remain literally and conceptually in the realm of human instead of allowing for a larger diversity of nonlinguistic attunements.

In *Le Lac*, director Nyasha Kadandara explores Lake Chad, a freshwater oasis that provides food and water to over 30 million people living in Chad, Cameroon, Niger, and Nigeria. From 1960 to 1990, the lake lost 90 percent of its water due to desertification, industrial irrigation practices, governmental mismanagement, and climate change. Since then, in part due to climate instability, insurgent groups such as Boko Haram have caused intense violence and conflict in the region, displacing upward of 10 million people. In her VR piece, Kadandara explores this political upheaval and environmental instability through various landscapes around the lake with a poetic voice-over that is supposed to represent the point of view of the lake itself:

> A mild itch turned into what seems like a virus. Invading my shores, eating away at me. Leaving me feeling depleted, wary, and forever insecure. Boko Haram came to my shores at dusk, stealing children, burning villages, destroying everything they came across, leaving Mohammed and Nassuri vulnerable and displaced, and me? Completely helpless.

A musical soundtrack clearly spells out the emotional overtones the audience is supposed to feel while experiencing these different immersive landscapes; the voice-over is a heavy-handed addition that repeatedly reinforces in both form (a linguistic rendition of the lake) and content (the lake's supposed concerns), an anthropocentric point of view. Nevertheless, the project is an important contribution to the world of VR and interactive documentaries in exploring a region that manifests, at the same time, a spectacular type of violence and a slow violence that is both environmental and political.

*The Great Animal Orchestra* (2016)[29] is an interactive web project based on Bernie Krause's 5,000 hours of recordings of natural habitats around the world – his life's work as a field recordist. The name is based on his concept of a "biophony," where animals occupy a type of unique acoustic habitat that is rooted in a collective sonority, where each animal has claimed, out of survival, their own frequency in the sonic spectrum.[30] The lower end is taken up usually by mammals, further up birds, further up insects, until the ultrasonics of bats. This approach to deep multilayered listening of an ecosystem can reveal surprising multispecies entanglements that are not "visible" in other ways. For one of his sites, Krause visited an area in the Sierra Nevada mountains, called Lincoln Meadow, both before and after a timber company had performed so-called "selective logging." Though the forest *looked* the same when he came back, the acoustic ecology was drastically different, with a huge decrease in the density and diversity of birds and other animals. In the 25+ years since, he has revisited the area multiple times, and it still has not recovered its original sonic richness. Krause's audio work demonstrates how a careful study of a multispecies soundscape can reveal the traces of slow violence that are otherwise imperceptible, yet so deeply important to attune to. Digital design studio Upian worked with five of Krause's sonic ecosystems and created interactive visual soundscapes that allow the user to explore different layers of frequencies and the songs unique within each of them.[31] One of these visual soundscapes features Lincoln Meadows. The result is a highly engaging interface that both visualizes the sounds we hear with different shapes and movements and also helps to focus our attunement to both individual and collective sounds.

My own critical practice during my fieldwork in Brazil extends some of the gestures made in these examples, documenting the long aftermath of the Rio Doce disaster. *The River Runs Red* (2018) is an interactive documentary that is a poetic dialectic, with an open-access interface attempting to make visible and audible the slow violence of the Rio Doce disaster through nonfiction film and sound (see Figure 8.1). Attempting to center the river in the project is a step toward avoiding human exceptionalism, as the i-doc brings to the fore multispecies entanglements, and highlights the interconnections within an ecosystem. Before discussing the project's fieldwork and interface, I will begin with the history that led to the Rio Doce disaster.

## The Rio Doce Disaster and Its Double Death

The name of the Brazilian state "Minas Gerais," where the Rio Doce is located, means "General Mines," and it is an accurate indicator of the region's extractive, colonial history. In 1693, Portuguese colonists discovered gold, and a gold rush ensued.[32] Though more than a hundred Indigenous groups inhabited the state of Minas Gerais at the time, a systematic regime of kidnapping and enslavement by bands of Portuguese enslavers drastically reduced their numbers.[33] Only five major groups remain today, and I stop to name them here as a small but important practice of recognition: the Xakriabá, the Krenak, the Maxakalis, the Pataxós,

**FIGURE 8.1**    An aerial drone image of Bento Rodriguez overlayed by a dialectic flood versus fauna from the interface of *The River Runs Red*.

*Source:* Photograph by Isabelle Carbonell and Lucas Bonetti; interface design by Isabelle Carbonell and Andres Camacho

and the Pankararus. The Krenak inhabit a stretch of the Rio Doce, and they were greatly affected by the disaster.

The Brazilian gold rush lasted two centuries, which provoked massive immigration from Europe and a large slave trade, with at least half a million persons kidnapped from Africa to work in the mines. Though the discovery of gold in 1693 was the trigger for European colonial invasion, mining activities expanded from gold extraction to many mineral resources such as platinum, diamonds, palladium, silver, lead, zinc, aluminum, uranium, and iron. In fact, the region is so rich in iron that it is called the "Quadrilatero Ferrifero" or "Iron Quadrangle," one of the largest iron-ore deposits in the world. In 1942, the Brazilian government obtained the support of the United States and Great Britain to form the Companhia Vale do Rio Doce (Vale) to mine and export iron.[34] Vale is the largest source of iron in the world, and, additionally, it runs nine hydroelectric plants and a large network of railroads, ships, and ports to transport its products.

The Rio Doce disaster stands on the pillars of this history. Samarco Mineracao S.A., the company responsible for the disaster, is co-owned by Vale and the Anglo-Australian BHP Billiton, the world's largest mining company. The Fundão Dam that collapsed had been holding tailings from the Germano mine, an open-pit iron-ore operation. Raw iron ore needs to be purified for use, and the resulting waste from this process is called "tailings," which resembles a type of thick, chemical-laden sludge of fine particles which are highly toxic. Tailings are a permanent waste product, and tailings dams are meant to be the permanent "solution": structures built to withstand "forever,"[35] provided there is constant monitoring and upkeep,[36] even after a mine or a mining company dissolves. Given the volatility of extractive capitalism, the only surely permanent part of that situation is the waste itself, not the mitigation of it.

Despite a leaked memo revealing that Samarco was aware of a potential breakdown of the Fundão Dam in 2013, 2 years before the catastrophe, the company did nothing to prevent it. It took no measures to address the problem, not even to create a basic sound alarm to warn local inhabitants in case of an emergency.[3738]

In 2013, with iron prices declining, Samarco tried to expand the area of the tailings disposal by merging neighboring dams in order to reduce costs, despite the operation being more destructive and more precarious than building a new dam. Dam failure was a known issue, with six occurrences in the state of Minas Gerais alone since 1986,[39] never mind the numerous other disasters worldwide. This disregard to actual, and potential, threat of lethality for the environment and for human communities matches the post-boom period of commodity prices dropping.[40]

Samarco exculpates itself by declaring the Rio Doce disaster an "accident,"[41] while fewer than 4 years later as mentioned earlier, on January 25, 2019, a repeat disaster occurred less than 60 km away on the river Paraopeba, in the town of Brumadinho.[42] This new "accident" while "only" releasing 12 million m³ of tailings, instead of 60 million m³ in the Rio Doce incident, killed nearly 300 people in the mud tidal wave, which, as mentioned earlier, made it the world's worst tailings tragedy in terms of human loss.[43] Both disasters were knowingly allowed to happen because of corporate greed; this could be called a "planned disaster," while many have more plainly called it a crime.[44]

Halfway down the Rio Doce is Indigenous Krenak land. There I met Lucia Krenak by the banks of the Rio Doce, where she and her community lived. I inquired whether Samarco was still delivering freshwater to Indigenous land, like they promised to do. She was silent a long time before answering, then explained they bring some, but none for the cattle, and none for the land, so they cannot live as they used to. Then she sang a song in Krenakan, which she ended with despair: "The river is our lives, our mother, our father. The day that dam burst they destroyed our lives."

The Krenak, including Lucia, have already gone through several massive brutal displacements in the long, and still ongoing, suppression of Indigenous people in Brazil. However, the river has never been a death they've had to mourn, and yet now this is not just one but a "double death," when "cascades of death . . . curtail the future and unmake the living presence of the past."[45] Put otherwise, a double death is when a damaged ecosystem loses its ability for resilience and renewal: when the fish are all gone, and the river has been buried under sediment and poisoned with toxic tailings, preventing healthy regeneration. Lucia may have despaired the day I spoke to her, yet the Krenak have no choice but to invent new futures in the face of a double death.

## Making *The River Runs Red* and Attunements

Making a multilinear interactive documentary seemed a natural fit with the subject material, as the disaster spanned more than 800 km of water and land. It was multilinear, multi-spatial, poly-vocal, and multi-landscape by its very nature. This, combined with investigating the slow violence of the disaster for both humans and more-than-humans, led me to using both traditional and experimental filmmaking methods, set within an interactive interface's unique capabilities, to explore the effects of a disaster on an ecosystem. Though the project is based on my dissertation research, and as such I was the director who oversaw the project from start to finish, I had a dedicated production team on the ground, and a lot of important contributions by various collaborators along the way. My co-cinematographer in the field was documentary filmmaker Lucas Bonetti, who grew up in the closest large city to the disaster, Belo Horizonte. Additionally, we had two more crew members with us, L. Assis, a film student from São Paulo, and Antonio Peluso, an American anthropology student who specializes in Brazilian Indigenous studies. Though we were a team, we each had our own experiences and approaches in the field, and as such I go back and forth in my writing between "we" and "I." We cultivated a relationship with MAB, or Movement of People Affected by Dams, who had a grassroots network with all the various towns and cities connected to the river, with Antonio and Assis attending many of their community meetings in Mariana for our pre-production research. Given limited funding, we decided on an intensive shooting schedule that spanned a month down the river, beginning in Bento Rodriguez and ending in Regência, with constant stops along the river.

We were at times split in two, with Lucas and Antonio taking the lead on more traditional documentary coverage, interviewing affected residents for their testimony, whereas I made experimental filmic or sonic interventions as I encountered new assemblages around the river of humans or animals, landscapes, and other more-than-humans. For example, I made daily durational recordings of the river with a hydrophone, an underwater microphone. These recordings, made 9 months after the disaster, revealed zones of complete silence that should have been teeming with fish, the silence being the loudest evidence of the far-reaching aftermath of the chemical-laden sediments. These hydrophone recordings ended up being our main sonic texture for many of our films later on, and they are the sound one hears on the homepage of our interface.[46]

Echoing Easterson's *Animal Cams*, we used portable cameras to strap to a dog who wandered through Paracatu de Baixo, the second town buried in the mud tidal wave. After we left her alone for quite some time – because otherwise she kept close to us likely from curiosity and hunger – the dog wandered through the ruins, wary of other dogs, searching for something we never discovered. Strapping a GoPro to this dog allowed us to notice – to attune – for a few hours to her paths through the landscape in a manner that was very different from our own. The destroyed buildings she trots by were our focus when we arrived, but the dog seems to ignore or want to bypass them, and instead pays attention to the ground, to different smells, and to what remaining life she notices (a man walking by, a lone cow, bees by a bush, other dogs). She does not enter a single building and sticks to the road, perhaps an echo of previous lifeways; thirsty, she laps water at the edge of the river, not knowing it is highly toxic, or perhaps in the extreme heat, not having the luxury of choice. The footage offers a very different sensorial input that goes beyond just a "dog's POV," of a place where the disaster is still an open wound.

We did the same again with a cow in Santana do Deserto while she went out to pasture by the river for half the day. Again, multispecies cinema is about experimentation, speculation, and trying to attune to more-than-human ways of being – even domesticated beings that live with and whose behavior is influenced by – humans. The cow herd is highly social, interacting with one another via sounds and gestures we do not understand. They nip at each other, saddle up close to our cow but then walk away, vocalize different types of sounds (these have been found to be a type of language[47]). It turns out our particular cow was also the bull's favorite companion as he comes over to lick her affectionately, as well as the camera. The herd eventually ambles over to the river to drink the water. I resist here the temptation to aim solely for Knowledge (what facts did we learn from spending a few hours with cows?) but rather lean into also gaining a layer of nonlinguistic attunement – with the cows and with these cows in this particular landscape, with its particular history.

One woman kept a plastic jug full of scorpions who had entered her home right after the tidal wave, escaping the river for better places on land.[48] We arrived 9 months after the disaster, so though we tried to find smaller creatures to attune to – no scorpions to be found, but perhaps a snail? – none were to be found on the banks of the river, a sign that the microbiome had not recovered. Most of the fauna we saw were either previously domesticated and now abandoned (dogs) or livestock with a human caretaker (cows, chickens, mules) or birds such as terns or plovers; no fish, no amphibians, no crabs, no mollusks, etc. Granted, we did not make an extensive catalogue, but I made a practice of searching out life in or by the river every day I was filming, and it was immensely difficult to find. If anything, left to meditate on the waterway itself, I developed a type of attunement with the river as an autonomous entity, through the previously mentioned hydrophone recordings.

Just north of the small town of Bento Rodrigues, ground zero of the dam failure, sat several massive pools of water holding a concentrated number of tailings. The town is often photographed for the story of disaster plainly written on its walls: a red line neatly meeting white, ten feet high. This testimony is repeated on the light gray bark of the trees on the banks and again in the color of these pools, a bright orange depth. Placing a camera under the water found only stillness; every rock covered by a layer of orange silt at least an inch thick. Scraping at the silt with a stick created a suspension that lasted hours, which made visible the temporal nature of the turbidity; the same silt suffocated all the fish at the onset of the disaster. Trying to attune to the ecosystem sometimes became an exercise of *detuning*, as these violent and haunted spatiotemporalities are disorienting.[49] Attunement here "speaks not only to relations but also the absence of relation . . . with lost futures and haunted presents."[50]

In Regência, where the river connects with the Atlantic Ocean, I left a camera at the break (see Figure 8.2). Waves crash into the device with a violent force, only to recede with the same suddenness, burying the camera in sand with each successive stroke. This sand turned black in patches, evidence of ongoing sediment deposition from the mouth of the river. Each of these examples is an attempt at Rangan's cinema of "surrender," where we purposefully let go of controlling the frame, with only the barest amount of editing afterward, as an attempt to deanthropocentrize the narratives of the river, a nonlinguistic attunement with the more-than-human.

It took 2 years and many iterations for us to arrive at a working interface. Again, Lucas and I split our energies: he edited the more traditional documentary pieces, and I edited the experimental pieces while overseeing and designing the i-doc interface. A new collaborator, Andres Camacho, was brought on to help build out the interface. As we were primarily filmmakers without advanced coding abilities and a very low budget, it was essential to use a digital storytelling interface program such as Klynt that could provide a solid framework from which to build out our project. However, this imposed some severe limitations in our ability to be more unique and inventive with the interface. Today, *The River Runs Red* is a constellation of films arranged in a poetic multilinear dialectic. Methodologically, taking a multilinear narrative approach to documenting a disaster helps to undo the myth of one unifying story and instead allows for a polyphony of multiple ideas, narratives, and perspectives to exist at the same time. To this end, instead of a single film, the project is made up of 43 short films. The interface presents three major paths to choose from, and each film proposes a dialectic between two opposing concepts, ideas, words, or worlds. Each new film is the synthesis of this dialectic, and, at the end of the short film, a new set of word choices appear, further opening up the possible paths. There are many possible combinations of the material, and a viewer may never watch all 43 films/dialectics; but, each time they revisit, they will experience a new set of films, and gain something new from the previous journey. With these, and other methodologies employed, *The River Runs Red* tries to reveal other perspectives, ontologies, and temporalities, while attending to a multispecies multilinear narrative of the Rio Doce. In short, the project attempts a nonconclusive portrait of an ecosystem and tries to trace how the river, the humans,

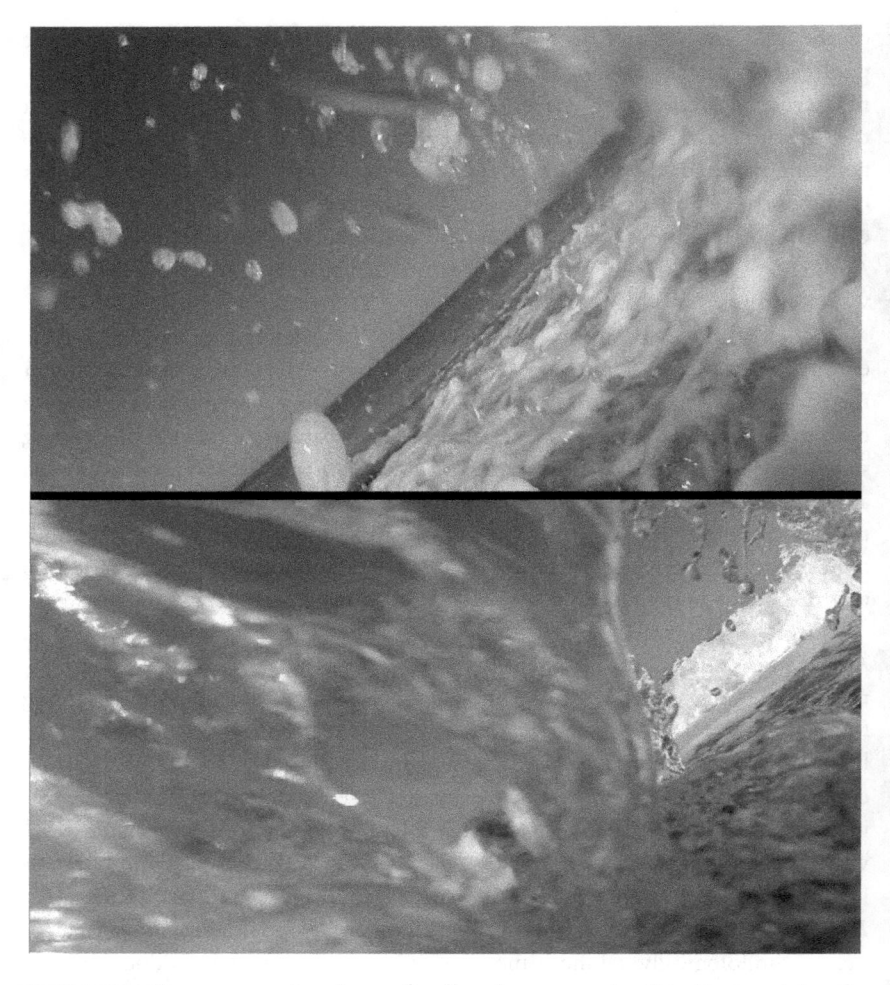

**FIGURE 8.2** Two consecutive shots of polluted water as the Rio Doce rejoins the Atlantic Ocean on the beach of Regência, from one of the short films featured in the i-doc *The River Runs Red*.

*Source:* Photograph by Isabelle Carbonell

and more-than-humans are learning to live with one another in what futures are possible given the irreversible present.

How can we get beyond the end of the Rio Doce? How can we learn to, as Donna Haraway explains, "stay with the trouble of living and dying together on a damaged earth" in order to "provide the means to building more livable futures"?[51] Joseph Masco argues that when the atomic bomb was invented, the possibility of instantaneous total death from nuclear war caused a systemic shift in thinking in America that changed our ability to define catastrophe and the apocalypse, such that we are no longer even able to configure or pay attention to a slower crisis, no matter the evidence at hand.[52] The Rio Doce has this same quality: a spectacular sudden event of total death is seen as the ultimate crisis, versus the slower, long-term effects. To learn how to perceive slow violence, a new attunement is needed. This was the lodestar for *The River Runs Red*: using multispecies cinema, I centered the river in the approach, the questions, the film-making methods. What worlds existed underwater, aboveground, and everything in between? How could these river worlds survive their double death, and what futures could they imagine? Centering the river celebrates the possibility for ongoingness, to stay with the trouble of figuring out how the Rio Doce, and other affected rivers, can survive beyond the end of the world.

## Notes

1. "Tailings" are the waste product from iron mining and purification, a combination of water, fine particles, and various chemicals.
2. Sections of this chapter are adapted from my dissertation. Please visit www.theriver runsred.com to experience the i-doc first hand.
3. Samarco, co-owned by Vale and BHP Billiton; Vale is the largest iron company in the world, while BHP, of Anglo-Australian origin, is the largest mining company in the world.
4. See: Lynn Margulis and Rene Fester, eds., *Symbiosis as a Source of Evolutionary Innovation*, 1st ed. (Cambridge, MA: The MIT Press, 1991).
5. See: Naomi Klein, *Let Them Drown – The Violence of Othering* (London: Edward W Said London Lecture, Southbank Center, May 4, 2016).
6. See: Eduardo Galeano, *El Libro de Los Abrazos*, 5th ed. (México, DF: Siglo XXI, 2001).
7. See: Eduardo Viveiros de Castro and Déborah Danowski, "Humans and Terrans in the Gaia War," in *A World of Many Worlds*, eds. Marisol de la Cadena and Mario Blaser (Durham, NC: Duke University Press, 2018), 172–204.
8. See: Sigma Colon, "Watershed Colonialism and Popular Geographies of North American Rivers," *Open Rivers: Rethinking Water, Place, & Community* 8 (2017): 1.
9. Frantz Fannon, The Wretched of the Earth, trans. Contance Farrington, (New York, NY: Grove Press, 1965).
10. Ros Gray and Shela Sheikh, "The Wretched Earth: Introduction," *Third Text: Critical Perspectives on Contemporary Art and Culture*, 203, no. 151–152 (March–May 2018): 164.
11. A "non-linguistic attunement" implies film can bypass human speech in both inter-action with and interpretation of the world, potentially opening up new forms of attunement with nonhumans.
12. See: Rob Nixon, *Slow Violence and the Environmentalism of the Poor*, Gld ed. (Cambridge, MA: Harvard University Press, 2013).
13. See: Jason W. Moore, "The Capitalocene, Part I," *The Journal of Peasant Studies* 44, no. 3 (May 4, 2017): 594–630.
14. See: Donna Haraway, *Staying with the Trouble: Making Kin in the Chthulucene* (Durham: Duke University Press Books, 2016).
15. Haraway, *Staying with the Trouble*, 55.
16. Haraway, *Staying with the Trouble*.
17. Keiichi Omura et al., eds., *The World Multiple: The Quotidian Politics of Knowing and Generating Entangled Worlds*, 1st ed. (Abingdon, Oxon and New York, NY: Routledge, 2018), 1.

18. Anna Lowenhaupt Tsing, *The Mushroom at the End of the World: On the Possibility of Life in Capitalist Ruins* (Princeton: Princeton University Press, 2015).

19. A longer discussion on the origins of multispecies cinema can be found in my dissertation.

20. Pooja Rangan, *Immediations: The Humanitarian Impulse in Documentary* (Durham, NC: Duke University Press Books, 2017), 178.

21. Laura U. Marks, *The Skin of the Film: Intercultural Cinema, Embodiment, and the Senses*, 1st ed. (Durham, NC: Duke University Press Books, 2000), 141.

22. See: Sarah Pink, "From Embodiment to Emplacement," *Sport Education and Society* 16, no. 3 (2011): 343–55.

23. Alberto Fernandez, Cesar Vallejo, and Charo Marcos, *Guadalquivir*, Interactive Documentary (RTVE, 2013), http://lab.rtve.es/guadalquivir/.

24. Two more important river projects that deserve a lengthier discussion: Jesikah Maria Ross and Vicki Funari's, *Troubled Waters: Tracing Waste in the Delaware River* (2014) and Brian Holmes' and Alexander Meitin's interactive map-based interface *Living Rivers/ Rios Vivos*. See https://troubledwaters2014.tumblr.com/; https://www.casariolab. art/2018/07/21/el-artista-alejandro-meitin-hace-un-mapa-del-delta-del-parana-y-los-problemas-que-enfrenta-la-region/.

25. "Films | Swampscape," accessed March 3, 2021, www.swampscapes.org/guides.html; Nyasha Kadandara, *Le Lac*, Interactive Documentary, 2019, www.nyashakadandara. com/le-lac.

26. S. E. Ingebritsen, "Florida Everglades: Subsidence Threatens Agriculture and Complicates Ecosystem Restoration," *Land Subsidence in the United States: U.S. Geological Survey Circular* 1182 (1999).

27. Patrick Brodie, Lisa Han, and Weixian Pan, "Becoming Environmental: Media, Logistics, and Environmental Change," *SYNOPTIQUE* 8, no. 1 (2019): 6.

28. See: Patricia R, Zimmermann, "Thirty Speculations Toward a Polyphonic Model for New Media Documentary," *Alphaville: Journal of Film and Screen Media* 15 (Summer 2018): 9–15.

29. *The Great Animal Orchestra*, Interactive documentary (Foundation Cartier, 2016), www.legrandorchestredesanimaux.com/en.

30. Tobias Fischer and Lara Cory, eds., *Animal Music: Sound and Song in the Natural World*, 1st ed. (London: Strange Attractor Press, 2015), 124.

31. An installation version, as well as the web project of The Great Animal Orchestra, was commissioned by the corporate philanthropy arm of the Cartier diamond company, FoundationCartier for Contemporary Art.

32. See: Laura de Mello e Souza, *Norma e conflito: Aspectos da história de Minas no Século XVIII* (Belo Horizonte, Brazil: Editora UFMG, 1999).

33. See: Oiliam José, *Indígenas de Minas Gerais* (Belo Horizonte, Brazil: Edições Movimento-Perspectiva, 1965).

34. See: Haruf Salmen Espindola and Cláudio Bueno Guerra, "The Ongoing Danger of Large-Scale Mining on the Rio Doce: An Account of Brazil's Largest Biocultural Disaster," in *From Biocultural Homogenization to Biocultural Conservation*, eds. Ricardo Rozzi et al., Ecology and Ethics (Cham: Springer International Publishing, 2018), 97–108.

35. Gretchen Gavett, "Tailings Dams: Where Mining Waste Is Stored Forever," *PBS FRONTLINE* (blog) (July 30, 2012).

36. Samarco built the Fundão Dam in a style called "upstream dam;" while some scholars debate that the upstream-style dams can be safe, it needs constant monitoring.

37. Andréa Zhouri et al., "The Rio Doce Mining Disaster in Brazil: Between Policies of Reparation and the Politics of Affectations," *Vibrant – Virtual Brazilian Anthropology* 14, no. 2 (August 2017): 9.

38. Samarco's track record before the Rio Doce disaster reveals, between the years of 1996 and 2015, the company had been fined at least 18 times for environmental

contamination. A study by sociologist Rodrigo Salles Pereira dos Santos revealed that Brazilian environmental agencies issue new licenses all the time even to repeat offenders, as mining is considered vital to economic development. Samarco denied most of the fines, and they went largely unpaid by delaying tactics through lawsuits, as after five years the statute of limitations expires and the lawsuit is shelved. See: "Samarco Mineração S.A. Mina de Alegria e Germano.," Parecer Técnico DIMIM (FEAM, 2006).

39. See: Bruno Milanez, Raquel Oliveira, and Clarissa Reis, "Capacidade Ambiental No Nível Subnacional: O Caso Do Estado de Minas Gerais, Brasil," *Planejamento e Políticas Públicas* 44 (2015): 317–42.

40. Rodrigo Santos and Bruno Milanez, "The Construction of the Disaster and the 'Privatization' of Mining Regulation: Reflections on the Tragedy of the Rio Doce Basin, Brazil," *Vibrant* 14 (August 16, 2017): 9.

41. "Results of the Independent Investigation into the Accident at Samarco's Fundão Dam," Corporation, Vale, August 29, 2016, www.vale.com.

42. Marina Novaes, "Brumadinho: as últimas notícias sobre o rompimento de barragem da Vale," *EL PAÍS* (January 28, 2019).

43. Charles Armada, "The Environmental Disasters of Mariana and Brumadinho and the Brazilian Social Environmental Law State," *SSRN Electronic Journal* (January 1, 2019): 4.

44. See: Espindola and Guerra, "The Ongoing Danger of Large-Scale Mining on the Rio Doce."

45. Deborah Bird Rose, "Double Death," *The Multispecies Salon* (blog) (November 17, 2014).

46. Additionally, I also later made a sound installation with collaborator Duane Peterson called *Songs of Mud*, which features five sonic riverscapes from the Rio Doce.

47. Alexandra Green et al., "Vocal Individuality of Holstein-Friesian Cattle Is Maintained across Putatively Positive and Negative Farming Contexts," *Scientific Reports* 9, no. 1 (December 5, 2019): 18468.

48. Rose Senna, The Scorpions of the Rio Doce, interview by Andres Camacho (March 2016).

49. See: Isabelle Carbonell, "Expanding the Interview: A Panesthetic Attunement to More-Than-Human Worlds," *Cultural Anthropology Journal* (September 14, 2021), https://culanth.org/fieldsights/attunements.

50. Julian Brigstocke and Tehseen Noorani, "Posthuman Attunements: Aesthetics, Authority and the Arts of Creative Listening," *GeoHumanities* 2, no. 1 (January 2, 2016): 3, https://doi.org/10.1080/2373566X.2016.1167618.

51. Donna Haraway, *Staying with the Trouble: Making Kin in the Chthulucene* (Durham: Duke University Press Books, 2016), 21.

52. Joe Masco, "Catastrophe's Apocalypse," in *The Time of Catastrophe: Multidisciplinary Approaches to the Age of Catastrophe*, ed. Christopher Dole (Farnham, UK: Ashgate, 2015), 19–46.

# 9

# ON HISTORIES OF DISPERSAL, THE MISSING PICTURES, AND WAYS OF KNOWING

## The Artist's Space Redefined for a Plural Art Practice

*Alexandra Sophia Handal in conversation with Rania Al Namara. Edited by Rania Al Namara*

Alexandra Sophia Handal[1] was born in 1975 in Port-au-Prince to a Palestinian family from Bethlehem. Like many countries in the Caribbean and Latin America during the tense Cold War years, the Haiti of her youth was under a dictatorship. She recalls being home-schooled as a child when curfews were imposed to suppress the protest movements that led to the ousting of Jean Claude Duvalier and the end of his regime in 1986. With relatives dispersed throughout the region, Handal especially remembers summers in Mexico. Forbidden to return to their native Palestine, her family considered moving to Santiago, Chile where there is the largest Palestinian community outside the Arab world but ended up relocating to Santo Domingo, Dominican Republic. These stories of displacement are numerous in Handal's family. Theirs is a history of south–south migration that is intergenerational, transregional and interregional, where the political, economic, and social struggles of the twentieth-century Levant, Latin America, and Caribbean intertwine.

Handal obtained a studio-based undergraduate education at Boston University in 1997, doing summer programs in language and culture in Madrid and Paris. She completed a theory-oriented graduate degree in art at New York University in 2001. After her studies, she taught, exhibited, and traveled in the Mediterranean and Caribbean for a couple of years. In search for an alternative to the art market and artist residencies, in 2004 she applied for practice-based PhDs in London, which were fairly new then and offered the kind of in-depth engagement she was seeking. Her thesis proposal drew the attention of a cross-disciplinary hub called TrAIN (Transnational Art, Identity and Nation) that was being founded that year at the University of the Arts London (UAL). She was granted a Chelsea College of Art and Design Studentship Award to undertake her postgraduate[2] studies at UAL and affiliated to TrAIN, which she completed in 2010.

DOI: 10.4324/9781003174509-12

For nearly twenty years, Handal has been working between Palestine and Europe, spending the first ten years in London, moving for a few years to Amsterdam before establishing her atelier in Berlin and Marseille. Currently, she is a commissioned researcher for the Latin American and Caribbean component of *PalREAD: Country of Words* – a Palestinian cultural project led by principal investigator, Prof. Dr. Refqa Abu-Remaileh at Freie Universität, Berlin. Handal works at the intersection of the visual arts, film, literature, and history. Her interactive web documentary art, *Dream Homes Property Consultants (DHPC)*,[3] is based on original oral history fieldwork[4] that she conducted with Palestinian refugees and exiles from West Jerusalem who lived through the 1948 Nakba.[5] In this interview, Handal describes the role and meaning of documentary to her pluridisciplinary practice as a whole, touching on education, language, translation, and personal and collective histories.

RA: How did you start the i-doc projects in the first place? What is your founding story?

ASH: From an early age, I enjoyed dance, literature, music, and theater but I was particularly drawn to the visual arts, especially painting. What I was unable to articulate through spoken or written words, I expressed through mark-making, color, and gestures. Painting was the first medium that I dedicated myself to. I became aware as a young girl of ten that in the solitude of a painter's practice, I could be connected to the universe. It was giving me new eyes to listen with and new ears to see. The notion of the artist for me then, like now, is that of the truth seekers and interpreters of our society. Every artist inherits a world from which they can build from. Mine was difficult for me to see, as it is characterized by fragmentation, erasure, disruption, rupture, and destruction.

During my childhood in the 1970s and 1980s, I recall that our relatives from Bethlehem were scattered throughout the world, especially in the Francophone, Hispanophone, and Creolophone parts of the Caribbean and Latin America where I was raised. Many upheld a transregional existence from the late Ottoman rule until the end of the British Mandate, their personal stories reflecting the varying political, social, and economic struggles that Palestinians faced in the turbulent decades that led to Al-Nakba. Their lives were being shaped by the challenges of a south–south migration. While countries in the Caribbean and Latin America were confronting the impact of European colonialism and slavery, those in the Levant were dealing with European colonialism and the residues of the Ottoman Empire. This intergenerational and transregional diasporic experience gave rise to my social and political consciousness.

As a young artist, searching through art history books, encyclopedic museums, and art collections fascinated me, but it also left me with a sense of alienation because I did not have the know-how to peel the multiple layers of history that the narrative of power overrode. To surmount the gap, I learned to read between the lines of colonial, imperial, civilizational, and national histories to fill in the missing pictures, until it was no longer sufficient. My paintings obliged a more fertile ground to thrive. Without a critical spoken and written language for them to evolve, I felt silenced. This led me to turn to documentary and archival practices that involved fieldwork and scholarly research. This strand of my work enabled me to possess knowledge and acquire skills in multiple specialized disciplines that I did not have access to when I was an art student.[6] By wandering outside the parameters of disciplinary borders, I was able to construct a foundation from which all my creative practice could expand on.

RA: How did you get inspired on producing this genre of filmmaking?

ASH: Fifteen years ago, when I started working on *Dream Homes Property Consultants (DHPC)*,[7] I had no idea what the outcome would be (see Figure 9.1). There were no precedents for this kind of web-based art that I was engaged in that was making use of the polarity between creativity and scholarly research. I came to what is being referred to today as interactive,

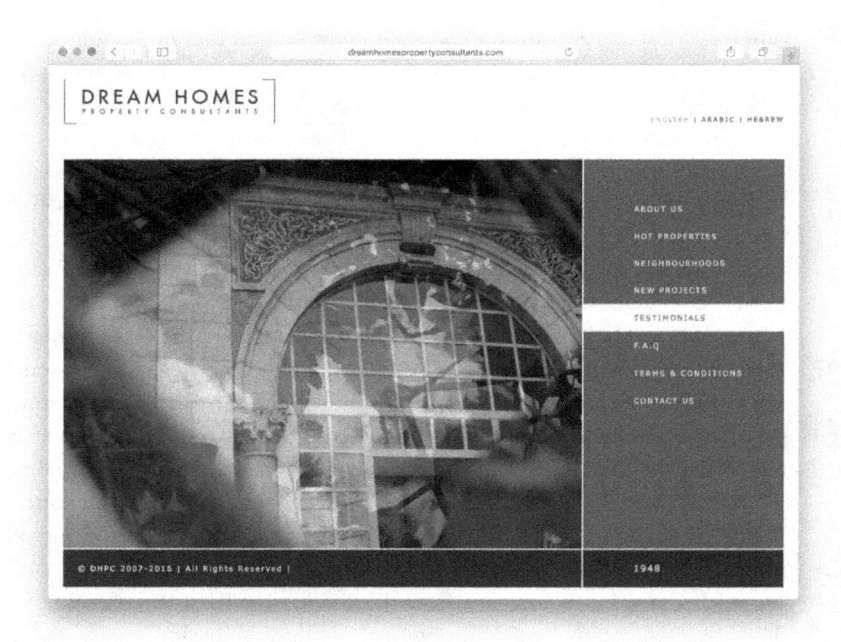

**FIGURE 9.1** Alexandra Sophia Handal, *Dream Homes Property Consultants (DHPC)*, interactive web documentary art, screenshot of homepage, 2007–ongoing.

*Source:* Courtesy the artist

participatory, or web documentaries through experimentation. Being in a new creative territory meant that I had to learn skills from various trades as it became necessary for the artwork.

A flow of ideas referencing varying artistic traditions would move between the different roles I was assuming, as they interacted with other spheres be it law, architecture, anthropology, geography, philosophy, archaeology, cartography, and history. I was aware of my crossings, as I could feel when my creative terrain was opening up. It involved having to negotiate my artistic and intellectual needs. Straddling between disciplines made me into a sharper reader, listener, and viewer. A freedom of thinking and being came about from the redefining of my space as an artist.

RA: Would you tell us more about your artistic process as you were developing the site?

ASH: The initial concept behind *Dream Homes Property Consultants (DHPC)* was to create an art intervention in cyberspace to disrupt the Zionist imagining of Jerusalem and Palestine. The idea came about after I discovered that expropriated Palestinian homes in West Jerusalem were being ironically repackaged on the Israeli real estate market as "Arab-style," an architectural terminology that conceals their factual history. Today, these confiscated Palestinian houses are considered the most sought-after properties in the upscale Israeli Jewish international real estate market, especially among the French, English, and American Jews. I compiled as many of these digital advertisements of "Arab-style" houses that I was able to find in order to study the spectacle of power.

Another approach I used to familiarize myself with present-day West Jerusalem was drifting in the parts of the city that had been emptied of their Palestinian Arab inhabitants. This prepared me for my oral history fieldwork with Palestinian refugees and exiles who came from these areas. Most of them were from the middle class, with some from the working class and upper class. Unlike the majority of Palestinian refugees, they did not end up in camps in 1948, but they still had to rebuild their life from scratch, as they had been uprooted and dispossessed. I started the oral history research with the refugees and exiles who now lived in East Jerusalem and Bethlehem instead of those in the diaspora, as remaining local meant that I could go see firsthand the neighborhoods, streets, houses, and gardens in West Jerusalem that were being depicted to me from memory.

During the process of conducting oral history fieldwork, the emphasis on the artwork shifted. The idea of making an online intervention was no longer at its core. The new starting point became the oral history, which guided me inward. It redirected the energy of the artwork into a source for illumination, while keeping the gesture of protest as an integral part of the work's DNA. My attention now rested on preserving Palestinian Indigenous knowledge. I approached the fieldwork following the rigorous ethical protocols of academia, which came to give the art a scholarly dimension. With the focus of the work changing, I began to view it as documentary.

The oral history fieldwork provided me with the material that *DHPC* would be based on. The experience of gathering the material and the various methods I used to document it gave *DHPC* its polyphonic narrative approach, whereby stories unfold nonlinearly through an interplay of oral, written, and visual components. By making them dependent on one another, I wanted to break down the hierarchies of form in the construction of historical knowledge, as they have been used as a tool for colonial and imperial conquest.

RA: How do you think i-doc filmmaking practices differ from traditional documentary films?

ASH: The difference that I would like to highlight between web documentaries and documentary films is how they were intended to be experienced. There are numerous approaches to documentary filmmaking, but when I think of those that are observational, essayistic, or lyrically inclined, the cinema with its large format screen and dark silent environment remains the most suitable place to appreciate them. I have made the experience of seeing such documentaries on the big screen and later re-seen them on online platforms or vice versa. Some of them barely translated emotionally or sensorially between the big and small screens. I find that the relationship between experience and meaning can also be hindered by the context in which the film is seen. By this, I mean the social space of the cinema and the private space of a home.

As far as web documentaries are concerned, they have many beginnings and endings. Depending on the project, they are conceived to be seen on a tablet, computer, and/or phone screen. Some web documentaries are evolving works, so this informs how they are experienced over time. One can view them at home, at an airport, or at a café (see Figure 9.2). They are portable and sharable across borders, although there is censorship to take into account. Their duration is limitless due to their nonlinearity, so the time the viewer stays on site relies on the experience they wish to have. Web documentaries are not compromised when viewed online like some documentary films. What can be impacted is the quality and experience of the user depending on the internet connection but more importantly the inequalities it raises on matters of participation and accessibility to knowledge.

RA: What do you think are the most innovative features of this genre of film production?

ASH: To create documentaries specifically for the web is to work in a branch of nonfiction that is still undefined and diverse in its scope. Some projects are initiated from cross-disciplinary collaborations, while others come

**FIGURE 9.2** Alexandra Sophia Handal, *Dream Homes Property Consultants (DHPC)*, installation view from solo exhibition: Memory Flows like the Tide at Dusk, Museet for Samtidskunst (Museum of Contemporary Art), Roskilde, Denmark, 2016.

*Source:* Photography by Léa Nielsen

from makers that have multiple professional identities. Then, there are those projects that stem from activism and those that arise from a technological impulse. The open-endedness and inclusiveness are what makes it most innovative, as there are so many reference points and possibilities for experimentation and none so far has been privileged, making conversations lively. This has broadened the realm of storytellers. It has substantially transformed and expanded what a documentary could be. This is reflected in the sheer number of terms that have been used to try and describe the different kinds of projects being realized as documentary takes flight in new directions that are immersive, interactive, and participatory.

RA: In what ways do you think this Indigenous filmmaking would give a voice authority to underrepresented groups? Do you have a specific story to share?

ASH: Palestinians, regardless of where we live or the citizenships we hold, struggle in one way or another to remain in physical contact with our ancestral land and to each other. We need to keep coming up with creative ways to sustain our relationships with people, places, and our environment. Every time I am in Palestine, I do not know if it will be the last. There is always this constant threat of loss. Creating a work that was conceived for the web allowed me to imagine its circulation beyond the restrictions of the physical borders that are imposed on us.

Contrary to the norm where artists strive to have an international audience, our greater struggle as Palestinians is having access to our own culture, which is fragmented in historic Palestine and dispersed globally. Given the nature of web-based documentaries, I could share it immediately with people and they could then continue to share it with others, creating an audience outside the conventional cultural circles. As a result, I have not had to rely exclusively on cultural establishments. I feel I am only beginning to understand the best ways to create a discursive platform for this kind of documentary. There is still so much room to imagine what this might involve. Maybe this is what makes it most hopeful.

RA: How do these films production practices lead/inform us to new things of practice and theory?

ASH: I initially went to French school, but then my parents decided to switch me to a non-sectarian American school. International English was the principal language of instruction, and it was complemented with French, the national one. They believed that studying in the emerging lingua franca of our times would provide me with more professional opportunities, especially given the volatile political and economic climate of the global south. The menace of another dislocation always felt near, and given our family history of intergenerational migration there was this need to be as well-prepared as possible and this meant having access to the Anglophone world, especially the United States which kept up an image then as an inviting country to immigrants. As a result, a foreign language was introduced to the cluster of other languages we were communicating in as a family that had native, colonial, and diasporic significance.

It was while working on *DHPC* that I began to reflect more profoundly on language and my own relationship to them, as my artistic practice had come to include creative nonfiction writing[8] and film. This made me pay attention to the particular ways that the act of reading, listening, and speaking was individually informing how I come to know the world through the various languages that I have ties to, namely French, Spanish, English, Italian, German, Kreyòl, and Arabic. In doing so, I was studying how my knowledge of the world was being constructed beyond the paradigm of national identities, as I have no first tongue that holds greater importance to my sense of cultural and social identity.

My relationship to language is kaleidoscopic in that all are equally significant to how I think and see the world. I do not measure my affection or intimacy to them based on my fluency or which I learned before the other. Perhaps this has to do with the fact that growing up, I traveled daily between my home culture, school culture, and local culture, where different languages could be heard or were spoken. This way of being has shaped how I continue to move today between diverse reference points that make up my family, work, and social life. Within this disjointed multilingual and multicultural context, the process of translation is an integral part of the construction of knowledge. Working in documentary and archival practices has been helpful for me to reflect, question, and examine different types of epistemologies, especially looking more closely at southern global perspectives.[9]

RA: How do you define the relations between the producers, the audience, and subject in i-doc production versus documentary films?

ASH: Documentary film has an already-established production model, whereas web-based documentary does not. When I started working in documentary practices, I founded my own production[10] and distribution platform to think through what this might entail for me the next time. It really was a learn-as-you-go process as I did not know what the final project would be like, what my preferred way of showing it would be and how to distribute it. The model one chooses to produce their web-based documentary matters from the beginning because funding in the visual arts, film, literature, and academia all have their own protocols.

With documentary films, one is working within a pre-existing system; however, with web-based documentary, one is working their way through various established systems. My own projects require fostering "inter," "trans," and "cross" cultural alliances between regions, continents, disciplines, and institutions. I therefore have to invent an infrastructure that best considers the subject matter of my work and its audience to preserve their artistic integrity. This has led me to thinking about ways to use a mixed-system cultural production model so as not to be dependent on any one of them.

More recently, what has been helpful is having learned about the work process of women whose fieldwork and scholarly research was of great significance to their artistic development, their revolutionary pedagogic approach, and their contribution to education. Although Katherine Dunham, Pearl Primus, and Zora Neal Hurston do not come from film or the visual arts, the way in which their fieldwork served as the original source for making their pioneering works in dance and literature, as well as transforming anthropology is a source of inspiration for me today. Dunham and Primus established their own dance schools, while Hurston founded a school of dramatic arts within a college. I admire how their fieldwork provided the footing for imagining a system of interconnectedness between art, life, education, pedagogy, and activism.

RA: How do users' experiences of interactive and non-interactive stories differ?

ASH: To have new tools that make possible what was once inconceivable is certainly exciting, especially when it concerns qualities that provide more inclusive ways to participate and contribute. Interactive features that allow for narrating co-authored documentaries can be empowering, but they also can be superficial. Just because emerging technologies offer us a level of unprecedented connectivity does not mean that their use necessarily leads to meaningful, reliable, and transformative documentary storytelling. I believe that it is not about choosing one direction over another, as there are so many potential levels of interactivity that can be applied to documentary. It is a matter of tapping into their attributes in times when such features can give semblance of closeness in a gratuitous manner. And while these new technologies change what can be done, they do not eliminate the necessity for documentary films and web documentaries that are reliant on human interaction. Many stories can never be told in any other way.

RA: What are the most useful technologies/tools you choose or recommend?

ASH: There is no special equipment I would recommend, but there are some that are necessary. Having a computer with internet connection is essential for an autonomous workspace. External hard drives are mandatory for making sure that there are copies of all digital content at all times. Virtual backups are imperative. Although these steps for ensuring the safety of one's work seem obvious, nonetheless they have an added significance for Palestinians and foreign creatives who work in the Occupied West Bank and the besieged Gaza Strip, for instance. Therefore, it is crucial under the circumstances to store copies of all digital content in multiple locations. Everything else that is required technology-wise changes each time one works on a new project.

What is most important is to start. It is to go places spiritually, mentally, and emotionally that one has not been to before. It is to create the conditions for independent thinking and radical imagining.

# Notes

1. The introduction is based on an unpublished text that Handal wrote to describe her background to Rania.
2. *Dream Home Property Consultants (DHPC)* is one of 15 projects mentioned in a chapter by Ian Biggs in James Elkins' 2014 guide on artists with PhDs. See: Ian Biggs, "Singing Across the Threshold," in *Artists with PhDs: On the New Doctoral Degree in Studio Art*, ed. James Elkins, 2nd ed. (Washington, DC: New Academia Publishing, 2014), 159–167.
3. *Dream Homes Property Consultants (DHPC)* is an ongoing interactive web documentary art that Handal began in 2007. It was a 2013 Official Selection of IDFA DocLab, the new media programme of the International Documentary Film Festival Amsterdam. The 2016 version of *DHPC* is part of the collection of Museet for Samtidskunst (Museum of Contemporary Art) in Roskilde, Denmark.
4. See: Alexandra Sophia Handal, "Chronicle from the Field" in *Oral History in the Visual Arts*, eds. Linda Sandino and Matthew Partington (London and New York: Bloomsbury Academic, 2013), 45–53.
5. See: Tamari, Salim, ed. *Jerusalem 1948: The Arab Neighbourhoods and Their Fate in the War*, 2nd rev.ed. (Jerusalem: The Institute of Jerusalem Studies and Badil Resource Center, 2002).
6. See: "Charting Terrains From Outside the Grid: Alexandra Sophia Handal in Conversation with Alia Rayyan" in *Memory Flows Like a Tide at Dusk*, Exhibition Catalogue (Roskilde, Denmark: Museum of Contemporary Art, 2016), -20-10.
7. To view *Dream Home Property Consultants (DHPC)*: http://dreamhomesproperty consultants.com.
8. See: Alexandra Sophia Handal, "A Passage from a Diary of Echoes," *Jerusalem Quarterly* 69 (Spring 2017): 16–20.
9. See: Boaventura de Sousa Santos, *The End of the Cognitive Empire: The Coming of Age of Epistemologies of the South* (Durham: Duke University Press, 2018).
10. Alexandra Sophia Handal, "C-D Beginnings," *Ciné-Dérive: Cinema and New Media Production House*, www.cine-derive.com/beginnings.

# 10

# DECOLONIZING TRANSMEDIA PRACTICES

## An Essay on Editing

*Anita Wen-Shin Chang*

## Prologue[1]

A new cinematic language can mean a new social imaginary – one that offers a projection of solidarities that acknowledge planetary effects, connections, interdependence, and a utopian guide for change grounded in depictions of daily struggles. The complex subject of language identity and revitalization in Taiwan, and later, along with Hawai'i, calls for a new social imaginary, and therefore, a new form of media arts practice that contributes to the dynamic processes of decolonization efforts.

This essay on editing focuses on the *Tongues of Heaven* (*TOH*) documentary, a key component of the i-doc web application and activist art platform, *Root Tongue: Sharing Stories of Language Identity and Revival* (root-tongue.com). *TOH* was produced and edited by the author and co-directed with Indigenous media makers An-Chi Chen, Shin-Lan Yu, Kainoa Kaupu, and Hao'oli Waiau. Set in Taiwan and Hawai'i, the documentary focuses on the questions, desires, and challenges of young Indigenous peoples to learn the languages of their forebears – languages that are endangered or facing extinction. As part of the women's process of personal reconciliation with what role their heritage languages play in their lives, each woman recorded their conversations with peers, family, and community members. They ask: What do you lose when you lose your native language? The production methodology of the women's collaborative personal camerawork reflects, refracts, and complicates notions of "native," "authenticity," "belonging," and "identity" necessary in the grappling with (post)colonial language identities. Scenes from the women's personal camerawork serve to inspire participation from those visiting *Root Tongue*, a web application designed to extend audience engagement motivated by the issues raised in the documentary

DOI: 10.4324/9781003174509-13

through online dialogue and uploads of creative user-generated content. Themes such as "teacher," "will," and "importance" were major discussion points during Q&A sessions at screening events of *TOH* that eventually inspired the web application design. Moreover, these online "film acts" or dialogic events enact a Third Cinema praxis, hence a *third digital documentary* aspect, for emergent new publics in the era of ongoing decolonizing actions.[2] This research initially resulted in an article I wrote, "In the Realm of the Indigenous: Local, National and Global Articulations in *Fishing Luck*," and evolved into the creative practice with *TOH* that would attempt to address the issues critiqued in the article.[3] As a result, the *TOH* documentary offers an aesthetics and model of collaboration combined with mentoring in the field of documentary production while putting into practice a decolonizing filmmaking methodology within the context of transcultural exchange across territorial boundaries. A "postnational cultural imaginary from the margins" would shape our presence together as women, socially defined as minorities in the land of our citizenship, with interest in bringing attention to our neglected histories and experiences.[4]

In writing about the editing of *TOH*, I have chosen the essayistic format because it lends itself to self-reflexive engagement with topics that usually relate to some forms of sociopolitical crises or aporias. Editing an experimental documentary about language, identity, and culture involves complex negotiations around issues of decolonization, recognition, essentialism, marginalization, inclusion, and exclusion, theoretically and in practice. These negotiations are often wrought with anxieties, ambivalences, discontent, and anger, as well as potentialities. Thus, the essayistic allows a relationship to form between the self and the public in such contested situations of (post)coloniality.

The following essay on editing assays or weighs my personal reflections as filmmaker/editor during the editing stage, along with the writings of students enrolled in the Multilingualism and Ethnic Groups course at NDHU in Taiwan during Fall 2014 upon viewing *TOH*. In juxtaposing their reflections as "watchers" with mine as "maker," I also aim to produce not so much a comparison of intention and reception, but a survey of "directions" and "orientations" that Christian Metz refers to as the "figures of enunciation" in a film. In pointing out the inadequacy of using narratology's notions of "enunciator" and "addressee" in the context of film viewing, Metz proposes that films' enunciators are more like "directions (belonging to the geography of the film)" and "orientations discovered by the analyst."[5] These students, as analysts, offer key insight into the predicament of young people in Taiwan as they consider the future of their language and identity in relation to personhood and nationhood.

## Essay on Editing

*Before viewing the film, I was thinking about its title, "The Language of Heaven." Is this language already in heaven and gone, or is this language as beautiful as heaven?*

*The world's languages are gradually being replaced by more powerful languages, thus beautiful languages that carry culture are heading to heaven.*

*– Chaoyi Ding*

FLUX. Editing is organizing time. Footage that was shot in the past is brought into the present, to be seen in the future. Some images still refer to their corresponding matter in the present, but some images do not, because the matter has been transformed beyond recognition or has simply disappeared. The image, without its originary corresponding matter, can now bask in its own aura. The wall along which An-Chi glided her fingers and the carvings above the wall, the chief's home where we peered in to catch glimpses of ceremonial objects and heirlooms, the rolling fields of millet are all destroyed by the forces of nature.[6] Many blame global warming for wiping out hundreds of years of these ancestral lands inhabited mostly by Indigenous peoples. I did not know that when I shot footage at Wutai Village, that it would become an act of preservation. Something as casual as having fun with your camera becomes a historical homage. I now understand why every time my father would project old super-8 home movies when growing up, my mother's eyes would glisten in the flickering dark.

*Saving Indigenous languages is like trying to save it from the violent waves. Take for example the Pingpu people. They were once the largest ethnic group in Taiwan but have been washed out throughout history and with no language, so what are they left with?*

*– Chao-Yi Ding*

So, here I sit in front of the editing timeline and wonder what is the purpose of this footage, to me, to the film, and more so, to An-Chi and the people she knows who once lived there. There is no there over there anymore, only a was-there over here. This is what I have to work with. Or not. I can find images from there transmitted via bits signals shooting through space, almost at the speed of light. The present is always becoming past, so editing is about organizing the past for the future experience of viewing immersed in the present. Being aware of the past-ness of the audio-visual recordings offers the framework from which to engage with it in the present.

*Why use the mother tongue? My body doesn't want to learn my mother tongue but my heart wants to. I've been struggling with this for a long time. After watching this movie, I understand that the mother language is me, my life, my culture, and I cannot lose it.*

*– Hao-Jun Chen*

*Perhaps I'm still walking towards the path to becoming Amis. I have to make big efforts to walk every step, and I know on this path I will have few companions. But I'll still continue to step forward. If we don't do it, nobody will.*

*– Shi-Ming Ruo*

*For me, am I really dreaming about saving a language, or is it that I really want to learn a language?*

*— Liang-Ying Hu*

As time moves forward, a slow death always seems to set upon us when we think of endangered languages. We seem to only hear about them when news stories tell of linguists rushing to the ends of the earth to record a sole surviving speaker. When we visited An-Chi and Shin-Lan's peer, Yan-Fen, who is actively learning Tsou Kanakanabu from her grandfather, one of ten speakers of this language (who is now deceased), we positioned him at the center of the frame in a close-up shot. We turned the camera on and silently listened as he addressed the camera. Only the cicadas dared to interrupt him. When he stopped, Yan-Fen asked if he could translate what he just said since none of us understood what he said. "Oh yes," said grandpa. "I said my name, I said that I lived here, and the downside is that my parents did not diligently teach us our language." When I am in Taiwan, the pace of transformation is quick and steady, but when I am in the United States, the pace is much slower. Time is ticking, change is happening, but transformation into what? How about what is right now?

*What must we do to reduce the rate of diminishment? The previous generation is getting older and is leaving this world. I'm afraid to think of when my mother language will disappear. Who am I going to be? Will my life be affected? Will our culture diminish just like our mother language? . . . Maybe I cannot put into action to recover my mother tongue, but I hope we will all keep this consciousness alive.*

*— Hao-Jun Chen*

*I'm going to find people to get together and find our roots so we can accomplish the mission of passing down our cultural heritage.*

*— Yan-Shi Chu*

VISION. I have tasked myself with how to let "reality" speak for itself, not so much in the observational sense only but to put pressure on our act of seeing and believing. The cameraperson instigates the field of vision, and I as the editor must figure out how to bring gazing, spectatorship, our desire in seeing, and our choice in seeing, to the foreground of the film frame, hence the mind. Selection is happening, enacting itself, and choosing what viewers can see. As viewers, we naturally browse and gaze, search for meaning, manage our feelings, and at moments we let go of these tendencies, letting ourselves go. I would not know how to make a didactic film about language endangerment, nor do I want to. Rather, as social philosopher Theodor Adorno, in writing about the essay form, eloquently puts it:

The pleasures which rhetoric wants to provide to its audience are sublimated in the essay into the idea of the pleasure of freedom vis-à-vis the object, freedom that gives the object more of itself than if it were mercilessly incorporated into the order of ideas.[7]

In fact, the "pleasures of freedom vis-à-vis the object" is quite a seductive notion, and feels like what I really want to do, or is it? Does not freedom have its dangers, especially the freedom of referentiality? According to Rey Chow,

> [r]eferentiality may in the end require us to accept it more precisely as a limit – as the imperfect yet irreducible condition that is not pure difference but a hierarchized differential, one that is thoroughly immersed in and corrupted by the errors and delusions of history.[8]

In identifying the limits of poststructuralism's main theoretical tenets, that of temporality as indefinite deferment of the signified, and that time does not coincide with itself, Chow demonstrates that in "rewriting referentiality as an illusory effect produced by the play of temporal differences," poststructuralism's motivity is one of a "compulsive interiorization – so much so that even what is excluded, as well as the act of exclusion, has to be cast by way of (or mediated through) interiorization, as a trace, an inscription and so forth," leading to the foreclosure of "X," which Chow marks as marginalized groups and non-Western cultures.[9] Thus, Chow argues that what is more productive is:

> to let the problematic of referentiality interrupt – to reopen the poststructuralist foreclosure of this issue, to acknowledge the inevitability of reference even in the most avant-garde of theoretical undertakings, and to make way for a thorough reassessment of an originary act of repudiation and expulsion (of referentiality) in terms that can begin to address . . . the scandal of domination and exploitation of one part of mankind by another.[10]

While Chow and Adorno are referring to linguistic operations, an interesting challenge is how a filmmaker might heed Chow's call "to let the problematic of referentiality interrupt." How could cinema bring some of its tools to bear in facing this challenge, tools that exceed that of language alone?

First, back to the idea of how to make a film that addresses language loss – what are the forces that lead to language endangerment and loss? The majority of languages endangered and lost are minority languages. Therefore, one cannot talk about language endangerment without talking about the minority, who is most often the marginalized other, hence "X." Besides death, what would cause X to stop passing down their language? What material and immaterial barriers prevented X's language from being passed onto the next generation of speakers? There are no simple answers to these questions, but one barrier is definite, and that is will, the will of the speaker to pass it down and the will of the receiver to learn it. What is shaping or pressing on this will? One factor to explore is how a nation or society treats minority groups, including how it sees the function and value of indigeneity within it. Put another way, how are minorities or indigeneity capitalized upon (or not) and for whose benefit?

> *I don't speak the Amis language and didn't know much about the culture, so my sense of identity is diminished. I didn't volunteer to tell people I'm Indigenous and I didn't want to be perceived as Indigenous. I also didn't want to know about my culture because I felt that the elders didn't know how to protect themselves, speak their minds, and I thought they were ignorant.*
>
> — Yan-Shi Chu

> *The film gave me the feeling of puzzlement, helplessness and sadness because young people are moving away from the village to the city to live and work for economic reason causing the village population to be reduced to only the elders and children. And the situation is worsening. Just like me, I was not born in the tribal village as my parents moved away and severed ties with the tribe.*
>
> — Jing-En Wu

Various "contact zones" are available to the general public in Taiwan as they engage their curiosity and interest in Taiwan's Indigenous peoples.[11] Some of these zones are institutionally supported, such as museums and national parks. Others are privately run, such as theme parks, while others are family-run businesses located on the family's tribal lands. Each zone produces different kinds of spectatorial engagements. By juxtaposing these various scenes of spectatorship, including the documentary itself through the women's camerawork, the viewing dynamics and its power relations can be discerned, hence certain values repeated.

Yet within these multiple settings of looking, lurks the reference, such that each transition to another setting of looking "lets the problematic of referentiality interrupt." One of the most obvious interruptions occurs within a segment at the Aboriginal Culture Village theme park, between the cut from wax figures staged within a ceremonial event, to a stationary figure of a man sitting on a stump. As this wax-like stillness uncannily becomes real, this living simulacrum confuses viewers, returning us back to our "compulsive interiorization." But where do we go to in this interior territory of ours? However subtle or dramatic they may be, these repeated interruptions of the referenced object through various terrains of spectatorship and knowledge are enacted, juxtaposed between scenes of An-Chi and Shin-Lan's personal expressions and voices. This allows for the question: Where does real value lie?

> *There is a section in the movie that moved me: "You have to think of a way to market yourself." I knew that my identity among Taiwan's mainstream society is a very little worthwhile group. I used to feel self-pity as an Indigenous person, especially when I lived with my Han Chinese relatives. I was aware that my skin color is*

*darker and was teased by my relatives because of it. In class and other places, I would find ways to hide my identity. I denied my Indigenous identity. But later, I started to deeply understand Indigenous culture, and discovered the precious value and mission of being an Indigenous person.*

*— Jing-En Wu*

*My tribal village is a tourist recreation area. During the summer tourists flock there for fun and visit our shop. When they ask about us, I will happily talk about our ethnic group, our culture and language. I tell them that Truku people are an optimistic, generous and cheerful people.*

*— Shen-Hua Liao*

VOICE. Amid the flurry of tourists flocking to get their pictures taken with the live Indigenous models in full costume, Shin-Lan is first introduced in the film via voice-over. Her introduction to us as a "pure" Truku woman is set against the visible differences between tourist and performer. Because she is often asked whether she is of mixed non-Indigenous Taiwanese and Indigenous descent, which means she can often pass as non-Indigenous in society-at-large, she is compelled to tell people that she is "pure." What does it mean to deliberately claim your heritage when it is not obviously visible to others? What does it mean to voice and mark oneself? From pure surface to enunciation from elsewhere, this scene aims to contrast the various forms of indigeneity – from an impersonal situation of being a photo backdrop to an intimate documentary voice-over. Hence, the work moves from public display to the personal, back to another type of public display, that is, the documentary presented before us.

*How to make society see us without calling us names, without being magnified to be examined, without stereotyping, without any prejudice (in terms of drinking), but to be truly respected? Especially when I see the Aboriginal Culture Village scene, I felt very sad.*

*— Chu-You Yang*

Meandering through a wax display of Indigenous sorcery, its display panel caught my attention (see Figure 10.4). There were buttons to push. Instructions prompted me: "Push the button to hear the Aboriginal voice." I pushed the button, but nothing was heard. I pushed it again, the same: silence. The button was broken, perhaps by overuse. We want to hear the aboriginal voice, but no one knows it is broken or they do know but haven't gotten around to fixing it.

*I see my grandfather learn our native language and his attitude touches me. The elders are living teaching material. Grab the current time that you still have to learn. It is the duty of native speakers to pass down their language, and keep our culture.*

*— You-Shien Shen*

*If our generation of young people really want to learn our mother tongue, we must be industrious, like grinding the black rose stone. We must carefully carve it to produce a perfectly smooth and bright rose stone.*

*– Shen-Hua Liao*

SURVIVAL. My grandmother had always emphasized to my mother that in order to survive, one must learn the language of a strong, prosperous country, a "sunrise language" as opposed to one of a declining country or society, a "sunset language." As a result, my mother was keen on having her children become fluent in English and speak standard English without an Asian accent. The benefits are clear, but what are the costs of being accent-free? With about 6,000 or so languages spoken in the world, and an estimated two disappearing every month, one may say to oneself, "So what? There are still thousands left." Or one may be shocked at the rate of this loss. Even my immigrant parents who still speak their native language challenged me. My father asked me: "What exactly do you lose when you lose your native language? Your soul?" How could I fashion an adequate response at that moment? Overwhelmed with emotion, I was rendered speechless.

*On learning their native language, many young people will feel, "The heart has desire but power is lacking." They do not know where to begin. Where can they learn it? I say keep expressing yourself in your language even if you don't say it correctly. Keep on trying and you will learn. Making the attempt is most important. Let the surging waves that continue to beat on the obstructing stones remind you not to give up.*

*– Shen-Hua Liao*

*Culture forms what I am today, and language lets me understand our ancestor's wisdom and mountain world.*

*– Hua-Wei Lu*

ENDING. Editors collect their favorite images and sounds, and at times think of the right moment to bring these recordings into the work. Sometimes the entire work or a major section is structured around these images. I have been advised to not let these favorite recordings dictate or distract editors from the pacing, style, information, argument, and discourse they have set out or are tasked to assemble. However, when working with greater creative freedom, these recordings say something about editors' – or more so – filmmaker-editors' desires. I was keenly aware of the ambivalence surrounding language revival and cultural preservation, especially through An-Chi's story as I was creating the script for the documentary. However, when I viewed Shin-Lan's recordings of her mother, I was curious at first about her mother's face, prominently filling the frame, and her direct address to the camera in the Truku language. I wondered why Shin-Lan chose to frame her mother in, what seemed to me, a striking composition? After I received the

Chinese translation of the Truku, I began translating the Chinese into English myself. As I deciphered each phrase and the meaning surfaced, I found myself moved to tears. I was so powerfully affected that my immediate thought was this would be the final scene of the movie. No matter how much I was focused on the complexity of the issues through youth perspectives on will, the fluctuations of culture and language or the "natural" phenomenon of extinction – all the factors that would go against or make the task of language revival an enormously challenging task – here was a middle-aged mother answering her daughter's question about why her Truku language is important to her. Later, after my emotional surge subsided, I struggled with whether I should end the film with this recording, as it may mute the frank admission from young people, like An-Chi, of no longer having the will to learn their heritage languages despite an awareness that they are critically endangered. However, the mother's eloquence, her earnestness, her lived reality, and her corporeality compelled me to end the film with her cogent plea. That despite foregrounding the perspectives of young Indigenous peoples, the fact that Shin-Lan initiated this interview with her mother highlights the importance of intergenerational relations as key to thinking about language survival.

> *When I asked my father why he did not speak Amis to us he replied, "What's the point? You should learn English and that way you will find a good job." . . . But now times are changing, and my father's thinking has changed . . . he will speak some Amis to us and let us remember it slowly.*
>
> – Shi-Ming Ruo

> *My cousin wanted to learn the Saisiyat language and so he returned to the tribe. He spends everyday to do so and everyday he improves a lot. I'm impressed by his diligence. To learn one's language, attitude is very important.*
>
> – Yan-Shi Zhu

## Editing and the Interval

Film and video practitioners who theorize and write about their editing do so to advocate exploring the potentials of the time-based medium to which they are dedicated. They put pressure on analog and digital cinematic tools to create new and energetic experiences of movie-watching that go beyond what has become clichéd or habitual viewing. Instead of "display[ing] things as everyone is in the habit of seeing them,"[12] or producing the feeling of traditional dramas driven by three-act structures, these film practitioner–theorists aim to "shift our perception of reality and experience of cinema."[13]

In *TOH*, I was interested in re-enacting through editing certain kinds of habitual seeing within touristic settings and allowing the skillful work of intellectual montage to let the problematics of referentiality interrupt as detailed earlier.

Montage theories of editing continue to be a critically viable technique for my work and particularly for certain key sections in *TOH*, particularly when montage alone achieves something greater than when voice-over narration is used. The early Soviet film practitioner and theorist Sergei Eisenstein believed that cinema, more than any other art, is able to reveal or enlarge the "mutual work of frame and montage."[14] He considered the period from 1920 to 1935 to be one during which film language developed as an expression of "cinema-thinking" meant to embody philosophies and ideologies that spoke directly to the proletarian experience.[15] Therefore, the technique of intellectual montage, whereby filmed shots or montage cells are edited together to produce a collision that gives rise to a concept, was conceived according to its social mission. As Eisenstein writes, this montage technique is "to form equitable views by stirring up contradictions within the spectator's mind, and to forge accurate intellectual concepts from the dynamic clash of opposing passions."[16] The resulting "intellectual dynamization" of such montage work is executed in the service of the Soviet socialist project. Thus, a major function of intellectual montage is that it does the work of ideology and discursive engagement, and in my case with the editing of the Aboriginal Culture Village segment, the work of discourses on authenticity, commodity fetishism, and nation-building can be activated and dynamically engaged.

Since the lifting of martial law in 1987, and in response to China's continued insistence that Taiwan is part of its territories, advocates for self-determination have mobilized Taiwan's histories, ethnicities, cultures, and languages to assert Taiwan's distinction from China. Part of proving such distinctions or differences requires the labor of not just the researchers but those in the public and private realms of identity production and performance. This has led to a sort of renaissance of cultural revitalization activities, much of it, government-funded, aimed at fostering and deepening pride in Taiwan's ethnic diversity. Indigenous peoples in Taiwan, however, continue to be presented in a hyper-visible manner relative to their population numbers (2.4 percent of the total population), as they are perceived to possess greater markers of difference, such as language and cultural practices, but most of all they are not perceived to be Chinese. For example, since the early 2000s during the beginnings of the Democratic Progressive Party governance and the rise of foregrounding Taiwanese subjectivity, Taiwan's major local and global tourism advertisements were largely Indigenous-themed (still so today but not as prominent).[17] This usually entails the word "Naruwan," which is a greeting in the Amis language, along with an image of an Indigenous cartoon character graphic, creating a new national brand so to speak. While this culturalism is certainly a key activity in Taiwan's (post)colonial milieu, commodification of culture is inevitable, particularly as it pertains to Indigenous peoples.

One example is the Formosan Aboriginal Culture Village, founded in 1986 by non-Indigenous businessmen as a commercial enterprise. In 1987, the park drew 808,628 visitors, and in 2010, it drew over 2 million visitors.[18] The park originally consisted of the Aboriginal Culture Village and the European Garden, with Joy World Amusement Park and the Cable Car added later on. The Aboriginal Culture Village is currently operated by Indigenous peoples though it is not clear if this has always been the case. In a study conducted in 2010, tourism researcher William Hunter showed that the Indigenous performers "consider their performance of culture to be a cornerstone of their identity and a mode for self improvement" and believed it strengthened their culture.[19] The study further concludes: "The key principle is that whereas ownership of the performance commodity might not be totally controlled by the people who perform, the culture itself is."[20] While I do not contest the study's conclusion, the small sample of interviewees does not fully represent the complexities of making a living working and literally living at the park and the nature of its entertainment and spectacular enterprise. My interest would be to consider the structural conditions in Taiwan that compel Indigenous performers to choose to work at this particular park as opposed to somewhere else, and in general the culture of spectatorship in relation to indigeneity.

Therefore, the mise-en-scène (or what is contained within the frame) is also critical to this work, as is thinking and working through temporality, as to form and content, within the act of editing in the broadest Vertovian sense of the term. While Eisenstein's montage theory conceived of shots as "*depictive*, single in meaning, neutral in content" until they are juxtaposed through editing "into *intellectual* contexts and series,"[21] his contemporary, Dziga Vertov, conceived of editing in broader terms that encompassed the time of observation without a camera, post-observation reflections, during filming, after filming and during the actual splicing, which include the "hunting for montage fragments."[22] He writes:

> I make the viewer see in the manner best suited to my presentation of this or that visual phenomenon. The eye submits to the will of the camera and is directed by it to those successive points of the action that, most succinctly and vividly, bring the film phrase to the height or depth of resolution.[23]

In the particular segment at the theme park, I am interested in not so much "points of action," as in showing what Vertov refers to as the "most advantageous sequence" of subjects in motion but the points of transaction from one touristic site to another. That is, each touristic site offers a certain type of sensory transaction in exchange for the payment the tourist gives.

This segment begins at the entrance with an image of tourists walking in a topiary garden against a backdrop of a large European-style building. The scene then cuts to a larger-than-life crab topiary. The audio track is the voice of Auntie Lai, a Rukai activist and cultural worker, as she expresses her opinion about how the government can actively ensure the protection of Indigenous lands and their resources. In the decision to create this segment, I think about how juxtaposing the concept of topiary traditions as the art of training a plant into a desired form and the enterprise of staging indigeneity at a commercial park could foreground and connect these different forms of desire and control. Therefore, as the segment moves from one section of the park to another, questions may arise in the film viewer's mind: How can we equate a crab topiary to Taiwan's Indigenous lands? How did the vision for this theme park come about and for whose benefit? Through a montaging of oppositions that creates points and counterpoints –"directions" and "orientations" – various facets of key issues have potential for being stimulated.[24]

The rhythm and pacing within each shot and the movement to another shot is critical to re-enacting the touring gaze (and in many ways to reproduce how I experienced this gaze), and this required thinking and working through temporality, as to form and content. In Vertov's theory of intervals, the space between each cut, "are the material, the elements of the art of movement, and by no means the movements themselves. It is they (the intervals) which draw the movement to a kinetic resolution."[25] Trinh T. Minh-ha further elaborates on Vertov's concept of intervals as constituting

> interruptions and irruptions in a uniform series of surface; they designate a temporal hiatus, an intermission, a distance, a pause, a lapse, or gap between different states; and they are what comes up at the threshold of representation and communication.[26]

For this segment, the distance or gap of the intervals connecting each tourist area of the park could not be too wide, in order that the "interval" is not made obvious. The pacing and switching of tourist sites are evenly timed in an attempt to put viewers into a simulated state of touristic viewing, in order to make the following intervening sequences more dramatic. After a series of Indigenous wax figures, where the segment then cuts to the Indigenous man sitting on the stump in a slumped over posture (see Figures 10.1, 10.2, and 10.3). Even if the man is not seemingly wax-like, his stillness, whether resting, tired, or sick makes his slight movements interrupt the touristic gazing of the Aboriginal Culture Village segment. This scene cuts to Indigenous performers who are neatly lined up as photo companions for tourists. This cut also creates a counterpoint, broadly, to the animated work of the Indigenous performers within the entire theme park segment.

In addition to the "temporal hiatus" of intervals, I would add the time interval occurring within the mise-en-scène as a key formal element to notions of *framing* as perspective and as a way of being in the world. Gilles Deleuze's film philosophy is a useful conceptual tool in this regard to expand the notions of intervals from in-between shots to the mise-en-scène itself. In particular, Deleuze's notion of the time image, as seen in post-war modern cinemas such as neo-realism and the new waves, foregrounds temporality over movement. He explains that the destructions of war had left in its wake "empty or disconnected any-space-whatevers replacing qualified extended space."[27] In such situations, characters no longer react and

**FIGURE 10.1** Aboriginal Culture Village in *Tongues of Heaven* (2013).

*Source:* Reproduced with permission from author

**FIGURE 10.2** Aboriginal Culture Village in *Tongues of Heaven* (2013).

*Source:* Reproduced with permission from author

**FIGURE 10.3** Aboriginal Culture Village in *Tongues of Heaven* (2013).

*Source:* Reproduced with permission from author

act as they would in the movement-image. Rather, these situations have become "pure optical and sound situations, in which the character does not know how to respond, abandoned spaces in which he ceases to experience and to act so that he enters into flight."[28] But the time-image character "has gained in an ability to see what he has lost in action or reaction: he SEES so that the viewer's problem becomes 'What is there to see in the image?'"[29] While Deleuze's analysis is focused on narrative cinema, I find his notion of time image to be applicable to the documentary genre, especially given that many of the post-war cinemas he is referring to index the real, or the world as is. Further, his theory on the time image can extend to other situations of destruction and, I would add, reconstruction, such as that which occurred as a result of colonialism's violence and its current manifestations today, as exemplified by the existence of the Aboriginal Culture Village.

In response to the (post)colonial conditions, such as cultural destruction, of Taiwan, the theme park was essentially created to commodify the celebration of diversity and difference. Moving through the park as a tourist and filmmaker, I was not only disoriented but also was left to "see" the various points of transaction and movement of bodies from one section to another. The moment I saw the Indigenous man sitting on the stump, the time image came into being, beginning from my perception–imagination, to become a digital moving image. Such metamorphosis is made palpable through making temporal the act of framing. Up to the moment when the image of the man on the stump appears, the pace of browsing, what is seen and how it is seen or framed becomes evident. Temporality, as a character, is used to create viewing conditions, whereby viewers' thoughts have the space to resonate with themselves. This includes Chow's heed to expose the limits of poststructuralism's notion of temporality as indefinite deferment or suspension of the signified leading to a compulsive interiorization that forecloses marginalized groups and non-Western cultures. Viewers of this segment are given an opportunity to see and feel how capital animates exterior and interior realities, but only in relation to experiencing the "aberrant movement" of the man on the stump. As Deleuze has articulated, the everydayness of aberrant movements is one where time is anterior "over all normal movement defined by motivity" or "controlled flow of action" and in this theme park segment, activating this motivity is capital in the broadest sense of the term: monetary, social, cultural, and visual.[30]

On movie-making, film director Robert Bresson once asked: "What is – face-to-face with the real – this intermediary work of the imagination?"[31] As tourist, camera operator, and editor, I noticed and subsequently made visible the abandoned affect I imagined of a man in Indigenous dress sitting slumped over on a stump. Through the interval, as it exists between each shot and within each shot, a mutual space is created for pause, reflection, and sometimes a disruption of the imagination, leading further to an awareness of the interval existing within as viewers and spectators (see Figure 10.4).

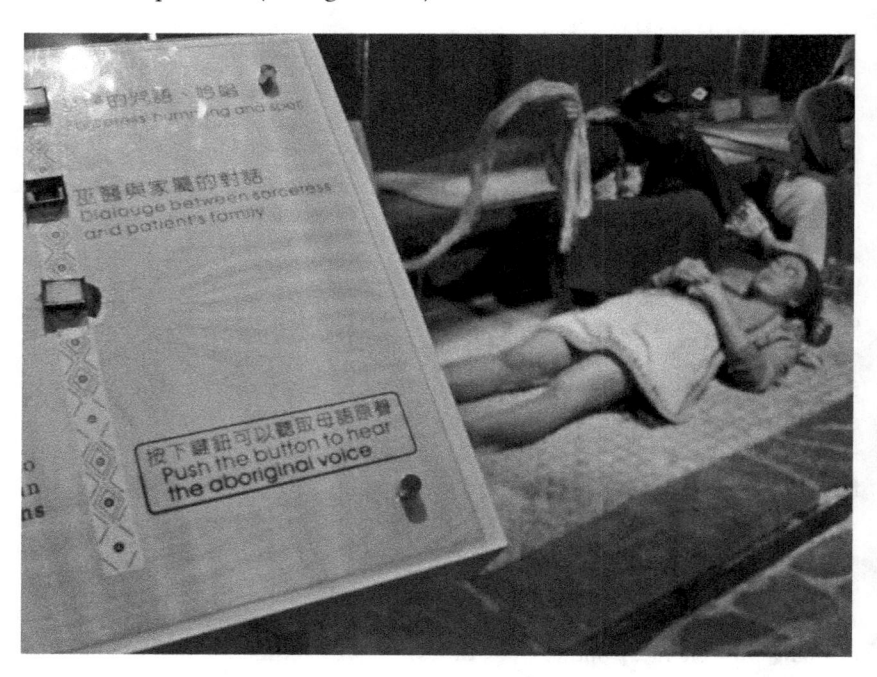

**FIGURE 10.4** Aboriginal Culture Village production still for *Tongues of Heaven* (2013).

*Source:* Photograph by author and reproduced with permission by author

## Coda

In the last scene from *TOH*, Shin-Lan and her mother are sitting on the couch. Shin-Lan asks her mother, "Just speak about the importance of the mother tongue. Any thoughts?" Her mother responds, "Yes, I already said it." "Nothing too long, something shorter," Shin-Lan says. "You can edit it," her mother retorts while pointing at the camera and us, the viewers. Shin-Lan sighs. In the next shot, Shin-Lan's mother's face fills the frame, her eyes cast down. She raises her head slightly and looks directly at the camera. In the Truku language she says:

Qurung nami mniq dxgal Teywan ka yami seediq tnpusu
只要我們這些原住民住在台灣的土地上
So long as we Indigenous peoples live here on the land of Taiwan,

Hncian rudan ka kari o,
長者們留下來的族語，
each language left by the elderly,

Iya bi shngii.
我希望你們不要忘記
I hope you do not forget.

Nasi ungat ka kari rudan do o, hawan bi kida
因為若是長者們的話語失落了將會是一種遺憾
Because it will be a pity when the words of the elders disappear.

Kari rudan o gnarang paah rudan sbiyaw
母語是原住民世世代代地傳承下來的
The mother tongue originated from successive generations of Indigenous peoples.

Niqan gaya rudan ka ga kska kari hiya
語言中蘊含了文化傳統的重要性
Language contains the significance of cultural norms,

Saw ta aji empeydang ni, duwa ta kgdhug mhiyug
幫助我們不會迷失，幫助我們站穩腳步
so that we will not get lost, will not get tripped.

Ga miniq kska kari rudan hiya kana ka knkla nii
這些就存在於長者的智慧話語中
This is all contained in the fine words of the elders.

Nasi saw nii ungat ka kari Truku do o
如果就這樣讓賽德克太魯閣語消失了
If you let the Truku language slip away,

Maha ungat ka gaya aji uri o gaya rudan ta uri da
我們就失去了「gaya」，也就是我們的文化傳統
we will lose our "gaya," our cultural norms,

Maha ungat ka kari uri da, yasa ga mniq kska gaya ka kari nii.
也失去了語言和文化，因為它們就存在於「gaya」之中
and lose the language and culture because they are all contained in "gaya."

Nasi su ini shngii ka kari o, qmlqa su dxgal siida
如果你沒有忘記，那麼當你踏上了土地
If you do not forget it, and when you walk on the land,

Maha su qmlahang balay ni, aji maha niqan sunu ka dxgal uri
你就不會魯莽大意，土地也就不會崩塌
you will not be reckless, and the land will not fall.

Aji su empeydang ni emptakur, maha malu bi ka daun su.
你就不會迷失，不會被絆倒，你可以順利的通過
You will not get lost, not get tripped over, you will squarely pass through.

Brahaw misu balay, iya bi shngii ka kari ta.
我希望你不會遺忘我們的族語
I hope you will not lose our native language.

Saw ga matas ka lqlaqi o
還在讀書的兒女們，
Those sons and daughters who are studying,

Usa ni, sai bi miying duri ka kari namu nanak.
你們一定要回頭去尋找你們的母語
you must turn around and find your mother tongue.

Psai bi qsahur namu ni, ptasi ka kari namu.
在心中記住，然後用筆寫下來
Remember it in your heart and use a pen to record it.

Saw maha tduwa mniq ana bitaq knuwan ka kari ta ni gaya ta nanak uri.
我的願望是我們的「gaya」和語言能永遠流傳
My hope is that our "gaya" and language will last forever.[32]

# Notes

1. This essay is a chapter in Anita Wen-Shin Chang, *Third Digital Documentary: A Theory and Practice of Transmedia Arts Activism, Critical Design and Ethics* (Oxford: Peter Lang, 2020) and reprinted courtesy of Peter Lang. The prologue has been revised.

2. For more on third digital documentary as a critical media practice, see: Chang, *Third Digital Documentary*.

3. One of the main points of the essay is to argue for a sustainable training and funding infrastructure to nurture Indigenous talent in Taiwan's film industry, despite its own economic vulnerabilities. As a personal response, I developed a mentorship opportunity for Indigenous women through the *TOH* documentary project. The essay was first published in the *Taiwan Journal of Indigenous Studies* 2, no. 2 (2009): 97–114, and re-printed in *Positions: East Asia Cultures Critique* 17, no. 3 (2009): 643–53.

4. Kuan-Hsing Chen, "The Imperialist Eye: The Cultural Imaginary of a Subempire and a Nation-State," *Positions: East Asia Cultures Critique* 8, no. 1 (2000): 66.

5. Christian Metz, "The Impersonal Enunciation: Or, The Site of Film (In the Margin of Recent Works on Enunciation in Cinema)," *New Literary History: A Journal of Theory and Interpretation* 22, no. 3 (1991): 765.

6. An-Chi's village, where we had filmed, was located in the mountainous region that was worst hit by Typhoon Marokot on August 8, 2009. The record-breaking rainfall produced landslides that resulted in 700 dead or missing. See: Shou-Hao Chiang and Kang-Taung Chang, "The Potential Impact of Climate Change on Typhoon-Triggered Landslides in Taiwan, 2010–2099," *Geomorphology* 133, no. 3–4 (2011): 143–51.

7. Theodor W. Adorno, "Essay as Form," tr. Hullot-Kentor, and Fredic Will, *Telos* 40 (Summer 1984): 168.

8. Rey Chow, *The Age of the World Target: Self-Referentiality in War, Theory, and Comparative Work* (Durham: Duke University Press, 2006), 69.

9. Chow, *The Age of the World Target*, 63.

10. Chow, *The Age of the World Target*, 69.

11. Pratt defines "contact zones" as the space of colonial encounters, the space in which peoples geographically and historically separated come into contact with each other and establish ongoing relations, usually involving conditions of coercion, radical inequality, and intractable conflict. Mary L. Pratt, *Imperial Eyes: Travel Writing and Transculturation* (London: Routledge, 1992), 6.

12. Robert Bresson, *Notes on the Cinematographer* (London: Quartet Books, 1986), 46.

13. Trinh Minh-ha, *D-passage: The Digital Way* (Durham: Duke University Press, 2013), 146.

14. Sergei Eisenstein, *Film Form: Essays in Film Theory*, trans. Jay Leyda (San Diego: Harcourt, Brace, Jovanovich, 1977), 5.

15. Eisenstein, *Film Form*, 17.

16. Eisenstein, *Film Form*, 46.

17. Bi-Yu Chang, "From Taiwanisation to De-Sinification: Culture Construction in Taiwan Since the 1990s," *China Perspectives* 56 (2004): 44.

18. William C. Hunter, "Performing Culture at the Formosan Aboriginal Culture Village in Taiwan: Exploring Performers' Subjectivities Using Q Method," *International Journal of Tourism Research* 15, no. 4 (2013): 406.

19. Hunter, Performing Culture at the Formosan Aboriginal Culture Village in Taiwan, 413.

20. Hunter, Performing Culture at the Formosan Aboriginal Culture Village in Taiwan, 414.

21. Eisenstein, *Film Form*, 30.

22. Dziga Vertov, Annette Michelson, and Kevin O'Brien, *Kino-eye: The Writings of Dziga Vertov* (Berkeley, CA: University of California Press, 1984), 72.

23. Vertov, Michelson, O'Brien, *Kino-eye*, 16.

24. Metz, "The Impersonal Enunciation," 765.
25. Vertov et al., *Kino-eye,* 8.
26. Trinh T. Minh-ha, *Cinema Interval* (New York: Routledge, 1999), xii.
27. Gilles Deleuze, *Cinema 2: The Time-Image* (Minneapolis: University of Minnesota Press, 1997), 272.
28. Deleuze, *Cinema 2,* 272.
29. Deleuze, *Cinema 2.*
30. Deleuze, *Cinema 2,* 37.
31. Bresson, *Notes,* 72.
32. Translated by Apay Ai-Yu Tang.

# PART FOUR

# Technologies

# 11

# BETWEEN SELF AND OTHER

## Propositions for Non-Dualistic Research on VR

*Eva Theunissen and Paolo Silvio Harald Favero*

Virtual reality (VR) is a technology and a practice of viewing that foregrounds a break from "flatties," that is, from rectangular, framed, controlled, and "distant" cinematographic screens. VR also brings us back to many other, older, and – to use the Gramscian term – "counterhegemonic" forms of viewing. Immersive forms of viewing have characterized many image-making and image-viewing practices of the past, from Etruscan tombs, to Roman bas-relief, stereo photography, (multi)lenticular images, 3D, etc. However, these forms of viewing have become marginalized by the hegemonic force of the flat rectangular photographic image. Embodying the principles of Renaissance perspective, the photographic image was to be recognized as a "natural" model of vision.[1]

In this chapter, we take these reflections further and argue that debates on VR are characterized by a simultaneous claim of novelty and a reduction of the unknown to the known (continuity). Scholars and critics alike often address VR as a new way of making and viewing images. At the same time, they "colonize" VR by reducing it to established categories of analysis imported from the world of "flatties," such as photography, documentary, and fiction film. When it comes to documentary practices, VR poses challenges that are larger than the shift from one type of screen to another.

In what follows, we offer a brief overview of some of the ways VR has been characterized in scholarship over the past roughly 30 years. Next, we offer two vignettes of the VR documentaries that have caught the attention of the authors of this chapter. The third section goes into the various definitions of VR as proposed by other scholars. Arguing that VR documentaries are not merely films, but rather another kind of documentary practice, this section offers a typology that can be useful for unpacking this terrain. In the fourth section, we look

DOI: 10.4324/9781003174509-15

at VR from the angle of embodiment. The core of VR scholarship addresses embodiment in VR as a paradoxical experience that goes back and forth between two extreme ends of embodiment and disembodiment. Looking through the lens of Buddhist philosophy and feminist new materialism, we wonder whether we might conceive of different frameworks for understanding what happens, phenomenologically speaking, when a participant is in VR space.[2] VR experiences (and characterizations) are paradoxical only insofar as one adopts a Western epistemology sustained by dualistic ways of looking at the world. This way of looking at the world can be summarized as the view that "one thing cannot be one and another at the same time and no degree of being one thing and another can exist."[3] We argue that VR is a neither/nor/and terrain that defies simple dualistic categorization. Rather than closing down the question of what VR *truly is*, this chapter concludes with a set of propositions for research formulated within a non-dualistic conceptual framework. Addressing the key categories on which our understanding of moving images is built, we're undertaking an act of epistemological decolonization.

## Views on VR

Definitions and characterizations of VR in scholarship are multiple. Most commonly, they are centered on the distinctive technologies, techniques, and (additional) tools used in making up a VR project, and/or on the perceptual processes and responses that being inside a virtual space elicits. Early characterizations range from "a particular type of experience, rather than as a collection of hardware,"[4] to "a computer technology that presents sensory information producing a convincing illusion that the user is immersed in an artificial world."[5] Mark Hansen focuses primarily on perceptual response and defines virtual reality as the "first properly 'postimagistic' technology" that wipes out the distinction between image and reality.[6] Jay David Bolter and Richard Grusin tackle the question of medium and genre. They argue that VR remediates "the subjective style of film" and consider it a "technology for putting on new selves as one takes on a new visual perspective."[7] The latter definition is very close to the famous view of VR as the ultimate "empathy machine."[8] This view has in recent years been criticized by many.[9] According to Robert Hassan (2020), "the VR commodity-spectacle is fundamentally just that: a sophisticated camera apparatus that produces an integrated spectacle."[10] Characterizations of VR are often riddled with hopes as well as fears. As with the advent of any "new"[11] technology, scholars find themselves divided along the lines of either hopeful optimism or bleak cynicism, and juggle between perspectives of seamless continuity and radical novelty. In Anne Balsamo's words: "the virtual reality industry actually disseminates a certain mythology and a set of metaphors and concepts that cannot help but reproduce the anxieties and preoccupations of contemporary culture."[12]

## Experiences With VR: Two Vignettes

Our interest in VR documentaries comes from two parallel experiences. Here, Paolo explores his encounter with *6x9* (2016), a VR documentary produced by *The Guardian*. *6x9* is a journalistic VR project that "simulates the conditions of solitary confinement and its impact on prisoners."[13]

> Entering this claustrophobic cell space, I was forced to challenge my claustrophobia. While in this room in I experienced the discomfort that comes along with the feeling of being caught in a narrow, enclosed space.[14] I started sweating, my heart accelerated. Yet, I also discovered that that I could easily interrupt the feeling. By accident, I touched the table in front of where I was seated. The act of touching the table with my hand immediately took me out. It was as if my hand brought me away from the virtual space into the physical space where I was seated (in front of a computer). Yet, a part of me (was it my vision or my mind or what was it?) was still inside the virtual space. At a certain point I realized how relief from claustrophobia could also be achieved, so to speak, filmically.
>
> In fact, when I suddenly started levitating in the room, as according to the script of *6x9*, I managed to look out of the window, towards the corridor. That small gesture brought relief and allowed me to breathe, and so did also the act of looking down. The absence of the vision of my legs interrupted my connection to realist representation and therefore brought me relief from panic.
>
> So, I wondered *Where am I exactly*? It would have been easy to fall back on Cartesian dualism to explain the first interruption. My mind was inside and my body on the outside. Yet, what about the sweat? That was, after all, very much internal to the machine. It was on top of it physically contained by a part of the VR apparatus: the goggles. And similarly, my vision, which is per definition embodied, was also contained by the machine.

What story could we get out of this? Was this an experience of another human being's life in solitary confinement, or something quite different altogether? Was it an exploration of a space of "the Other" or an inner exploration, an exploration of the Self in all its affective transformations? Was it inserting me, Paolo, into someone else's shoes or rather anchoring me in my own? Was it a space to tell a story or simply to have an experience? None of these neither-nor choices seem to make real good sense.

Eva's interest in VR was triggered in parallel to Paolo's experience, after first seeing the VR documentary *Notes on Blindness* (*NOB*). *NOB* is an immersive reality project that was released alongside the eponymous documentary/feature film, in 2016. The official web page says that the "interactive experience [the

VR project] complements the story world of the feature film."[15] Eva's notes continue:

> I first experienced this documentary at *DocLab*, a branch of the yearly International Documentary Festival Amsterdam (*IDFA*), in 2016. Even though I had already "seen" a number of VR projects during previous festival editions, what I experienced with *NOB* somehow felt different, much more intense and overall more engaging. *NOB* is made up of six chapters that guide the participant through a number of experiences the narrator of the story, John Hull, went through in the process of becoming blind. Through a poetic voice-over, the participant listens to fragments of original audio tapes that tell Hull's first-person journey into what he calls *deep blindness*. Each chapter addresses a specific memory from Hull's diary and uses binaural audio and 3D animations. Along this journey, participants are introduced to the distressing and mournful as well as the delightful and sublime emotions that come along with losing one's sight. In the documentary, sound guides the participant's perspective. The objects in the VR space, rather than being represented as fully delineated shapes, are instead made visible as drifting clusters of energy with an unstable (and often-disappearing) form. It seems that they aim to suggest a way for the participant to *feel* and perceive the world.

In an interview, one of the authors of the project says that in *NOB* "all is black and every sound is a point of activity, and when there is no sound, then the world dies."[16] This idea was taken from the original audio diaries of John Hull.

> The first chapter of the VR still felt calm and appealing: "I am relatively at home with the feeling of being at the edges of a dark field, and as Hull narrates a story of 'the nature of acoustic space,' I witness small glowing lights steadily form the boundaries of an observable space in concert with the sound of his voice."[17] Chapter 3, however, threw me into the middle of a dark and scary space. No longer just observing, it felt as though I was being sucked into a black void. At one point, I started to panic when I could not find a way to move from this chapter to the next: "I can't see my body when I glance down looking for the promised footsteps. My senses go into overdrive. I feel hyper-alert and visually aware. Indeed, I may not be able to see it but I feel my body acutely."[18]

In these vignettes, we have described (our experiences with) two VR documentaries that enthralled us and remained with us because of the deeply embodied, affective, and sensory responses they triggered. However, when Eva later also experienced *6x9*, she felt hardly impressed. Paolo, too, would on a later occasion also find *6x9* less impressive. What works powerfully for one does not guarantee a similarly affective response in another person. Nor does VR trigger the same effect every time. VR experiences are in fact highly individualized and contextual.[19] Behind the label "VR" goes not only a plethora of different technologies, tools, and techniques[20] but also a plethora of situated responses.

Balsamo writes that the body in VR disappears "representationally," yet it remains present "materially . . . in the phenomenological frame of the user."[21] Following the idea that "forms of experiential engagement involved in VR challenge analytical tools of visual culture,"[22] we suggest that we need to engage with VR in a double direction: for further exploring the phenomenological and embodied dimensions of engagement with the world of images in our analysis of image-making techniques, and to use these insights for a critical reflection on contemporary visual culture theory. VR research needs to take into better account the experiential dimension in the engagement with VR. We suggest doing so by bringing our attention to matters of embodiment within a non-dualistic epistemological account that does not aim to pull the body away from the mind. But first, let us have a look into:

## "New" Vocabularies and Typologies for VR

Defining VR is a complicated matter. As mentioned earlier, the field is divided between scholars such as Bolter and Grusin who address VR within the space of filmic practices, and others for whom VR is *not* the same as film. Janet Murray notes that "VR is not a film to be watched but a virtual space to be visited and navigated through."[23] She builds her argument foremost on the different aesthetical principles and techniques central in the (post)production of a VR project, for instance, the fact that "[t]he focus of VR design is not the camera frame, but the embodied visitor."[24] William Uricchio extends this argument by pointing to the different (and often heterogeneous) underlying technologies, techniques, and tools that make up VR projects.[25] Murray and Uricchio are not the first to define VR away from film theory. Johan Hoorn, Elly A. Konijn, and Gerrit C. van der Veer argue that VR "is not technology and is not new. VR is fiction and fiction is as old as humanity."[26] Reflecting on this matter without falling into the trap of terminology is important. Indeed, VR is not "film" but it is also not entirely "not-film," as it contains evident elements of cinematic conventions. We believe that a terminological debate is useful only insofar as it helps us open our understanding of the unknown, and for tracing new as well as old connections.

We agree with Uricchio's suggestion that VR scholarship needs to "[develop] new expressive vocabularies."[27] One example is that we often go back and forth between terms such as "film," "installation," "project," and "experience" when discussing VR projects. Similarly, we alternate between the terms "viewing," "sensing," and "experiencing"; and between the terms "viewer," "user," "observer," and "participant." Each of these terms suggests a new conceptual space, which may be the key to enter a new set of theoretical challenges. In parallel to this, a number of theoretical concepts need to be rethought. Among them are the notions of the "frame" and "projection," which carry along with them the politics of Renaissance perspective with their separation of mind and body, of self and other, of human and the world surrounding them. We do not aim to go further in depth with this here; others have done so elsewhere.[28] Instead, our aim is to address a question not too often explored in the context of VR documentaries. After all, what *type* of documentary form, style, or, following Bill Nichols' terminology, "mode"[29] are these? And more so, where does this analytical exercise take us?

## Defining Documentaries: Between Truth and Lie

Conventionally considered to be the visual form that has kept alive "the myth of photographic truth,"[30] documentary is expected to maintain a strong adherence to what is conventionally referred to as pre-filmic and profilmic reality – that is, the reality that exists beyond and before the camera.[31] However, the two documentaries addressed earlier do not adhere to this vision. They do not seem to aim at "representing" the pre-filmic world. They break the spell of "photographic truth," as their key concern is not realist representation but something else. They have a different mission. Yet we consider them, nevertheless, to be documentaries. We build our understanding of the distinction between what a documentary *is* and what it *is not* in Dirk Eitzen's article "When Is a Documentary?" There, Eitzen insists that a documentary is a visual form that stimulates in the viewer an exploration of the border between truthfulness and lie. "Might it be lying"? is the question that according to Eitzen identifies the moment in which a viewer enters the space of a documentary.[32] Moreover, this question "is posed by *viewers*, not texts."[33] This is what happened to us when viewing *6x9* and *NOB*, where we both asked ourselves "did this *actually* happen?"

## Documentary Modes

To unpack this further, let us have a look at Nichols' typology of documentary modes. Reacting against the notion of genre, a category that dominates film studies, Nichols has suggested that documentaries can be divided based on a typology with six different "modes" of representation, and also of diverse types of engagement with viewers. The choice of modes, rather than genres, has to do with the fact that one can often find several modes combined in the space of a single documentary film. In Nichols' words, documentary modes "overlap and intermingle."[34] So, while genre tends to lock down aesthetic choices to define a film in its totality, the notion of "mode" provides us with a greater degree of flexibility. This is of fundamental importance once we move into the terrain of VR.

The typology we offer in the following combines Nichols' typology with typologies offered by other scholars,[35] updating them with attention to more recent, participatory, and immersive forms of documentary practice. Nichols' work builds on the existence of six modes: the "expository," the "poetic," the "observational," the "reflexive," "the performative," and the "participatory" mode. Paolo's work on i-docs[36] supplements Nichols' typology with two more modes: the "active" and the "immersive." This brings us to a total of eight documentary modes.

The "expository" documentary mode centers around a narrative. This mode finds continuity in the story rather than in the images, with the voice-over functioning as the spine on which the rest is built. Many TV documentaries (as well as early anthropological and activist films) are dominated by this mode. The expository mode stresses a vertical relationship between filmmaker and film viewer, and often carries a didactic or explanatory ambition. It does not leave much room for reciprocity. The "poetic" mode has a lyrical tone. Rather than explaining, this mode aims at evoking, and rather than stating it implies. Exploiting openness and polysemy (of both image and text), it foregrounds an aestheticized form and is characterized by a more subjective and emotional tone. The "observational" mode is the one that, together with the expository mode, is most commonly associated with documentary film. Often symbolizing the purest form of documentary film, the observational mode aims to promote a sense of unmediated reality, a feeling of *being there*. Not surprisingly, this is also the preferred mode in ethnographic film. "Reflexive" is the mode of representation that makes the conventions (and often also the technologies) of representation visible. Repositioning the relationship between film and subjects, the reflexive mode challenges representation itself. Emphasizing epistemological doubt, reflexive documentaries easily also become a political/ethical statement that aims to close the gap between viewers and the viewed. The "performative" mode invites emotional engagement and directly addresses the viewers. This mode underscores the "affective dimensions"[37] of the documentary's subject matter and explores issues such as personal experience, memory, imagination, and embodied knowledge. Finally, the "participatory" mode is one in which the gap between makers, images, and viewers comes under attack. This happens through a negotiation or dialogue with viewers enacted through their active participation.

In his work on i-docs, Paolo has expanded Nichols' typology by adding two documentary modes, the "active" and the "immersive." The "active"[38] mode of representation concerns documentaries that offer viewers a variety of angles from which to explore the materials that make up the documentary itself. Conventionally using a variety of different media (such as still and moving images, sound files, maps, etc.), these documentaries constitute a creative archive. In this context, viewers are, however, not able to actively change or expand on the materials on display (unless minimally, for instance, by adding comments). Finally, "immersive" documentaries aim to close the gap between the image and the everyday lived experiences of the viewers. Potentially experiential, haptic, and/or emphatic, such documentaries move along a continuum that goes from expanded emplaced participation (bordering on augmented reality) to XR and 360° documentaries.

Following this typology, both *6x9* and *NOB* are simultaneously expository, poetic, performative, active, and immersive works. This shows that the potential of VR lies somewhere in between these categories. In VR, the modalities of engaging the viewer/user/participant do not only build on matters of representation and narrative but also on strategies of engaging and involving bodies. However, these categories do not allow us to unpack any further the multiple and situated negotiations between body and mind, self and other, here and there that take place when entering a VR environment. Responding to our aim to acknowledge the constructive limits of categorizations and typologies, we therefore suggest a move into the terrain of experience and non-dualism.

## Leaving Your Body at the Door: On Being Self/Other/ Not-Self

As described in the vignettes given earlier, the VR documentaries we experienced triggered strong sensory responses. These sensations were intensified by a sense of bewilderment over how something "unreal" can feel so frighteningly real, and even incite feelings of panic. Similar types of "uncanny"[39] experiences have been described by other scholars, many of whom also focus on the type of embodiment of their experiences in and with VR. Mandy Rose notes that VR experiences are of a "paradoxical nature."[40] In contrast to the experience of viewing a film through a screen, in VR the entire medium and hardware (the headset or interface, headphones, cables, the screen/frame, etc.) disappear from the participant's view. VR participants are confronted with "the optical illusion of *being there* within events depicted while at the same time being fully aware of *not being there*."[41]

For the most part, this is because the VR participant no longer has visual access to their body and finds their body "dispersed"[42] in multiple places at once. Some authors have described this process as though they are leaving their bodies behind. Simon Penny argues that "[o]ne does not take one's body into VR, one leaves it at the door while the mind goes wandering."[43] John Barlow offers a similar description: "I've been reduced to a point of view . . . [a]t least I know where I *left* my body."[44] VR has also been addressed as an "empathy machine,"[45] a space where participants may enter someone else's story and body and similarly leave their own body and life story (momentarily) aside.

### *Questioning Our Selves*

What happens when we enter a VR space? Do we truly leave our bodies behind? Are we truly entering the lives of someone else? We claim that the assumptions behind these questions are sustained on dualistic thinking, through a logic of either/or and neither/nor. Looking through a non-dualistic lens, instead, we can ask start to ask different questions. We consider this a decolonizing operation: one that can help us identify the limits of conventional assumptions. While VR has been addressed as an empathy machine, what happens in many cases is that the self is interpellated, in a way in which it is not really "self."

Let us explain this more clearly. When we enter *6x9*, we are also asked to enter the space and experience of an inmate. We can indeed identify with this experience (as we would do in a film) through the story. To some extent, we can also feel that we are entering someone else's body (the person caught in there); for the duration of the VR experience, it feels as though we are actually on the inside of a prison cell. Yet the sensory responses the VR experience enact in the participant speak very much about the participant themselves. Paolo's claustrophobia in fact got interpellated in his experience, providing an entrance into the various short circuits that *6x9* provoked. So, does the experience make us focus on ourselves or on another?

VR offers us a unique opportunity for addressing this question, one which also underlines our engagement with the world of cinema (at least to a certain extent). During these experiences, we are neither exclusively self nor other, neither body nor mind, and neither here nor really there. We are a bit of both yet none. Like looking at an old photograph of yourself from when you were a baby. How much of that person is you? How much is perhaps no longer you? We believe that the conventional dualisms on which Western visuality builds (inner/outer, self/world, self/other, body/mind) do not help us in grasping the subtlety of this experience. VR projects often make participants feel as though they are oscillating between different experiential poles, such as presence/absence, here/there, embodied/disembodied, close by/remote, and self/other. This is the crux of what Rose describes as the "paradoxical nature"[46] of VR. Yet would it be possible to *think differently* in relation to VR experiences? Is the very notion of "the paradoxical" also nothing but a sign of an incapacity to move beyond Western dualisms? Could it be that too much of an emphasis on so-called contradictory experiences merely obfuscates what takes place experientially when a VR participant is present in VR? Following Buddhist and feminist new materialist epistemologies, we argue that VR is a neither/nor/and terrain that defies simple dualistic categorization. These non-dualistic lenses may help us in formulating a constructive critique of the assumptions on which dominant understandings of VR are built.

## *Seeing Differently: Two Non-Dualistic Lenses*

Buddhist philosophy offers us one option for moving beyond dualistic oppositions and for realizing their cultural situatedness. One of the pillars on which Buddhism builds is the resistance to dualistic reductions. Looking upon life, the "self" and the world as impermanent, fleeting, and in constant becoming, Buddhism builds its own theory of knowledge on the principle of non-duality or of double negation.[47] This principle fundamentally states that between opposite poles such as self and other (or not-self), for instance, there is also another possibility: that of being simultaneously both "self" and "not-self" and also "neither self" nor "non-self." Such resistance to dualistic reductions is key to the Buddhist (agnostic and ethics/practice-driven) way of addressing the world. Buddhism engages with the world and with knowledge through a constant act of "confrontation"[48] rather than through a search for solid, stable answers. It can hence be seen as a method, rather than a coherent system of knowledge[49] and one that builds on the impossibility of fully knowing.

The principle of double negation crafts a circular space with four extremes, or four sets of possibilities that can be postulated: being, non-being, both being and non-being, neither being and non-being. Translated into matters of the self, this entails that "I" can be simultaneously "self" and "not-self" and also "neither self" nor "non-self." "I" can be simultaneously "here" and "not-here." This particular space of propositions inevitably forces us to move beyond the meaning of each of these categories and rather focus on their interrelatedness. As Thich Nhất Hạnh (2002) postulates, "[n]othing can exist by itself alone. It has to depend on every other thing. That is called inter-being. To be means to inter-be."[50] The distinction between self and not self, subject and object, viewer and viewed brings to the fore the space-in-between dualisms.

There are some parallels between Buddhist philosophy and postmodern theory. Schools of thought that derive from postmodern theory such as queer theory, science, and technology studies (STS), posthumanism, and (feminist) new materialism also emphasize non-dualistic concepts such as becoming, flow, difference, partiality, and multiplicity. New materialism stands for a "theoretical turn away from the persistent dualisms in modern and humanist traditions whose influences are present in much of cultural theory."[51] Among the binaries this field attacks and aims to rewrite are body/mind, subject/object, meaning/matter, culture/nature, inside/outside, and self/other. New materialism considers matter, materiality, and the body as central. Mind and body are entangled, and rather than disconnected and inseparable, they are smoothly transforming into another like a "Möbius strip where the 'outside' and the 'inside' become one another and are topologically 'unorientable.'"[52] The body is not "autonomous, independent, separated," and "discrete"[53] but instead is relationally involved with the outside world. The body has "*affective potentials*, that is, the potential . . . to affect and to be affected, to move and to be moved, to feel and to arouse feeling."[54] Since the body is never fixed, but instead, "multiple,"[55] it is also "never one, but part of open systems (always already in plural)."[56]

In addition to this, the body is deeply entangled with the world around it. Therefore, the body should not be addressed as separate from the world it seeks to understand.[57] Overall, new materialism engages a world view that centralizes partiality, instability, relationality, and difference. Favoring relationality and multiplicity over separateness and unity, we can borrow from new materialism concepts that may be "good to think with"[58] when studying VR. The concepts and ways of thinking new materialism proposes seem fitting for making sense of the "contradictory" experiences of VR. Yet how do we make the move from theory to research practice?

## Some Propositions for Non-Dualistic Research on VR

In his seminal work *After Method*, John Law writes that: "[i]f the world is complex and messy, then at least some of the time we're going to have to give up some of the simplicities."[59] Responding to the notion that VR experiences are highly individualized and situated, we make a call for qualitative, small-scale, and in-depth research on VR. As Paolo argues, "the struggle" with this space is that it hosts "experiences that can be conceptualized and lived differently by different viewers depending on their own choices, contexts, and viewing positions."[60] In this section, we aim to propose a number of questions and topics that may be addressed in the context of qualitative interviews and may also guide researchers in tackling the "strangeness," heterogeneity, and individual nature of VR experiences.

One central question we propose VR scholarship to focus on is: "what type[s] of body"[61] or put differently, which types of embodiment does VR produce? One way of attending to the participants' ways of feeling (dis)embodied during the VR experience is by interrogating moments of presence and absence that stood out (inspired by Eitzen,[62] the *when* and not the *what*). Were there moments during the VR experience in which the participant felt deeply *affected*? How did this feel in/to their body? Were there also instances of boredom, of drifting off, of being pulled out of the experience? Related to this, as we have shown, is the task of interrogating how dominant Western epistemologies interfere with our understanding by imposing dualistic conceptual frameworks such as body/mind, here/there, present/absent, inside/outside, and self/other. An example of such a practice is Sita Popat, who in her article on the embodied experience of VR uses concepts like "absent-present" to indicate "more than just an apparent duality of experience of both being visually absent and proprioceptively present at the same time."[63] Let us remind readers that in addressing the types of embodiment VR produces, it is important to also consider the ways in which VR systems build on assumptions of an able-bodied and neurotypical participant. Doing this, such systems enable, constrain, or hinder the participant's specific embodied experiences.[64]

A second issue relates to the experience of space and location in VR. Where did the participant feel they were during the viewing? How did the VR space feel, and how did they move through and within it? Did they feel as though they were merely observing or also participating? Did they feel that they were able to navigate the space and interact with it? Which spaces did they visit? Did the participant at moments also experience "breaks in presence?"[65] Breaks in presence are exemplified in Paolo's experience of touching the table at which he was seated and suddenly exiting the virtual space. In such moments, "the participant stops responding to the virtual stream and instead responds to the real sensory system [i.e. from the outside world]."[66] One way to qualitatively explore the participant's sense of location is by interrogating their experiences and interpretations of here and there, inside and outside, intimate and distant in VR space.

Last, and more generally, we propose moving away from fixed and dualistic categories of social science research toward an approach that foregrounds the existential before the epistemological. Foregrounding that existential sense of being that translates into reciprocity, performativity, relationality, and materiality, images do more than merely represent. They act and perform upon us. More than ever today images are "present" in human life.[67] Rather than carrying meaning, they simply *are*.

## Notes

1. See: Paolo S. H. Favero, *The Present Image: Visible Stories in a Digital Habitat* (Basingstoke: Palgrave MacMillan, 2018); Paolo S. H. Favero, "Rediscovering 'Wonder' through I-Docs: Reflections on 'Immersive' Viewing in the Context of Contemporary Digital/Visual Practices," *Alphaville: Journal of Film and Screen Media* 15 (2018): 49–62.
2. With "in VR space," we refer to the experience of being elsewhere, "being there," being "present," or "spatial immersion." The word "in" is key in this sentence: it could be argued – yet also debated – that the immersive and distance-breaking effect and effect of VR are one of the main characteristics that set it apart from previous screen-based media and technologies. Much has been written about the multisensory, spatial, and emotional presence VR participants experience while in VR space. See: Luna Dolezal, "The Remote Body: The Phenomenology of Telepresence and Re-embodiment," *Human Technology: An Interdisciplinary Journal on Humans in ICT Environments* 52, no. 2 (2009): 208–26; Marie-Laure Ryan, *Narrative as Virtual Reality. Immersion and Interactivity in Literature and Electronic Media* (Baltimore and London: The John Hopkins University Press, 2001); Jonathan Steuer, "Defining Virtual Reality: Dimensions Determining Telepresence," *Journal of Communication* 42, no. 4 (1992).
3. Bernd Reiter, "Fuzzy Epistemology Decolonizing the Social Sciences," *Journal for the Theory of Social Behavior* 50 (2020): 107.
4. Steuer, "Defining Virtual Reality," 74.
5. Richard Coyne, "Heidegger and Virtual Reality: The Implications of Heidegger's Thinking for Computer Representations," *Leonardo* 27, no. 1 (1994): 65.
6. Mark Hansen, *New Philosophy for New Media* (Cambridge and London: MIT Press, 2004), 166.
7. Jay David Bolter and Richard Grusin, *Remediation. Understanding New Media* (Cambridge: MIT Press, 1999), 165–66.
8. See: John Constine, "Virtual Reality, the Empathy Machine," *Techcrunch* (February 1, 2015), https://techcrunch.com/2015/02/01/what-it-feels-like/; Chris Milk, "How Virtual Reality Can Create the Ultimate Empathy Machine," *Ted Talks* (2015), www.ted.com/talks/chris_milk_how_virtual_reality_can_create_the_ultimate_empathy_machine?language=en.
9. See: Robert Hassan, "Digitality, Virtual Reality and the 'Empathy Machine,'" *Digital Journalism* 8, no. 2 (2020): 209; Kate Nash, "Virtual Reality Witness: Exploring the Ethics of Mediated Presence," *Studies in Documentary Film* 11, no. 2 (2017): 1–13; Janet H Murray, "Not a Film and Not an Empathy Machine," *Immerse News* (2016), https://immerse.news/not-a-film-and-not-an-empathy-machine-48b63b0eda93;

William Uricchio, "VR is Not Film, So What Is It?" *Immerse News* (November 8, 2016), https://immerse.news/vr-is-not-film-so-what-is-it-36d58e59c030.

10. Robert Hassan, "Digitality," 209.
11. Indeed, VR is not that "new," we mean by "new" here the fact that VR has only in recent days become commercially available.
12. Anne Balsamo, *Technologies of the Gendered Body* (Durham and London: Duke University Press, 1995), 122.
13. Massachusetts Institute of Technology, Docubase, "6x9," accessed September 12, 2021, Docubase, https://docubase.mit.edu/project/6x9/.
14. See: Favero, "The Present Image."
15. "Virtual Reality – Notes on Blindness," Notes on Blindness, accessed September 12, 2021, www.notesonblindness.co.uk/vr/.
16. Sandra Gaudenzi, "Light into VR Darkness – An In-depth Interview with Arnaud Colinart," *i-Docs.org*, http://i-docs.org/light-into-vr-darkness-an-in-depth-interview-with-arnaud-colinart/.
17. Eva Theunissen, " 'Becoming Blind' in Virtual Reality," *Platypus: The CASTAC Blog*, http://blog.castac.org/2017/11/becoming-blind/.
18. Theunissen, " 'Becoming Blind.' "
19. See: Frederick Aardema, Kieron O'Connor, Sophie Côté, and Annie Taillon, "Virtual Reality Induces Dissociation and Lowers Sense of Presence in Objective Reality," *Cyberpsychology, Behavior and Social Networking* 13, no. 4 (2010); Steuer, "Defining Virtual Reality."
20. See: Mandy Rose, "Technologies of Seeing and Technologies of Corporeality: Currents in Nonfiction Virtual Reality," *World Records* 1, no. 1 (2018): 1–11, https://vols.worldrecordsjournal.org/#/01/11; Uricchio, "VR is not Film."
21. Balsamo, "Technologies of the Gendered Body," 126.
22. Rose, "Technologies of Seeing," 2.
23. Murray, "Not a Film."
24. Murray.
25. Uricchio, "VR is not Film."
26. Johan Hoorn, Elly A. Konijn, and Gerrit C. van der Veer, "Virtual Reality: Do Not Augment Realism, Augment Relevance," *Upgrade IV*, no. 1 (2003): 18.
27. Uricchio, "VR is not Film."
28. See for instance: Oliver Grau, *Virtual Art. From Illusion to Immersion* (London: MIT Press, 2003); Favero, *The Present Image*; Paolo S. H. Favero, "Visual Ethnography and Emerging Digital Technologies," in *The SAGE Handbook of Visual Research Methods*, eds. Luc Pauwels and Dawn Mannay (London: SAGE Publications, 2019), 641–58.
29. See: Bill Nichols, *Introduction to Documentary* (Bloomington: Indiana University Press, 2001).
30. See: Martia Sturkin and Lisa Cartwright, *Practices of Looking: An Introduction to Visual Culture* (Oxford: Oxford University Press, 2001).
31. See: Nichols, *Introduction to Documentary*; K. Beattie, *Documentary Display. Re-viewing Nonfiction Film and Video* (London: Wallflower Press: 2008).
32. Eitzen, "When Is a Documentary?" 89.
33. Eitzen, "When Is a Documentary?" 92, italics in original.
34. Nichols, "Introduction to Documentary," 34.
35. See: Nichols, "Introduction to Documentary"; Kate Nash, "Modes of Interactivity: Analyzing the Webdoc," *Media, Culture & Society* 34, no. 2 (2012); Judith Aston and Sandra Gaudenzi, "Interactive Documentary: Setting the Field," *Studies in Documentary Film* 6, no. 2 (2012); Favero, "The Present Image"; Eva Theunissen and Paolo S. H. Favero, "Between Automation and Agency: Curatorial Challenges in New Terrains of Digital/Visual Research," in *The Anthropologist as Curator*, ed. R Sansi (London: Bloomsbury Academic, 2020), 195–210.
36. Favero, "The Present Image."

37. Nichols, "Introduction to Documentary," 131.
38. See: Favero, "The Present Image"; Paolo S. H. Favero, "The Travelling i-doc: Reflections on the Meaning of Interactive Documentary-based Image-making Practices in Contemporary India," in *I-docs: The Evolving Practice of Interactive Documentary*, eds. Judith Aston, Sandra Gaudenzi, and Mandy Rose (New York: Columbia University Press, 2017), 1–26.
39. See: Sita Popat, "Missing in Action: Embodied Experience and Virtual Reality," *Theatre Journal* 68, no. 3 (2016): 357–78.
40. Rose, "Technologies of Seeing," 3.
41. Rose, "Technologies of Seeing," italics in original.
42. Grau, *Virtual Art*, 278.
43. See: Simon Penny, "Consumer Culture and the Technological Imperative: The Artist in Dataspace," *Simon Penny*, http://simonpenny.net/1990Writings/consumerculture.html.
44. John Perry Barlow, "Being in Nothingness," *Wired* (April 30, 2015), www.wired.com/2015/04/virtual-reality-and-the-pioneers-of-cyberspace/, own italics.
45. Constine, "Virtual Reality, the Empathy"; Milk, "How Virtual Reality."
46. Rose, "Technologies of Seeing," 3.
47. See: Jaysankar L. Shaw, "Negation and the Buddhist Theory of Meaning," *Journal of Indian Philosophy* 6, no. 1 (1978): 59–77.
48. Stephen Batchelor, *Buddhism without Beliefs: A Contemporary Guide to Awakening* (London: Penguin, 1998), 18.
49. See: Helmuth von Glanesapp, *Indiens Religioner* (Lund: Student Litteratur, 1967); Giuseppe Tucci, *Storia Della Filosofia* (Indiana, Bari: Laterza, 1992); Batchelor, "Buddhism without Beliefs."
50. Thich Nhất Hạnh, *No Death, No Fear: Comforting Wisdom for Life* (New York: Riverhead Books, 2002), 47.
51. See: Kameron Sanzo, "New Materialism(s)," *Critical Posthumanism* (2018), https://criticalposthumanism.net/new-materialisms/.
52. Monika Rogowska-Strangret, "Body," *New Materialism* (2017), https://newmaterialism.eu/almanac/body/body.html, citing Grosz (1987, 1994).
53. Rogowska-Strangret.
54. Rogowska-Strangret.
55. See: Annemarie Mol, *The Body Multiple: Ontology in Medical Practice* (Durham: Duke University Press, 2002).
56. Rogowska-Strangret, "Body."
57. Karen Barad, "Posthumanist Performativity: Toward an Understanding of How Matter Comes to Matter," *Signs: Journal of Women in Culture and Society* 28, no. 3 (2003).
58. Rick Dolphijn and Iris van der Tuin, *New Materialism: Interviews & Cartographies* (Ann Arbor: Open Humanities Press, 2013), 50, http://openhumanitiespress.org/books/download/Dolphijn-van-der-Tuin_2013_New-Materialism.pdf.
59. John Law, *After Method: Mess in Social Science Research* (London: Routledge, 2004), 3.
60. Favero, "The Present Image," 68.
61. See: I. Richardson and C. Harper, "Corporeal Virtuality: The Impossibility of a Fleshless Ontology," *Body, Space & Technology* 2, no. 2 (2002).
62. Eitzen, "When Is a Documentary?"
63. Popat, "Missing in Action," 371.
64. On various design levels, VR systems exclude individuals that experience physical, neurological, and mental challenges. VR systems construct an ideal type of embodied access to and presence in VR. As Maretz Mott *et al.* note, they are minimally accessible for visually impaired and hearing-impaired people. Also, various components of the VR infrastructure (head-mounted displays, hand-held controllers, etc.) "have largely ignored people with upper-body motor limitations" (452). However, at the

same time, VR systems have been inserted into a host of (mental) healthcare settings, testifying to the potential of VR systems to cater to individuals that cope with a wide range of (mental) health issues. See: Martez Mott et al., "Accessible by Design: An Opportunity for Virtual Reality," 2019 IEEE International Symposium on Mixed and Augmented Reality Adjunct (ISMAR-Adjunct) (2019).

65. See: Mel Slater, "A Note on Presence Terminology" (2003), http://www0.cs.ucl. ac.uk/research/vr/Projects/Presencia/ConsortiumPublications/ucl_cs_papers/pre sence-terminology.htm.

66. See: Mel Slater, Andrea Brogni and Anthony Steed, "Physiological Responses to Breaks in Presence: A Pilot Study" (2003), http://citeseerx.ist.psu.edu/viewdoc/ download?doi=10.1.1.2.9663&rep=rep1&type=pdf#:~:text=A%20'break%20in%20 presence'%20(,to%20the%20real%20sensory%20stream.

67. See: Favero, "The Present Image."

# 12

# BEYOND TECHNOLOGY'S PROMISE

## Building Trust, Owning Narrative, Self-Authorship, and the Power of Storytelling!

*Joel Kachi Benson in conversation with Rania Al Namara. Edited by Rania Al Namara*

After a decade working at production studios, Joel Kachi Benson started experimenting with the possibilities of producing different types of documentaries, using VR 360 technology for virtual reality storytelling.

In his documentary *Daughters of Chibok* (2019),[1] Benson covered and documented the trauma families continued to experience after the kidnapping of 200 girls from a girls' school in the Nigerian town of Chibok. Benson and his crew had no sophisticated technology but used a camera that lacked a monitor to capture testimonies, memories, and stories from the girls' mothers. His emotive films gained international support, making him the first Nigerian filmmaker to use VR in storytelling. Benson was awarded the Lion Award for Best Story of 2019 at the Venice International Film Festival.[2] That same year, *New African Magazine* named Benson one of the most influential people in Africa.[3]

In addition to *Daughters of Chibok*, Benson produced a number of other films as *J. D. 'Okhai Ojeikere* (2014), and another VR film *In Bakassi* (2018), which screened at the Berlin Film Festival.[4] In this interview, Benson talks about his experience with virtual reality production, shedding light on the most effective ways of storytelling, on top of which is connectivity, emotions, and bonding with the interviewees. His approach to storytelling lies on the premise of communities' ownership of stories to produce an impactful narrative, therefore, making a genuine change. He is inspired by the people whom he meets through his journey to chronologize emotional scenes and capture accounts of Indigenous storytellers.

RA: Would you please just start by introducing yourself and the company, the production company that you created and founded in the first place?

JB: My background story is that I've always been passionate about real stories, human stories; so, when I started off trying to get myself into the world of

DOI: 10.4324/9781003174509-16

video production, I tried my hands on making music videos and all those kinds of things. In many ways, it wasn't as exciting as the real personal stories that I found myself increasingly drawn to, so I started by telling stories, documentary stories. However, a couple of years ago, 3 years ago, a client of mine told me that she wanted to make a 360° video. Back then, I didn't quite know what she was talking about? She said to go and do some research and come back to me. So I did some research and I realized oh this is so cool but I don't do it and she said: "Well go and figure it out. I want you to be the one to do it. Because I love how you tell stories and I want to tell a story using this medium. We are going to do a lot of work together." I decided to go do more research and find out how those productions of 360°videos work. And the more I searched, the more intrigued and interested I became and for me it suddenly became like a sort of a new tool to push the envelope of storytelling. I've done a lot of documentary work in conflict zones, and I brought the stories back, and most of the time, I always feel like I didn't quite capture the essence of what I experienced. So, when I found VR and 360° videos, suddenly it became my dual goal tools: take the experience and take it anywhere. Have all the people experience what I experienced and that, for me, was a fascination with VR. I was able to take people to places that they ordinarily wouldn't be able to get access to.

RA: Would tell us about the innovative features and other creative ways that you bring into the storytelling?

JB: For me when people ask me why you use VR, cinematic VR, I'm more concerned about using virtual reality and 360° stories to amplify people's voices. So, that really was pretty cool for me. And to give all the people an opportunity to experience what they otherwise wouldn't have been able to experience, so I give voices to those of Chibok for instance. A lot of people have heard about the Chibok story, you've seen it on the news but you've never been there before. So, what we were able to do was to use this technology to take people there and give them this sort of a different experience of Chibok, you've heard about Chibok, now go to Chibok. Go and experience it. And I think that's in my opinion where the true power of VR lies: you can transfer people to places that they ordinarily wouldn't be able to get access to; while amplifying the voices of those whose voices need to be amplified. So, I am very much inspired by the impact of storytelling, and storytelling for the impact of change for the communities. Virtual reality plays an important role in that mission of amplifying people's voices.

RA: From your perspective how do you see the relations between the producers and the audience on interactive storytelling or interactive documentary?

JB: Well, I don't know if I truly give that a lot of thought! My question always is; is this story worth telling? Are these stories that need to be amplified? I feel like there is always an audience for every story. What I owe myself and what I owe my audience or the viewers are to be genuine about my intentions in telling the story. So, I go into every story with a genuineness of intention. This is what I'm trying to say with this story. This is the issue that I'm trying to address or issues and these are the voices I'm trying to amplify, and so once I go out there with that in mind and I tell the story that way, the rest is to fully put it out there to the universe. Whatever happens afterward, it is really not my call. And I'm being very honest that's how I really do about my stories. It might not be the classical way of doing things! You experience it. You need to find out what the audience wants, what the people want but I always ask what do I want first? I do what my heart tells me to do and then I put it out there.

RA: What kind of new practices would you introduce to filmmakers who might be passionate about following your path? How is this different from the traditional practices that filmmakers usually follow?

JB: Well, I mean in terms of storytelling, storytelling is storytelling. It is less tech and more creative in terms of how you go about telling a story. The usual plot points, the usual story points, and the usual arc of the story are the same regardless of the medium. There are learning curves that any filmmaker who does a sort of traditional and trying to migrate to interactive or virtual which could be more technical, like understanding that rule number one you can't be a present director on-site because the camera is 360°, you can't be there taking the shots, you have to be somewhere else. So just like the way we did in *Daughters of Chibok*; the camera that we used we couldn't even monitor every shot. I mean now obviously we have sort of better equipment and we can monitor but still can't be present on-site and be observing. You are going to observe from a monitor. So, those little technical details about how you approach it would be sort of like the learning curves but if you are a storyteller, you are a storyteller regardless of what medium you use whether it is audio, it is visual, whether it is 2D or interactive. It is about understanding how to keep the audience engaged over the length of the film whether it is 5 minutes or it is 50 minutes.

RA: Did you say you just used the camera without the monitor? Like you couldn't see the shots that you were capturing in the camera?

JB: When we did *Daughters of Chibok*, we couldn't see the monitor. So, what we did because I used the camera over and over again, we started calculating the length, what is the distance between the camera and the subjects and the distance between the subject and the background. So, we learned where to position our camera either put it as a portrait or landscape. I had these sorts of interesting discussions with my team and then we say yes this looks great, looks good, it will be fine and hit the record button and we stepped to the back. Because we couldn't afford the expensive cameras at that time which also brings me back to the issue about the power of the story itself. About the story and telling it by putting your emotions into it and telling it with a genuineness of intention like I said earlier. Now we've got better cameras and we can monitor and all of that but it still doesn't take away the fact that you need to understand what story you are trying to tell before you try to tell it.

RA: So, technology and expensive equipment won't stand as a barrier for you to tell a story?

JB: No, it shouldn't. It shouldn't. At a time, it does lend some advantage to the look and feel, but it is also about emotions, and if the stories connect, I mean people were still making shoots with mobile phones and they are able to engage with the audience. So, find the right story and tell it with whatever tool you have. I mean you never sit down and wait for a big fancy camera before you go out and tell that story. Stories don't have time to wait for who the audience would be and how to distribute it. The model one chooses to produce their web-based documentary matters from the beginning because funding in the visual arts, film, literature, and academia all have their own protocols. They are happening in real time so are you going to just allow that moment to pass or are you could to capture it? It's your own call.

RA: So what would be the best practices from your experience that you would share with people who are passionate now producing filmmaking using sometimes modest technology?

JB: Technology, finance all kinds of things are going to always keep telling you that it isn't the right time, it is not a right place, it is not a right gear, and it is not a right! That's all just noise. If you are convinced in your heart that this is a right story to tell, just go out there and tell that story and don't let anything stop you. And I would say that not because it sounds cool, just saying it! I say it because that's what I do. That's what I do. For every story that I want to tell, before I tell it people or go like "Oh hey look I'm telling a story I need some support." I've already started! And once I start, I'm fully committed to finishing it regardless of whatever happens along the way. So, my advice to young filmmakers or anyone who wants to go out there and start telling a story, you just have to do it, don't stop. If you make a mistake, then you learn from it and you don't repeat it again but at least you've made that attempt. So, yes, just go out there and do it.

RA: When you interview people in your stories, how would you approach your interviewees? The subject as we call them in journalism.

JB: Good question! Most of the stories that I've told by the end of the film we were like really good friends. I don't see them as subjects, they don't see me as a producer or a director, and they see me as a friend. And I like to keep it that way. So, for me it is very important to build trust with my subjects. If you don't trust me, you are not going to tell me stuff; you are not going to be afraid to be vulnerable in front of me. But then how do you build trust right? How do you get these people to trust you? Well, it is about the energy that you give out. If your intentions are genuine in telling that story they will know somehow; they will know and when they know they are more willing to open up to you and tell you things. So, yes, I usually spend and invest a lot of time in just building that trust and building that rapport, and really genuinely trying to understand what the story is. Because you see in understanding the story better that way, I'm able to convince myself about my "why"; why I'm telling the story.

The more I understand them, the more convinced I'm about why I need to tell this particular story. So, every new day of interviewing or hanging out with them is an opportunity to know more about them, to learn more about their lives, and even the things that are not directly connected to the story. Just some random stuff, like; what do you like for dinner, where do you like to visit? Do you have a girlfriend; you have a boyfriend? Just showing interest in their life, I tell them about my life as well. And a lot of times we usually end up as really good friends who are unafraid to share their stories and also respecting boundaries as well; respecting the things they don't want to share, the things that we are not comfortable sharing, and being open about your intentions; this is why I'm telling a story, this is why I want you to share your story with me, this is what I'm going to do with your story so if they understand fully what you are about to do and why you are in the space, I think it is easier for them to open up to you.

RA: So, you're thinking about the people you interview as building relations of trust and friendship do you think this is a best practice to let them own the story or have a voice authority in the film? Give them a space to give their own voice, more representations in the film?

JB: Yes, like I said it is their story. It is a story about them. Do I have, as a director or as a producer: editorial control over the final output? Yes, sure I do. But even in that there is still some level of consultation. Again, it goes back to the original emphasis, why am I trying to tell the story? And a lot of times most of the stories are targeted at impact. They are targeted at making a difference in their lives, amplifying their voices, and making a difference in their society. So, it is definitely important that they have a voice because it is their story, right? It is important that they are well represented and not misinterpreted. So, I'm not going to ask you a question and intentionally go out of my way to take you out of context or take what you say out of context. I'm not being honest when I do that. So, if people trust you, then do your best not to betray that trust. You are going to be able to navigate that and ensure that you retain as much as you can of your artistic integrity and the integrity of the project while respecting their boundaries and their sensibilities as well.

RA: Do you have any story that you'd like to share from the site, something that was so close to your heart? Like a story you felt so special when you did it?

JB: Yes. Every story is special. Every story is special. Since I'm talking about *Daughters of Chibok*; so we were interviewing Yana and that's a lead character in the film and we were asking her about her daughter who's still missing.

She was telling us about the story and at a point, she stopped talking and she stood up and walked away from the camera. Now, this is a 360 camera, so I'm in the other room and I see her standing up to leave, so I was a bit like do I go out and meet her? Do I wait? I'm not quite sure? I just sit there and then she went out, and then she came back in with a bag. In that bag, she brought out clothes and books and pencils and then she started saying that these are the clothes of her daughter whose been missing for 7 years and every other week or month she brings out all those clothes, she washes them, dries them, and keeps them in the box. And her books are intact, her pencils are intact, everything is intact. And she does that because she believes that one day her daughter is going to come back.

By the time that scene was done, there was not a dry eye in the room, but you know I think that was the strongest scene and toughest scene that we had to deal with in the film. But they also brought home to me why it was important to tell that story, because this is a woman who despite everything, she hasn't given up hope and has a very interesting way of showing her faith.

It was totally unexpected for all of us but yeah, I'm glad that we told that story. I'm glad that despite how tough it was for us to tell that story, we told the story. It is a few moments like that that reinforce my decision; why am I going to tell the stories and I remember that as a result of that film, yes, her daughter isn't back yet but some of the things that we talked about were some of the challenges in her community, the film was able to get some support for her and for other women in Chibok. And so, you see a film, like that, used as a tool to bring change to communities like that. I think that is the biggest gratification for me beyond the awards or the accolades or whatever; it is a fact that you made a film, and that film made a difference in someone's life, like in your lifetime you saw it, it made a difference in their lives. There is no bigger reward than that.

RA: I think this is perfect. I mean the way you described the scene and how the mother described which has then the rest of the narrative. I think that's powerful and passionate. And again, it goes back to the trust you built with the people that you work with it isn't only a subject that, you know, interview and it's gone. But you built that relation.

JB: Yes, when you do have that relationship when you get to the point where they fully trust you, I think they tell you stuff. They will not be afraid to be vulnerable in front of you. Because they don't see you as just an outsider, now you are a friend, and they are just talking to a friend.

## Notes

1. Gbenga Bada, "Daughters of Chibok Tells an Emotional Story of Rifkatu Yakubu," *Pulse Nigeria* (April 15, 2019), www.pulse.ng/entertainment/movies/daughters-of-chibok-tells-an-emotional-story-of-rifkatu-yakubu/rbww2sq.

2.  Chuck Nwanne, "Daughters of Chibok Puts Benson on Global Stage," *The Guardian Saturday Magazine – Guardian Nigeria and World News* (September 14, 2019), https://guardian.ng/saturday-magazine/daughters-of-chibok-puts-benson-on-global-stage/.
3.  Anver Versi, "100 Most Influential Africans," *New African Magazine* (2019) https://Newafricanmagazine.com/100/.
4.  *"In Bakassi* Lights Up Berlin Film Festival," *The Guardian Nigeria and World News* (February 2019), https://guardian.ng/life/film/in-bakassi-lights-up-berlin-film-festival/.

# 13

# DESERT STARS

## Effectuation and Co-Creation in a Research-Creation I-doc

*André Paz, Felipe Carrelli, and GalileoMobile and Amanar Task Force*

Over the past decade, a vast range of interactive documentaries (i-docs) have arisen, which use different technologies and media (websites, mobile applications, virtual reality, augmented reality, installations, artificial intelligence, audio 3D). International festival circuits, including Sundance New Frontier Lab and IDFA DocLab Academy, recognize the most innovative productions. These include a heterogeneous group of hybrid works in a constantly innovating environment: large, multiplatform productions such as *Highrise* (2009–2015); webdocs such as *Hollow, An Interactive Documentary* (2012); collaborative works, such as *The Quipu Project* (2014–2017); geolocation-based narratives on mobile applications, such as *Walking the Edit* (2010); immersive documentaries such as *6x9: A Virtual Experience of Solitary Confinement* (2016); and installations such as *In the Event of Moon Disaster* (2019).

These mainstream, international works are references for innovative and wider i-docs around the world from different producers (artists, non-governmental organizations, collectives, universities, startups) with diverse purposes. These innovations go beyond technology and format. The i-docs explore, represent, and critically engage reality through nonfictional narratives while taking advantage of newly available technologies. Behind their interfaces, these projects utilize different practices of creation, production, and agencies between creators, participants, and publics.[1] Developing a project in the field requires designing this unique *dispositif* that intertwines format, interface, practices, and relational processes. The dispositive directly influences the experience of the users – called *interactors* – and their affects, effects, and impacts.[2]

On the other hand, the productive process and project development require an intense level of collaboration between different specialties and technical and aesthetic capacities (audiovisual, design, programming, technology). This is why the most innovative work is carried out in *creative ecosystems*.[3] The process is closer to software development than traditional audiovisual production, and this requires strong research, ample resource investment (capacities, technologies, partnerships, finance), and time for project development to mature.

As André Paz and Sandra Gaudenzi have pointed out,[4] this has helped to unleash a *hackathon culture*, with workshops and programs aimed toward supporting project development in the field,[5] such as !F Lab (Interactive Factual Lab), designed and led by Gaudenzi.[6] In a certain way, this hackathon culture has extended into university research-creation programs geared toward the field, such as disLAB (digital and interactive storytelling MA LAB) from the University of Westminster, led by Gaudenzi; and the master's degree in the Creative Media Graduate Program (PPGMC) at the Federal University of Rio de Janeiro (UFRJ). Paz is a professor at the PPGMC where he teaches the Development of Immersive and Interactive Projects course. It's a long workshop that follows a specific methodology based on the perspectives of *design thinking, effectuation, co-creation,* and *research creation* – a result of the !F Lab methodology.[7]

This chapter discusses the strategic decisions on the project development of the research creation[8] led by Felipe Carrelli, as part of the master's degree in the PPGMC at the UFRJ, supervised by André Paz. The research aimed to explore the possibilities of using a virtual reality-based i-doc as a means of popularizing ethnoastronomy,[9] and it was connected to Carrelli's participation as a member of GalileoMobile (GM) since 2014.[10] GM is a volunteer astronomy outreach initiative that arose during the UN International Year of Astronomy 2009, composed of volunteers from different areas: astronomers, science reporters, filmmakers, and anthropologists. Since its foundation, GM has organized activities in 15 countries and shared astronomy with more than 20,000 people. The scope of the program includes activities with underrepresented groups, such as native people in Brazil or communities in territories in conflict.[11]

The initial research-creation project was focused on using virtual reality as a means of popularizing the ethnoastronomy of the Paiter Suruí, an Indigenous group from Rondônia, Brazil. However, Rondônia is too far from Rio de Janeiro and limited resources for fieldwork became a significant barrier. The research project was redirected to the Saharawi people in the first months, when the International Astronomical Union decided to fund GM to carry out the Amanar project.[12] Thus, Carrelli could collaborate with the GM team – science communicators, astronomers, refugee specialists, cultural astronomers. The research-creation project could leverage its resources (human, financial, technical, logistical).

From that moment on, *Desert Stars* became a wide research-creation i-doc about the sky of Sahrawi refugees in the Sahara Desert. *Desert Stars* was conceived in partnership with GM within the scope of the Amanar project. Amanar was organized by GM in collaboration with the Canary Islands Astrophysics Institute (IAC) and the Canary Association of Friendship with the Saharawi People (ACAPS). It was divided into two phases, both carried out during 2019. The first took place in July and August with Sahrawi children who visited the Canary

Islands, and the second stage took place in October when the team traveled to the camps near Tindouf, Algeria, for 2 weeks to work with local students and teachers and donate educational materials.

Guided by the Sustainable Development Goals defined by the United Nations, the Amanar project aimed to empower and inspire the Sahrawi refugee community through astronomy, as well as promote peace.[13] The initiative sought to achieve this by facilitating the development of scientific skills, such as critical thinking, and performing hands-on activities and sky observations. Moreover, the program promoted teacher workshops to encourage educators to use astronomy as a didactic tool to contribute to the improvement of teaching quality in the region.[14] Moreover, based on the perspective of decolonial studies and ethnoastronomical guidelines, the Amanar activities encouraged an exchange of astronomical knowledge with the Saharawi people.

*Desert Stars* was developed within this context, and it was based on interviews and audiovisual material from the field trips to Saharawi refugee camps in the Sahara Desert.[15] It is a transmedia project composed of six different products as well as interactive and immersive narratives: 1. *Desert Stars VR* (6DoF[16] virtual reality documentary for Quest 2 headset); 2. *Desert Stars 360°* (360° documentary piece with 3DoF); 3. *Searching for Stars* (360° interactive docugame for web browser); 4. *A Refuge in the Stars* (linear feature-length documentary); 5. *GalileoCast* (series of podcasts); and 6. *Irifi* (interactive installation). Each product explores a different approach and user experience, based on specific media and platform.

The objective of this chapter is to discuss four strategic decisions in the development path of the i-doc *Desert Stars*, based on the incorporation and adaptation of the research concepts. In this sense, item 2 presents the Saharawi historical and political context, as well as the principles of the Amanar project, based on the perspective of decolonial studies and the orientations of ethnoastronomy. Then, it points out how research creation opted and pursued the transmedia strategy (see Figure 13.1), as a response to the different purposes of the project. Item 3

**FIGURE 13.1** Different products of *Desert Stars.*

*Source:* Photograph by Felipe Carrelli

describes how the concept of co-creation guided the incorporation of the Sahrawi political issue in the i-doc *Desert Stars*, within the possibilities and resources available. Item 4 discusses how the effectuation perspective encouraged the development of *Desert Stars* within the available resources. Finally, considerations are made about the process of incorporating concepts into research creation.

## Amanar Project and Transmedia Strategy

Located at the Atlantic end of the African continent, the territory of Western Sahara has a total area of 266,000 km² and is part of the Sahara Desert – one of the most inhospitable regions on the planet. For centuries, the Saharawi people learned to live off the land. The stars guided the nomads across the desert plains and thus inspired many legends. All the knowledge based on this experience has been orally transmitted for generations.

The population's presence in the Saharawi territory dates back to prehistory, but Spanish colonization of the territory of present-day Western Sahara occurred in 1884/85, during the Berlin Conference and the distribution of the African continent among European powers.[17] On June 27, 1900, Spain and France signed an agreement, and the colonial borders of both countries were established in this region.[18]

Only in 1975, after pressure from the United Nations (UN) to decolonize the Sahara, did the Spanish government decide to carry out a census of the Sahrawi population in order to organize a referendum, under UN observation.[19] On November 6, 1975, however, Moroccan authorities sent 350,000 civilians and 25,000 soldiers to Western Sahara, in what became known as the Green March.[20] This movement achieved its main objective of intimidating and pressuring the Spanish government, and on Nov. 14, a tripartite agreement was signed in Madrid between Spain, Morocco, and Mauritania. Spain withdrew from Western Sahara without completing the decolonization process. In view of this legal vacuum, the Polisario Front[21] proclaimed the Sahrawi Arab Democratic Republic (RASD) in 1976 and declared war on the occupation of Morocco and Mauritania, initiating the armed conflict between the Saharawi and Morocco.

The Sahrawi population escaped toward the Algerian border, where the Algerian government provided land. The Saharawi built five refugee camps (*Wilayas*) in this territory and named after the main Saharawi cities under occupation in Morocco – Smara, Boujdour, Laayoune, Dakhla, and Awserd.[22] According to the March 2018 report by the UN Refugee Agency (UNHCR), 173,600 Sahrawi refugees still reside in these refugee camps, which are administered by the Saharawis themselves. Forty-five years since the beginning of the conflict, the Sahrawi population is still in this temporary-permanent condition,[23] which makes the Sahrawi refugee situation one of the most protracted in the world (see Figure 13.2).

In this context, the GalileoMobile (GM) team arrived at the Saharawi camps with telescopes, inflatable planets, and galaxy posters to carry out the Amanar

**FIGURE 13.2**   The Sahrawi Camp in Smara, 2019.

*Source:* Photograph by Felipe Carrelli

project in 2019. In parallel with the activities carried out in schools with teachers and students, Amanar also used astronomy to promote a cultural exchange to learn about the local population's worldview.[24] During their 10 days in the field, the team interviewed four sages (three men and one woman) in addition to 15 local employees, politicians, public officials, teachers, and students. Amanar's activities encouraged a cultural exchange based on the perspective of the decolonial studies and ethnoastronomical guidelines.

The decolonial perspective[25] points out the organization of a deep system of cultural domination, which controls the production and reproduction of subjectivities under the guidance of Eurocentrism and modern rationality. Culture is always intertwined with (and not derived from) the processes of political economy. According to Castro-Gómez and Grosfoguel, Eurocentrism is a colonial attitude toward knowledge, articulated simultaneously with the process of center-periphery relations and ethnic/racial hierarchies.[26] The superiority attributed to European knowledge in many areas of life was an important aspect of the coloniality of power in the world system. Subaltern knowledge was excluded, omitted, and ignored. Since the eighteenth century, this knowledge was silenced, legitimized by the idea that represented a mythical, inferior, pre-modern, and pre-scientific stage of human knowledge. Only the knowledge generated by Europe's scientific and philosophical elite was considered true knowledge, as it was able to abstract its spatiotemporal conditioning and be placed on a neutral observation platform.[27]

In line with the decolonial perspective, ethnoastronomy[28] is the discipline that studies the *other skies by* addressing astronomical knowledge in different cultures and the associated representations of the cosmos and other customs. An appreciation of different ways of understanding the world through something is as fundamental as interest in the sky.[29] Although most oral societies have adopted the written word as a tool for documentation, expression, and communication, many still depend on this tradition and place great value on the oral transmission of knowledge as an intrinsic aspect of their cultures.[30] For this reason, people who rely on orality to transmit their traditions suffer irreparable losses with the death of their sages, who hold most of this knowledge. Thus, to document the Saharawi astronomical knowledge is very significant (see Figure 13.3).

In this sense, initially, Desert Stars had two specific purposes. The first was to record the oral memory of the Saharawi through audiovisual resources (audio, photo, linear video, and 360° video) in order to help the local community to preserve their worldview. The second objective was to explore how VR could help popularize their knowledge. However, the collaboration with the Saharawi people in the field also showed the importance they placed on political issues and their refugee status. Thus, *Desert Stars* also needed to respond to the different purposes of Amanar: cultural exchange, documentation, and communication of local astronomical knowledge and attention to the refugee status of the Saharawi people. On the other hand, research creation sought to explore new narrative

**FIGURE 13.3**  Intercultural exchange at the refugee camp.

*Source:* Photograph by Felipe Carrelli

possibilities and the audiovisual material collected during the visit to the camps proved to be quite fruitful.

In this context, the research-creation *Desert Stars* opted for a *transmedia* strategy. This consists of developing different narrative products across various platforms that offer specific and complementary approaches, questions, and experiences for the users, aiming to promote a closer knowledge of the Sahrawi people's astronomical knowledge and of their refugee status.[31] Each product could thus approach and explore questions and dimensions that are more appropriate to the potential of their particular platform, format, and language. They should have narrative autonomy, but at the same time, feed the users' continued interest in other products, as they are part of a wider *transmedia narrative*.

Thus, *Desert Stars* created six products, developed from 360° footage, photos, videos, and audio recorded during Amanar. Beyond their complementary content, each product has a different approach and provides the public with a unique experience. By enabling a more aesthetic work, *Desert Stars VR* prioritizes the sky's splendor and the desert scenery in order to fully immerse the participant. *Desert Stars 360°* explores the possibilities of the equirectangular image to create a poetic transition between the narrative's elements. The docugame *Searching for Stars* uses gamification to place the interactor at the center of decisions. A *Refuge in the Stars*, on the other hand, provokes the viewer to reflect more deeply on the question of Sahrawi refugees. The *GalileoCast* (podcast) was specially developed to bring back the knowledge acquired on the field with Saharawi teachers. Finally, Irifi is an installation that seeks to transport the virtual experience to the physical world and immerse the participants within the work.

## Co-Creating With Saharawi People

The decolonial perspective and ethnoastronomy both value cultural exchange and attentive listening to traditional Saharawi knowledge. Still, how can the Saharawi be incorporated into the collaboration and development of the i-doc that came to be called *Desert Stars*? In this sense, the research was based on the concept of co-creation. This creative process incorporates other groups and voices outside the original project team. It is based on the team's dialogue and collaboration with users, representatives of social groups, and professionals from different specialties. Co-creation offers alternatives to the single-author view. It is a constellation of methods and frameworks. According to Katerina Cizek, William Uricchio et al:

> In co-creation, projects emerge from a process, and evolve from within communities and with people, rather than for or about them. Co-creation also spans across and beyond disciplines and organizations, and can also involve non-human or beyond human systems. The concept of co-creation reframes the ethics of who creates, how, and why. Our research shows that

co-creation interprets the world, and seeks to change it, through a lens of equity and justice.[32]

The authors highlight four types of co-creation: (1) with communities in person; (2) with communities online with emergent media; (3) between professionals from distinct specialties, disciplines, and organization; and (4) with non-human systems, such as artificial intelligence.[33] Regarding co-creation with communities, co-creation relies on an open dialogue for collaboration between participants/ researchers in the development of the project and in the creative process. In the words of Rose,[34] "not media about, but media with." The creation processes happen within communities and with people, instead of being made for or about them. After all, no one better to talk about an experience than the subject himself. In this movement of self-reflexivity, the subject speaks of his own empirical and subjective experience, aiming for the results to be applied for the benefit of the group.

Co-creation, however, is not based on a symmetrical relationship of power, nor do the different subjects occupy the same place or exercise the same functions. In practice, countless ways exercise this guiding approach to *creative collaboration*. Cizek, Uricchio et al.,[35] for example, point out some *best practices* to encourage dialogue and learning with attentive listening instead of arriving with a predetermined agenda. How can one exercise this co-creation within the possibilities of *Desert Stars*?

Cultural and linguistic differences limited the process of co-creation in the project. Examples include the physical distance between the GalileoMobile team and the Saharawis and, especially, the short duration of the visit due to limited financial resources. Even so, research creation established co-creation as a fundamental guiding principle and, in this regard, sought attentive listening and dialogue with representatives of the Saharawi during the interviews conducted by the GM team (see Figure 13.4).

The GM team adopted the following procedure for conducting the interviews: first, the group sits in a circle with the interviewees and starts the conversation by focusing on questions about ethnoastronomy. In the second part, the conversation opened up so that other team members could participate with non-directive questions for the interviewees. During the second part of the interviews, Carrelli explained, in a very transparent way, the general proposal of *Desert Stars*, the methodology, and the importance of listening to the Saharawi people. At this point in the field, the proposal was to co-create a virtual reality documentary for the dissemination of the Sahrawi people's worldview. During the interviews, this idea was discussed in order to listen to the participants' opinion. The GM team also opened the survey to suggestions and criticisms from the interviewees. As these interviews had the character of a chat, this procedure was dynamic and unpredictable in a certain way.

**FIGURE 13.4**   Interview with star experts in Auserd, 2019.

*Source:* Photograph by Felipe Carrelli

The interviews made it very clear that, to the Saharawi, the scientific theme could not be disconnected from the political issue. Mohammed Ali, for example, secretary of the oral memory department at the Saharawi Ministry of Culture, pointed out that, "The humanitarian part cannot be separated from the whole . . . This work must have a common basis. A common factor. It is a cultural, scientific work. It is political and social."[36] When asked how astronomy could help with the political issue, the sage Baruyemaa[37] reflects that, "Science is the mother of all. It is an instrument that you can use for many purposes. But the Sahara is liberated through war, from expelling Moroccans outside."

Attentively listening to the Saharawi people made it evident that the political issue and their status as refugees should be addressed and clarified in *Desert Stars*. It was not only a matter of listening to the Saharawi voice when valuing, documenting, and communicating their traditional knowledge revealed by the ethnoastronomy methodology. For effective co-creation, the project as a whole needed to listen to the presence and vulnerability of Saharawi otherness and incorporate the need to address the political context that gave them this refugee status into its products. Therefore, the idea was to approach the issue of refuge from the point of view of social injustice and not of piety.[38]

Although the co-creation process was not ideal, the solution was to respect the Saharawi demand to highlight the political issue as much as possible. In this sense, excerpts from the interviews were incorporated into the scripts, addressing the political and social contexts. Despite having many similarities, each piece has its distinctive characteristics, aesthetics, and themes. However, every product presents the theme in a certain way. In the 11'12" piece *Desert Stars 360°*, the political issue is addressed until 6 minutes and 20 seconds. The Saharawi worldview emerges just after that. The documentary *A Refuge in the Stars* delves into the historical issue of the war between Saharawis and Moroccans and also addresses other issues, such as interviews with members of GalileoMobile talking about the Amanar project and the activities carried out in the camps. The *Irifi* installation also prioritizes the political issue but presents Saharawi astronomical knowledge as a background. On the other hand, in *Desert Stars VR* and the *GalileoCast*, Sahrawi ethnoastronomical knowledge is prioritized, and the political and social issues permeate the discussion. Finally, in the docugame *Searching for Stars*, the player needs to find the Saharawi sages to learn about the local worldview, but first, he needs to travel the field in search of clues and find other characters who talk about the social–political issue.

## By the *Effectuation* Perspective

In the trajectory of the development of this research creation, the options for the Amanar project, transmedia strategy, and co-creation were largely based on the available resources. In this sense, the incorporation of Saras Sarasvhaty's effectuation perspective was decisive in legitimizing these choices and in leveraging the creative possibilities. *Effectuation* is the result of cognitive scientist Sarasvhaty's research into how highly successful, innovative entrepreneurs make decisions and take action while creating new products.

In high-risk ecosystems and with limited resources, she identified a specific logic of thinking: the *effectual logic*. They always design and produce products and projects with an awareness of the available resources – understood here: in a broad sense as team, capacities, equipment, financing, and partnerships.[39] This kind of logic prioritizes exploring the resources available in the trajectory of project and product development, to subsequently enter into resource expansion cycles in parallel with the redefinition of objectives.[40]

Sarasvathy[41] differentiates *effectuation* from what she calls *causation*. She affirms that *causation* idealizes an end (product) and is dedicated to leveraging the means (resources) to accomplish it. The *effectuation* process, however, is dedicated to developing and achieving ends from the means available. In her well-known metaphor:

> Imagine a chef assigned the task of cooking dinner. There are two ways the task can be organized. In the first. the host or client picks out a menu in advance. All the chef needs to do is list the ingredients needed, shop for them, and then actually cook the meal. This is a process of causation. . . . In

the second case, the host asks the chef to look through the cupboards in the kitchen for possible ingredients and utensils and then cook a meal. Here, the chef has to imagine possible menus based on the given ingredients and utensils, select the menu, and then prepare the meal. This is a process of effectuation.[42]

Both logical processes can occur simultaneously, but an effectuation-oriented product or design development process is best suited to a high-risk environment with limited resources, where planning cannot control the process. Effectuation triggers procedural, open, and indefinite development. It does not expect the perfect conditions for carrying out a pre-designed product. It initiates product development from the *bird in hand* principle – start with the resources available: who you are, what you know, and who you know. The process and directions are continuously reformulated to adapt to the circumstances. Leadership needs to be flexible and able to learn, improvise, and turn the unforeseen into something advantageous – the *lemonade principle*. Partnerships are not built to realize previously conceived products; they are a resource for the imaginative collaboration – co-creation – of goals and products.

In recent years, Paz has been carrying out a research and innovation project that incorporates the perspective of *effectuation* in a methodology for developing i-docs projects.[43] The methodology invites participants (creative project leaders in the field) to strategically think about their projects in light of the resources available. I-docs are fertile ground for *effectuation* for various reasons: no pre-established format or production process; it requires collaboration between different specialties and, often, with different social groups and communities; resources (financial, technical, human) are scarce in the field and there is a significant risk of the projects not being realized. These factors are even more intense when it comes to research-creation projects – by nature, indeterminate, open to research, and creative exploration, with even scarcer resources.

The development of projects and products by *effectuation* is procedural; it takes place during the exploration of the possibilities brought about by the resources available or leveraged along its trajectory. In *Desert Stars*, the incorporation of effectuation principles took place during Felipe Carrelli's participation in the Development of Immersive and Interactive Projects Course at PPGMC/UFRJ. Looking at research creation from the perspective of effectuation, co-creation is a way to expand resources and start an open creative collaboration, which brings unforeseen directions to the project's development. During the field trip to Argelia, Carrelli produced as much audiovisual material as possible, although he had not a complete idea of the possible products. Besides, the co-creation with Saharawi pointed out the necessity to disseminate their political and refugee condition.

After returning to Brazil, Carrelli led gradually the conception of new products within a transmedia strategy as the resource expansion, largely in collaboration with partners. Based on the logic of effectuation, *Desert Stars* started creating the products with the docugame,[44] *Searching for Stars*, taking advantage of the 360° images recorded in the refugee camps. *Desert Stars 360°* was developed next by using part of the material edited for the docugame and the experience gained from developing the software. Through the transmedia strategy, *Desert Stars* developed products with different experiences for a diverse audience, especially to people who do not know about Saharawi history. The wide interactive possibilities facilitated adaptation and distribution of the recorded audiovisual material.

*Desert Stars VR* was only possible after establishing the partnership to develop the 6DoF, since the creation process requires professionals from different areas of expertise such as a game designer, programmer, and developer. The project sought support in the network of the research-creation group Bug404. Thus, the project established a partnership with professor Joel dos Santos and his students (Victória Carvalhal and Rafael Lucas), from the Multimedia Research Group (GPMM) of the Federal Center for Technological Education Celso Suckow da Fonseca (CEFET/RJ), and with professor Leila Lobato Graef, from the Institute of Physics of the Fluminense Federal University (UFF). Throughout the process of creating *Desert Stars* VR, the boundaries between the initial functions gradually blended, and a new process of co-creation began, this time across different disciplines.[45] To enter the world of gamification means breaking narrative paradigms and facing a new universe of possibilities that were previously unknown. Thus, throughout the creation process, Joel, Victória, and Rafael contributed with references and narrative solutions.

Although some products of *Desert Stars* are free and available online, the technology also brings challenges to their reception and impact. On one hand, different experiences increase the capacity of the narrative to reach a diverse audience. On the other hand, the ephemerality of the interactive media still brings uncertainties about the long-term reception. Furthermore, the virtual reality piece is hard-to-access for the Saharawis because of the headsets. The team has not yet leveraged enough resources to come back to Argelia and show *Desert Stars VR* to them. From a decolonial perspective, this is problematic. For now, the solution was to share with them just the online accessible products. However, even in those products they have some cultural barriers to reception that must be yet researched.

In a way, every i-doc can only be made with the resources available to produce and distribute it. Nonetheless, *effectuation* legitimates and enhances the development path of the project and its products by prioritizing the exploration of the possibilities within the available resources. The *effectuation* perspective is opposed to a creative process that endeavors to carry out a project or product completely idealized a priori by a person or a group as an exclusively authorial process. Certainly, this process has moments of authorial creation. However, in large part it requires authorship based on a kind of leadership that merges production, creation, and research.

Research creation is an open process of experimentation, trial and error, and readjustment of directions, which opposes theory and practice and calls for improvisation. In this sense, from the effectuation perspective, the very concepts incorporated into a research-creation project can be also seen as resources. The reflection creatively incorporates the concepts – it appropriates, digests, and adapts to the conditions of practice. Thus, co-creation and transmedia strategy are tools used to guide *Desert Stars*, which informed the strategic decisions regarding where the project could go. On the other hand, the research experience unfolds into reflections upon the concepts themselves. It is a kind of dialectic that makes its path by walking. Texts are its footprints.

## Notes

1. See: André Paz and Kátia Augusta Maciel, "Beyond the Interface: Fundamental Concepts and Works in Interactive Narrative," in *Bug: Interactive and Immersive Narratives*, eds. André Paz and Sandra Gaudenzi (Rio de Janeiro: Automática / Letra e Imagem / Oi Futuro, 2019), 38–51.
2. See: Paz and Maciel.
3. See: André Paz and Julia Salles, "Brasil, Mostra a sua Cara: Aproximações ao Cenário Brasileiro de Cocumentários Interativos," *Doc On Line* 18 (September 2015): 101–36; André Paz and Mayra Jucá, "The Scenario of Interactive and Immersive Narratives," in *Bug: Interactive and Immersive Narratives*, eds. André Paz and Sandra Gaudenzi (Rio de Janeiro: Automática / Letra e Imagem / Oi Futuro, 2019), 10–18.
4. See: André Paz and Sandra Gaudenzi, "!F LAB: Experiência do Usuário e Recursos na Metodologia WHAT IF IT pra Desenvolvimento de Narrativas Interativas e Imersivas," *ANIMUS: Revista Interamericana de Comunicação Midiática* 18, no. 37 (2019): 18–42.
5. A few examples include: Tribeca Hacks, IDFA's DocLab Academy, POV Hackathons.
6. Produced by !DROPS, financed by the European Commission, and available for free at: www.iflab.net.
7. In 2018–2019, Paz and Gaudenzi adapted the *!F Lab* methodology to the Brazilian environment with the research project "'!F BUG LAB: an experimental methodology for developing interactive documentary projects in the Brazilian context," an international collaboration between UNIRIO/UFRJ and University of Westminster (UK), funded by the Newton Fund Mobility Grants and the British Academy. Since then, André has researched and developed the methodology using *Effectuation, co-creation and research-creation*, in order to create a new project developing methodology and adapting it for research-creation projects.
8. See: Owen Chapman and Kim Sawchu, "Research-Creation: Intervention, Analysis and 'Family resemblances'," *Canadian Journal of Communication* 37, no. 1 (2012): 5–26; Louis-Claude Paquin, *Méthodologie de la Recherche Création*, http://lcpaquin.com/methoRC/.
9. Science that studies the astronomical knowledge of a people through customs told through orality. See: Edmundo Magaña, "South American Etno-astronomy," in *Myths and the Imaginary in the New World*, eds. Edmundo Magaña and Peter Mason (Amsterdam, The Netherlands: Foris Publications, 1986), 459–98.
10. www.galileomobile.org/.
11. See: Sandra Benítez Herrera and Jorge Rivero González, "Under the Same Sky with Amanar," *Nat Astron* 4 (2020): 434–36.
12. Amanar was selected as a "Special Project" at the commemoration of the centennial of the International Astronomical Union (IAU100), as it is an example of how

astronomy can serve to motivate inhabitants of places in conflict and promote respect between cultures. Saharawi and Sahrawi are used interchangeably to refer to the nomadic people of the region.

13. See: Sandra Benítez Herrera et al., "AMANAR: Astronomía, Cooperación y Sensibilización con el Sáhara," *Astronomía, Madrid* 38, no. 248 (2020): 38–44.

14. See: Benítez Herrera and Rivero González, "Under the Same Sky."

15. Audiovisual material includes 360 footage, photos, videos, and audios.

16. The 6 degrees of freedom product (6DoF) allows the user to walk in and explore a virtual environment. Thus, beyond the 360° vision (3DoF), the participant can walk from side to side, forward and backward, as well as up and down. This kind of experience provides a more complex narrative where the user's impression of presence in the space is far more profound. See: Júlia Salles and Maria Laura Ruggiero, "Narrativas Imersivas: Imaginando Múltiplas Realidades," in *Bug: Interactive and Immersive Narratives*, eds. André Paz and Sandra Gaudenzi (Rio de Janeiro: Automática / Letra e Imagem / Oi Futuro, 2019), 82–91.

17. Carlos M. Beristan and Eloisa G. Hidalgo, *El Oasis de la Memoria: Memoria Histórica y Violaciones de Derechos Humanos en el Sáhara Occidental* (Tomo I. Sáhara Occidental: El Aaiún, 2012), 71.

18. See: Francisco Villar, *El Proceso de Autodeterminación del Sáhara* (Valencia: Editorial Fernando Torres, 1987).

19. See: Beristan and Hidalgo, *El Oasis de la Memoria*.

20. See: Antoni Segura, "A Propósito de la Regionalización en Marruecos y la Cuestión del Sáhara Occidental," *Quaders de la Mediterránea* 2–3 (2001): 101–4.

21. The Popular Front for the Liberation of el Hamra and Río de Oro (Polisario) is a political-revolutionary movement in favor of the autonomy of the territory of Western Saara and the self-determination of the Saharawi people.

22. See: Beristan and Hidalgo, *El Oasis de la Memoria*.

23. See: Abdelmalek Sayad, *A Imigração. Ou os Paradoxos da Alteridade* (São Paulo: EDUSP, 1998).

24. See: Andrea Rodríguez Antón, "Proyecto Amanar, la Astronomía como Herramienta de Intercambio Cultural con el Sáhara," *Turismo de Estrellas* (November 15, 2019), www.turismodeestrellas.com/proyecto-amanar-bajo-el-mismo-cielo-astronomia-cultural-en-el-sahara.

25. See: Santiago Castro-Gómez and Ramón Grosfoguel, coords., *El Giro Gecolonial: Reflexiones para una Diversidad Epistémica más allá del Capitalismo Global* (Bogotá: Siglo del Hombre Editores, 2007).

26. See: Castro-Gómez and Grosfoguel.

27. Castro-Gómez and Grosfoguel, 20.

28. See: Antón, "Proyecto Amanar."

29. See: Antón.

30. See: Erin Hanson, "Oral Traditions," in *Indigenous Foundations* (First Nations Studies Program, University of British Columbia, 2009), https://indigenousfoundations.arts.ubc.ca/oral_traditions/.

31. The meaning of *transmedia* strategy here is the result of creative reflection through the adaptation of concepts from key authors in the field to the research-creation project. See: Katia Augusta Maciel, "A Criação Transmídia no Contexto Cultural Brasileiro," in *Direção de arte e transmidialidade*, eds. by Amaury Fernandes and Katia Augusta Maciel (Rio de Janeiro: Editora UFRJ, 2018), 167–95.

32. Katerina Cizek et al., "Part 1: 'We Are Here': Starting Points in Co-Creation," in *Collective Wisdom: Co-Creating Media within Communities, Across Disciplines and with Algorithms*, eds. Katerina Cizek and William Uricchio (Cambridge: MIT Press, n.d.), https://wip.mitpress.mit.edu/pub/collective-wisdom-part-1/release/3.

33. See: Cizek et al., "We Are Here."

34. See: Mandy Rose, "Not Media About, but Media With: Co-creation for Activism," in *I-docs: the Evolving Practices of Interactive Documentary*, eds. Mandi Rose, Sandra Gaudenzi, and Judith Aston (New York: Wallflower Press, 2017), 49–65.
35. See: Cizek et al., "We Are Here."
36. See: Mohammed Ali, interview by Felipe Carrelli et al., translation by Hamdi Ahmed Aomar, Project Amanar of GalileoMobile, October 2019.
37. See: Mohammed Salek Mohammed Embarek Sidi Baruyemaa, interview by Felipe Carrelli et al., translation by Hamdi Ahmed Aomar, Project Amanar of GalileoMobile, October 2019.
38. See: Lilie Chouliaraki, "Solidarity in the Age of Post-humanitarianism," in *Humanitarianism, Communications, and Change*, eds. Simon Cottle and Glenda Cooper (New York: Peter Lang, 2015), 133-49.
39. See: Saras Sarasvathy, "Causation and Effectuation: Toward a Theoretical Shift from Economic Inevitability to Entrepreneurial Contingency," *Academy of Management Review* 26, no. 2 (April 2001): 243–63; Saras Sarasvathy, "Entrepreneurship as a Science of the Artificial," *Journal of Economic Psychology* 24, no. 2 (April 2003): 203–20.
40. See: Sarasvathy, "Causation and Effectuation"; Sarasvathy, "Entrepreneurship as a Science."
41. Sarasvathy, "Causation and Effectuation," 245.
42. Sarasvathy, 245.
43. See: Paz and Gaudenzi, "!F LAB."
44. Docugame is a Hybrid Game and Documentary. See: Felipe Carrelli, "Planeta Perdido: um Docugame para a Divulgação de Astronomia" (Post-Graduate Certificate Thesis, Fundação Oswaldo Cruz, 2019).
45. See: Cizek et al., "We Are Here."

# PART FIVE

# Expanding Boundaries

# 14

# GUERRILLA ARCHAEOLOGY AND ANCIENT ALIENS

## Countering the Mediascapes of Stigmatized Knowledge

*Jeb J. Card and Leighton C. Peterson*

In a world where pseudoscience and fake news are presented daily as fact in popular media, mermaids are real, Bigfoot lurks, and aliens built the Pyramids. These paranormal narratives are often substantiated with pseudoscientific discourses that proliferate in the North American mediascape in a variety of televisual forms including documentaries, reality shows, and genre-bending hybrids. Once, documentary films such as those on United States (U.S.) public television were the unquestioned harbingers of filmic truth presented by one of America's most trusted institutions. They were accepted as authoritative and accurate sources on historic or scientific topics and issues and remain vital as educational resources.[1] In recent decades, however, the "documentary" has been usurped. U.S. cable television outlets such as the Travel Channel and Animal Planet now rely on "documentaries" as programming staple through prolific series and specials produced for shock, spectacle, and entertainment. Social media and online televisual platforms have democratized media production and circulation. The genre, the outlets, and the audiences for documentaries have changed. So too has the documentary itself.

## Cold Open: Mediated Pseudoscience

Long-held assumptions of on-screen expert authority and the integration of vetted research are shifting. For example, History Channel's series *Ancient Aliens* (2009–2021) relies on shaky, pseudo-archeological science to bring the past to life. It purports to educate audiences in the "truth" about, for example, the extraterrestrial origins of the Pyramids or the creation of Inka civilization[2] by ancient astronauts. It accomplishes this through convincing representation of empirical "facts" framed in the genre markers of documentary films such as

DOI: 10.4324/9781003174509-19

realistic-sounding evidence substantiated by talking-head "experts" who have little-to-no scholastic knowledge of the subject matter. For the distributors, this serves a dedicated audience of millions per episode; for producers, this popularizes their version of science. Mainstream U.S. public television documentaries have their own complexities of production, reception, and entextualizing objectivity and "truth," and are complicit in, for example, perpetuating social stratifications.[3] But these new documentary trends are different. While ostensibly geared for entertainment, these shows present filmic elements and genre markers of traditional documentaries but the producers and televisual experts have a variety of motives including evangelizing, spiritual warfare, and the creation of alternate worlds and worldviews.

The origins of televised paranormal documentary can be traced to the series *In Search of . . .* (1977–1982) and the preceding special *In Search of Ancient Astronauts* (1973), based on the success of the book *Chariots of the Gods?* by Erich von Däniken and a subsequent documentary film adaptation.[4] These alternative narratives have seeped into other parts of the mediascape and emergent forms of "documentary" and evidentiary media. What is new are the larger social networks that amplify these narratives connected by an intertextual parallelism that links documentary and evidentiary media content to fake news, user-generated blogs, and political activist networks. Media personalities including Graham Hancock and von Däniken appear in numerous streaming productions and documentaries, including *Ancient Aliens*. Appearing with media superstars like Joe Rogan – a prolific podcaster whose streaming show *The Joe Rogan Experience* regularly engages alien theories and pseudoscience – they facilitate and spread interpretations of archaeological evidence outside of professional, scientific archaeology. This provides new publics and interconnections, where user/producers not only contribute original paranormal, pseudoscientific, and conspiratorial content but also spread these narratives into vast social media networks. Documentary and evidentiary media productions from media giants distributed over cable and user-generated content presented on individual streams or corporate YouTube channels all contribute to their amplification and spread.

In the broader sociocultural and political context of biblical theme parks, anti-science politicos, and "alternative fact" commentators, the consumption and spread of pseudoscience as "real" is dangerous. These phenomena allow space for alternative representations of truth. These alternative discourses, that we might consider simultaneously conspiratorial and pseudoscientific, originate and fall under the umbrella of what Michael Barkun calls *stigmatized knowledge*.[5] Stigmatized knowledge are "claims to truth that the claimants regard as verified despite the marginalization of those claims by the institutions that conventionally distinguish between knowledge and error – universities, communities of scientific researchers, and the like."[6] Paranormal media are ambiguous spaces that allow for negotiation of belief and skepticism among the audience. They offer a space to "play" with identity.[7] Fake news, conspiracy communities, and documentary films based on pseudoscience are part of mediascapes of stigmatized knowledge. They rely on non-expert "citizen scholars" and producers with ulterior motives. They provide alternative readings of facts and evidence, and on the idea of "conspiracy," that the "truth" is being withheld from publics, making the "real" story unknowable.[8] These are not innocuous beliefs as they claim the space of charter myths: "Pseudoarchaeology actively promotes myths that are routinely used in the service of White supremacy, racialized nationalism, colonialism, and the dispossession and oppression of indigenous peoples."[9]

Archaeologists and aligned citizen scholars have launched multiple responses to debunk some of the biggest and most dangerous myths of mediated pseudoscience. This chapter investigates the ramifications of pseudoscience in documentaries by following the [social] media trail of the 2021 UFO (Unidentified Flying Object) media uproar and its links to paranormal mediascapes. We also examine the i-doc as an interactive documentary practice with content driven by, and responding to, social media audience engagement. It is a productive toolkit when in the right hands, and also one used by those spreading myths. But why does it matter that citizen scientists are stepping into the social field? Is it a problem when the academy is decolonized in this way? We argue that structural decolonization that removes content creation from authoritative voices is the opposite of decolonization; rather, it serves to reify dominant colonial narratives. The "old paradigm" of high-concept public television documentaries as authoritative voices has structural limitations (e.g., relatively lower audiences), and yet some citizen-produced i-docs can colonize new spaces once reserved for experts. Guerrilla scholars should embrace i-docs and social media platforms like YouTube by adding their voices to a participatory, vetted, and recontextualized documentary mediascape.

## Act I: When Documentary Media Hits Critical Mass

A momentous event in human history allegedly happened in Spring 2021. North American television, streaming services, and print/online news outlets were inundated with the revelation that the U.S. government was taking UFOs (or UAPs, Unidentified Aerial Phenomena) seriously. News pieces from *The New Yorker*, *CBS This Morning* and *60 Minutes*, *Politico*, *The Washington Post*, NBC, CNN, and others all ran very similar stories with a roughly similar group of former government officials and contractors as well as related reporters and advocates. Their message? The U.S. government, specifically the U.S. Navy, had proof that "UFOs were real." This was not the first time these same claims, by these same people, had made mainstream news. *The New York Times* and *Politico* ran similar simultaneous stories in December 2017 from the same sources.

This revelation spurred a steady trickle of UFO stories in the press, including numerous appearances on Fox News personality Tucker Carlson's commentary show *Tucker Carlson Today* in May 2021 (in between discussing Scientology and psychology with actress Kirstie Alley,[10] mocking CDC recommendations with the help of a "chicken enthusiast,"[11] and attacking the Black Lives Matter movement[12]). Beyond established media, the story fueled a social media streaming and podcast movement subsumed under the general title of #UFOtwitter. The core message was excitement around a soon-to-be-released U.S. Department of Defense report on UFOs which largely was treated as a disappointment after its publication.[13] For #UFOtwitter, YouTube, podcasts, and professional producers, this was UFO disclosure, the long-awaited release of secrets hoarded by the U.S. government.

The social media community that emerged after the 2017 stories hailed every major media story but spent much of its time from 2017 to 2021 creating videos, podcasts, Twitter threads, and Facebook posts. People were "researching" every bit of minutiae about the characters that had worked first as government officials and contractors, and then as private paranormal researchers and promoters or for entertainment television about UFOs. Were they really in government programs? For whom did they work? What were they hiding? When would they reveal their secrets? While mass media stories were major goals, spectacles to be praised, the reality of the community that emerged from these media pushes was an interactive, if often repetitive and obsessive one, playing out in social media. Elders in UFO and paranormal communities were taken aback by the attitude and behavior of #UFOtwitter,[14] to the point that the term became shorthand for angry and aggressive believers and advocates that did not know the history of their "field" but simply made social media about the activities of each other in the years since 2017.

The sporadic and delayed nature of traditional media engagement, in contrast with a more engaged social media community that punished disbelievers and drove hopeful predictions, is one manifestation of the decentralized mediascape, especially on topics that are used to negotiate identity and order reality. The angry and mocking nature of the (mostly) White male #UFOtwitter is similar to the efforts of MAGA advocates in social media to "own the libs" and make them cry. Virtually identical language can be found regarding UFO skeptics who dare suggest alternative explanations for blurry videos. It is notable that there were serious discussions of holding the 2020 presidential debates on *The Joe Rogan Experience*,[15] a significant venue for UFO disclosure activists as well as major alternative archaeology and other science activists. The fundamentals are the same for stigmatized knowledge and broader conspiracies: 1. Someone (a government or institution) is hiding something from the public, and 2. We can show you the "real" story and the "real" path to truth. Social networks linked through conspirituality or stigmatized knowledge are seeking new epistemologies and social orders: "Proponents believe that the best strategy for dealing with the threat of a totalitarian 'new world order' is to act in accordance with an awakened 'new paradigm' worldview."[16]

Beliefs in paranormal phenomena are longstanding in North American culture and have only gained in adherents.[17] Henry Jenkins, Sam Ford, and Joshua Green's concept of "spreadability" explains how the multiplatform, multimodal circulation of media intersects with agency of producer/consumers in the recontextualization and spreading of media narratives, foundational to "participatory culture" that encompasses "shaping, sharing, reframing, and remixing media content."[18] As Mark Peterson notes, "Participatory cultures are created through practices of exchange, communal acts of giving and receiving that link people together into networks."[19] Spreadability is related to what folklorists call "amplification," which allows fake news narratives to spread and alter beyond the contexts of an original [non]event. Amplification accounts for not only the agency and participation of users but also the algorithms of social media platforms. "Through this process, communications that would have previously been one-offs, small-scale events, or local stories may become framed as major news stories, common occurrences, or issues of public concern."[20] The same processes are involved in the spreadability and amplification of stigmatized knowledge including alternative archaeology narratives.

## Act 2: Social Media Decolonizes the Documentary

A good example of social media documentary in this genre would be *Buzzfeed Unsolved* on YouTube. This recorded streaming show has been produced since 2016, and as it grew in popularity, split into *Buzzfeed Unsolved Supernatural* and *Buzzfeed Unsolved True Crime*. The parent entity *Buzzfeed* is a hybrid of pop culture and investigative journalism. It does not have the media legacy reputation of the programs discussed earlier, but like *The Joe Rogan Experience*, it has a much larger audience. For example, one episode of *Buzzfeed Unsolved*, "3 Creepy Cases for Ancient Aliens" from Season 2 Episode 3, has been viewed nearly 14 million times – unsurprising given that almost 5 million people subscribe to the channel – and has over 20,000 comments.[21] By contrast, *Ancient Aliens* continues on the History Channel despite having around one million television viewers on first run; comparable paranormal and other shows that top out at around three million viewers.[22] These programs have an afterlife of being re-broadcast officially on YouTube (or easily copied and unofficially uploaded) facilitating their global reach. Nonetheless, material designed exclusively for streaming is increasingly gaining ground for not only spreading specific content but also building community and identity.[23] Key to such programming is getting to "know" the hosts of streaming or podcast programming in a more engaged manner than traditional media. Comments, live chats, and question-and-answer sessions are common to these programs, including *Buzzfeed Unsolved*.

This particular episode matched in topic with a more "authoritative" (or so it would seem, see Act 3) response to the *Ancient Aliens* television series. The two

*Buzzfeed* hosts lay out evidence in a streaming chat style. Numerous times in the episode, animated text on a black background similar to chat or text punctuates spoken humorous argument or disagreement, which produces a parody or illusion of interactive discussion. While this can have the effect of telling the viewer to take none of this terribly seriously, the framing device of the show is that one host is more of a believer, and it is trying to convince the other host of paranormal phenomena through evidence. In a sense, *Buzzfeed Unsolved* puts the epistemological hook of not only this show but also the entire genre, on display, replicating the expected arguments of those who post, comment, and argue about such topics based on their "evidence," rather than hiding that part of the program's audience as in traditional documentary television. Notably, when such tactics have been employed in the past, it has often been on paranormal and true crime television programming. The first major paranormal television series *In Search of . . .* had a disclaimer that the theories presented by the producers were some but not the only possible explanations for the mysteries. In the 1980s, *America's Most Wanted* and *Unsolved Mysteries* on network television encouraged viewers to call in with possible tips to solve a crime or mystery (*Unsolved Mysteries* covered both true crime and the paranormal) and would provide updates if viewers did in fact provide helpful information or other evidence emerged. On cable television, paranormal and "weird" stories with re-enactment or viral videos could even be framed as possibly real or fake and designed for the viewer to decide the truth in shows such as *Beyond Belief: Fact or Fiction* (1997–2002) and *Fact or Faked: Paranormal Files* (2010).

The "Ancient Aliens" episode of *Buzzfeed Unsolved* uses several of the most common tropes found on the show *Ancient Aliens* as well as in related official and unofficial media (books, amateur videos, and social media memes). Images of Australian and Saharan rock art allegedly depicting aliens may be handled somewhat critically for a few seconds before a completely uncritical presentation of the Late Classic Maya sarcophagus of K'inich Hanaab' Pakal as a spaceship takes a few more seconds. This might be followed by the erroneously understood "helicopter" hieroglyphic inscription of New Kingdom Egyptian pharaoh Seti I (actually a subsequent partial recarving over earlier text, combining images). The three "creepy" cases include the Pyramids of Giza in Egypt, the allegedly mysterious astronomical knowledge of the Dogon people in Mali, and the architecture of Tiwanaku, Bolivia. These cases are handled in a light fashion and range from some critical approach (examining possible evidence for ethnographic interaction with Dogon knowledge) to largely uncritical assertion of mystery. Even an informed UFO proponent or believer would likely find some of the "pro" evidence presented in the video to be superficial or to have significant errors. Some books or proponents are mentioned in the video, which are a key element to viewers who wish to investigate further. (A key element in, for example, the *Hellier* streaming series, acclaimed by many within the paranormal community, which leads to Reddit communities and other online spaces where members obtain the books discussed in the show and seek to further understand the mysteries presented.) The *Buzzfeed Unsolved* discussion of the Dogon concludes with the "skeptical" host concluding that some of this is nonsense because famed popular astronomer Carl Sagan said it was nonsense. The "believer" complains that Sagan is critiquing paranormal proponents for lying, a conversation similar to those that play out every day in social media discussions of "mysteries." Sagan had died likely before the birth of the hosts of *Buzzfeed Unsolved* and much of their audience, but his video presentations from *Cosmos* (1980) have been broken down into small clips and widely posted on social media, making Sagan a memeable icon of "skepticism" and "science communication" online since the 2000s.

## Act 3: They Look Like "Documentaries," But . . .

Bill Nichols analyzed a variety of emergent documentary forms that invoke "irony," "paradox," and "double binds."[24] Beginning with the basics, as viewers he suggests we can ask questions such as "Does this film have its facts straight?" or "Is the film lying?" or "Does this film frame or label itself as something other than what it is?" (i.e., *Triumph of the Will*, 1935). The Animal Planet channel's widely popular *Mermaids* shows relied on conspiracy: The government is withholding information about the existence of mermaids, evidence only made public by a government whistleblower exposing the controversy. As Andrew Thaler notes, "By framing the villain in these productions as real, often nonpartisan, institutions like NOAA,[25] they don't just direct resources away from the agency's actual work by forcing it to respond to a phony controversy; they lend weight to other campaigns aimed at discrediting these organizations."[26] They contribute to the destabilization of the discourses of sobriety. They contribute to the idea that the "truth" is not knowable, yet the claimants possess the "truth" which multiplies exponentially: "If NOAA is lying to us about the existence of mermaids then they're definitely lying to us about climate change."[27]

Another question is "Does this film mock or play with familiar conventions to amuse, disturb, or provoke us by mocking them?" Here, Nichols cites *This is Spinal Tap* (1984) as the preeminent example of this genre. Certainly, the producers and executives at Animal Planet would argue that the *Mermaids* shows were a form of mockumentary. However, the "mocking" of the genre was subtle, and disclaimers barely and only briefly visible, as with the YouTube series discussed earlier. We have argued for a "myth and conspiracy" genre of documentary media, a genre that destabilizes knowledge, making the world "unknowable." The genre appropriates, rather than "mocks," documentary genre conventions, and it omits or trades "fact" as "evidence" for "relative facts" as evidentiary markers.[28] The genre is marked by the "obfuscated knowledge" plotline, explication of the "sins" of the ignorant and complicit governments, an elucidation of the power of reclaimed knowledge, and allowing the audience to find and reclaim this stigmatized knowledge.

One of the "creepy cases" of the aforementioned *Buzzfeed Unsolved* video, "Tiwanaku," is a major component of a key example of where decentering and decolonizing knowledge can create problematic results: the highly popular docuseries *Ancient Aliens Debunked*.[29] Different versions of this film, including breaking it into segments, have been popular online and routinely show up in undergraduate student research papers in the experience of the authors. The majority of the film is a point-by-point rebuttal and critique of early episodes of *Ancient Aliens*. One major focus of the film is the architecture of Tiwanaku, Bolivia (400–1000 CE). This site has been used and abused by non-Indigenous observers since the late nineteenth century; its cut-stone architecture high in the Andes led White Bolivian elites and outsiders to claim it as an ancient civilization, perhaps Atlantis, often identified with a lost White race.[30] One of the key investigators of the site partnered with a member of the *Ahnenerbe* – the occult division of the Nazi SS – and planned to lead a major Nazi archaeological expedition to the site until these plans were disrupted by the outbreak of war in 1939. The decades of focusing on Tiwanaku and other highland masonry in the Andes as lost advanced civilizations made Tiwanaku an easy inclusion into ancient aliens lore and an early and recurring topic of *Ancient Aliens* the series.[31]

*Ancient Aliens Debunked* particularly and effectively focused on the Tiwanaku claims by showing easily observable problems in the original *Ancient Aliens* footage, as well as using the work of professional archaeologists on Andean stone masonry to explain some of the "mysteries" claimed by ancient aliens proponents. The film's direct rebuttal to *Ancient Aliens* (a technique rarely found in mainstream science programming but very useful for viewer engagement in social media argument or "research") made it effective, as did breaking the film into shorter components familiar to social media viewers. This led to the film being promoted by "skeptical" "science communicators," and "thought leaders" as an antidote to perceived pseudoscientific nonsense, promoted by secular pro-science organizations committed to exposing non-scientific propaganda.[32] Except, a knowledgeable observer would note that in the very beginning of the film and in several latter parts, it argues for a Biblical literalist approach regarding a global deluge and giants. Giants of the Old Testament, fallen angels, or Nephilim who bring knowledge to humanity have become an obsession of paranormal and conspiratorial thought and were cited by the most famous ancient aliens proponent, von Däniken, as the beginning of his interest in the topic. The creators of *Ancient Aliens Debunked* deploy common-sense arguments against the television show *Ancient Aliens* but intend through initially veiled assertions to replace extraterrestrials with a literalist Biblical narrative.

One of the most egregious examples of streaming paranormal media interacting with archaeology, anthropology, and government institutions is the "Nazca Alien Mummy" affair. In 2017, a media buzz grew around alleged "alien" mummies surfacing in southern Peru, which relate to the Nazca culture of the First Intermediate period (100 BCE–800 CE). Since at least the 1950s, this cultural label has been associated with allegations of extraterrestrial visitation.[33] These claims were amplified by the streaming network *Gaia*, which made a series of videos about the alleged Nazca mummies.[34] *Gaia* was initially in the wellness and yoga business but, by the 2010s, had moved into alternative and paranormal video, and critics have suggested that *Gaia* is promoting harmful antisemitic, anti-vaccination, and other conspiracy culture content.[35] One of the first major "exclusives" by *Gaia* was the "Nazca mummy" case.

A key player in this drama was Mexican journalist Jaime Maussan, who had been involved in other dubious UFO or extraterrestrial claims, most famously the 2015 "Roswell Slides" affair.[36] In this case, a handful of "newly discovered" photographic slides of an "alien body" from the infamous Roswell, New Mexico, UFO crash of 1947 was to be revealed alongside alleged scientific analysis of the true nature of the remains. A series of online videos and announcements promoted an event on May 5 (the holiday *Cinco de Mayo*), streamed on pay-per-view, that would reveal analyses, including a holographic reconstruction of the alleged alien life form. UFO researchers and enthusiasts, also known as ufologists, were skeptical of these claims given that the first teaser images looked like mummified human remains in a museum. Within 36 hours of the streamed event, analysis of the images clearly demonstrated that they were images of a known set of Indigenous American human remains taken from Mesa Verde, placed in a museum, and subsequently repatriated.[37]

The Nazca Alien Mummy case had similar resonance: the creation/modification of "alien mummies" by individuals within the UFO community in Peru. This started small-scale and mushroomed, aided, and abetted by Maussan and the *Gaia* series. Ancient human remains were mutilated, removing the finger and toe bone and wiring of them into longer remaining appendages to appear "alien." A greyish plaster-like material was applied to another set of remains to produce an "alien" visage.[38] A Peruvian UFO/ancient aliens hoax turned into a major media event associated with a company (*Gaia*) intending to fashion itself as the major streaming source of paranormal and New Age content. As media interest prompted a greater investigation of the "aliens," professional archaeologists in Peru began to push for legal action, different paranormal and conspiracy factions began to vie for attention and authority, and the entire affair became a protracted mess. It has inspired other paranormal media productions, including a long-form pseudoscientific documentary available on YouTube.

Again, these kinds of claims – especially about ancient aliens in the archaeological record – are racist and perpetuate colonial narratives. Citizen scholars can have agendas that don't align with academic scholarship. Conspiracy theory is about what is wrong, not what is right. It is the inquiry of the alienated, though not necessarily of the (actually) oppressed. It selects elements of uncertainty from weird and mass media to create a bricolage to explain the coming apocalypse. The nature of this apocalypse can always change, and it is adaptable to different extremes of the political spectrum (the extreme is the key element, not left or right nor up or down) but the core truth is of the apocalypse.[39] With this moving target of reactionary opposition, simply reiterating our professional values is not sufficient. Our most concentrated form of this method is the classroom. Archaeology in particular – and anthropology and historical humanities more broadly – are particularly suited to this approach.[40]

## Act 4: Decolonization and "Guerrilla Archaeology"

The broader goal of guerrilla archaeology is to construct a *public* counternarrative with archaeological and anthropological data that debunks the myths of the televised, anti-science, Aryan-inspired, pseudo-Western historical imagination. One of the difficulties of engaging with conspiracy theory and "alternative science" is stepping outside of academic training. Social scientists tackle existing material and ideas, sometimes trying to overturn existing ideas. We marshal evidence and precedence. However, we generally do *not*, if we're competent, propose contradictory ideas or theories in the same publications.

Teaching critical thinking through examining paranormal and conspiracy ideas, whether throughout curriculum or in dedicated courses has yielded significant results.[41] Yet this is limited by the realities of university education such as tuition and paywalls. Open discussion of these topics on social media has its own perils. Instead, moving forward involves several steps. Not all are required at once, but an ideal approach would include first understanding the historiographical aspects of an academic field that impact popular perception, and then understanding the alternative claims that tie into popular perception. Finally, it involves producing new media content on social media, informed by popular perception, that educates with academic understandings. Here, we are suggesting the i-doc – an interactive documentary practice with content driven by, and responding to, audience engagement – as a productive outlet for guerrilla media activists. The social media-based i-doc, when combined with knowledge of popular perceptions, overcomes issues of access and the constraints of "old paradigm" documentary media practice. Let us explain.

Legitimate archaeological mass media is somewhat more common in, for example, the United Kingdom, with shows such as the *Time Team* (BBC4, 1994–2014). While successful, that series did not largely address topics enmeshed in pseudoscientific histories as it was aimed at an already invested "scientific literate" public. That has limited impact on audiences and producers uninterested in or unable to break out of pre-existing models and frames benefitting the shocking, the groundbreaking, or the sensational. Infotainment programs such as *Ancient Aliens*, *America Unearthed* (2012–2015), or *Expedition Unknown* (2015-present) are still more widely known, using sensationalistic Victorian approaches to scholarship which traditional media professionals and academics abandoned a century ago.[42] However, conspiracy and alternative ideas spread best via video, and increasing social media video. This high ground must be recentered to recognize this reality.

For example, the notion of ancient aliens dates back to at least the late nineteenth century, in a mixture of fiction and occultism, until going mainstream in the 1970s with the success of von Däniken and *Chariots of the Gods?* But the most prominent recent proponent of an alternative human past is British journalist Graham Hancock. In a series of books beginning in the mid-1990s, Hancock has offered various versions of the notion that an advanced super-civilization thrived in the Upper Pleistocene, which influenced subsequent ancient monuments and wisdom, but was destroyed by a cataclysm (early versions of this included a crustal displacement, but Hancock has largely settled on a massive comet swarm that scoured away this civilization). These ideas bear a strong resemblance to the nineteenth-century idea of Atlantis as the source of complex society.[43]

This claim may seem somewhat removed from ancient aliens but the topics are closer than they first appear. Hancock detailed the idea that humanity had an explosion of creativity due to contact via altered states aided by particular entheogenic plants, alternative planes of reality, and the non-human entities of those realms.[44] Hancock is not arguing for entities arriving on Earth physically, but existing in a realm we cannot normally access due to materialist and problem-solving forms of behavior. Hancock cites concepts from UFO and paranormal circles, especially those related to alien abduction, that compares these entities to the lore of European fairies and other non-human spirits or entities.[45] A compacted form of this argument can be found in a lecture by Hancock in 2010 from the pop culture convention Dragon Con Atlanta.[46]

In 2019, Jeb participated in a Society for American Archaeology effort to address alternative archaeology, particularly related to Hancock's recent book *America Before*.[47] Rather than focus on material claims, Jeb covered the non-material aspect of Hancock's work and how it fits into broader paranormal culture, present in his books but often ignored by critics and many supporters alike. This approach led to Hancock praising this approach as a serious assessment of his work, even though there are clear points of disagreement.[48]

> Attempting to critique . . . [Hancock] using the criteria of professional archaeology is doomed to failure, as his goals are outside of the materialist practice of scientific archaeology. In a nutshell, Hancock argues that an ancient civilization of the Pleistocene emerged in North America that was based not on material technology but on psychic/spiritual knowledge. It became a global sea-based society comparable with the late pre-Industrial British Empire. These Ice Age Americans (spoiler: Atlanteans) foresaw a cosmic disaster and spread memetic seeds of sacred knowledge of geometry, astronomy, and the Otherworld and how souls may navigate it around the world. After this civilization was destroyed by impact events from a comet during the Younger Dryas, these advanced people came to be remembered as magicians and gods. Seeking this knowledge today is a path to truly understanding reality and the spiritual elements denied by materialist science.[49]

It was with some surprise that we noticed this same paragraph appearing in a 2021 YouTube video titled "Fundamental Objections to Graham Hancock." The quote – as well as Hancock's approval of it – formed the core definition in an 18-minute long critique of Hancock's more outrageous ideas.[50]

The video was produced by Stefan Milosavljevich (Milo), one of the best practitioners of i-doc guerilla archaeology. Milo has a degree in Archaeology and Anthropology from University of Sheffield,[51] and goes by the public moniker "Stefan Milo." Milo is the creator of a popular self-named YouTube channel with an emphasis on the prehistoric archaeology of Europe; his channel has over 4.5 million YouTube views (as of October 2020). The channel description includes "three golden rules":

1.   *Use only academic sources for my videos.*
2.   *List all my sources so people can read and discuss the evidence for themselves.*
3.   *Try explicitly to mention when I'm giving my personal opinion.*[52]

His channel is also tagged with a public disclaimer: "No aliens, no atlantis, no bollocks." In an interview, Milo acknowledges the difficulties in countering the outrageous claims and media dominance of alternative archaeologies because,

> their topics are so sensational: Lost civilization blown apart by asteroid. They don't need clickbait. Their whole idea is clickbait. It's not enough to be correct or know the archaeology, you have to be good at making the videos. And it's through videos that people are really engaging this content.

He's been making videos on history, and increasingly archaeology, since 2018, and notes that people aren't necessarily reading Hancock's books – "they're coming into contact with them through YouTube."

Most of the content on Milo's channel is aimed at exploring the human past for a broader audience, but as he began to make videos that touched on topics of particular interest to alternative archaeology, viewer comments increased:

> The first video where I thought there was some big potential here was . . . "How Long Have People lived in America,"[53] and I put on the thumbnail 15,000 Years? and that's 83K views now, and I think at the time it immediately shot up to the most popular video I had made up to that time. And virtually everyone in the comments wanted me to talk about the Solutrean Hypothesis.[54]

He says that experience made him realize he could address fringe ideas held by a lot of his viewers on YouTube. This reaction led Milo to begin making videos that addressed this and other alternative ideas.[55]

Another example of engaging a conversation on alternative archaeology can be found in Milo's video on the Pyramids of Giza, Egypt.[56] This video was based on mainstream evidence and ideas, but many comments began to reference, often disapprovingly, the age of the Sphinx. A more ancient Sphinx is a key aspect of alternative archaeology and esoterica given substantial material and ideological support by followers of the "Sleeping Prophet" Edgar Cayce. It leapt into broader popular consciousness following a geological paper suggesting water erosion that many associated with the growing popularity of Hancock and his book *Fingerprints of the Gods*.[57] As Milo notes

> I had no idea how popular he was until I made that video on the Pyramids. And again it's so predictable. If I made a topic about something Graham Hancock doesn't mention, the comments section will be people just curious about archaeology, "That's interesting." If I make a video about anything that he's mentioned, then the comments section is full of people who believe in pseudo archaeology.

This kind of immediate response by explaining broader ideas but directly related to popular alternative archaeology is not commonly made by academics or professional archaeologists in print or other mediascapes. But it is at the heart of a guerilla-informed i-doc approach.

## Stinger

We live in a guerrilla age in which the trustworthiness of media is based less on trust in institutions than in subversion, inversion, and parody of old institutions. By signaling one does not possess traditional icons of authority, social media producers build authenticity. Epistemological approaches based on uncertainty and contradictory evidence, such as conspiracy and paranormal claims, thrive in such an environment. Harry Collins long ago called for more scientific programming on television to counter emerging pseudoscientific discourses;[58] Sparks and Miller explain that "If the media plays a central role in encouraging people to adopt beliefs about reality that are unsubstantiated, there may well be widespread implications for future society that are incalculable at the present time."[59] With access to traditional media closed by bias for sensation and cheap predictable production costs, and American public television roiled in its own issues,[60] one clear avenue forward is the i-doc. Yes, it is also used by alternative "sources" and disingenuous citizen scholars. For guerrilla scholars, producing new ideas that incorporate popular perceptions rather than angrily reacting to them, and doing it in a way that embraces social media rather than being decontextualized by it, is the only way forward.

This is not new for archaeology. Prior to television and prior to the expansion of university tenure and professionalization systems, scholars like archaeologists would potentially write in text for a broad audience and accompany their scholarship with appearances on radio, and later, the early years of television.[61] However concomitant with the emergence of television, academic scholars were either relegated to the genre-marking "talking-head interview" in documentary television or incentivized to stop speaking to the public and write for peers for purposes of promotion. The expansion of an industry of "alternative" scholars willing to wear the lab coats of science on-camera is a direct result of the colonization of academic knowledge. The old documentary and academic paradigms are no longer valid. Milo and others have learned lessons from other decolonizing (yet dangerous) producers: provide shorter videos, engage with the audience, and build social media personas. This also includes and emphasizes sensational – even colonial – topics, but then owning and reframing them in a representation of decolonized academic knowledge. This i-doc approach is the best practice for the future of advocates and scholars providing their work and their concerns in a popular medium to new generations of audiences.

## Notes

1. See: Leighton C. Peterson, "Made Impossible by Viewers Like You: The Politics and Poetics of Native American Voices in Us Public Television," in *How Television Shapes Our Worldview: Media Representations of Social Trends and Change*, eds. Deborah A. Macey, Kathleen M. Ryan, and Noah J. Springer (New York: Lexington Books, 2014), 247–266.
2. Inka is the proper decolonized orthographic representation of what was formerly "Inca."
3. Peterson, "Made Impossible," 247.
4. See: Erich von Däniken, *Chariots of the Gods? Unsolved Mysteries of the Past* (London: Souvenir, 1969).
5. See: Michael Barkun, *A Culture of Conspiracy: Apocalyptic Visions in Contemporary America* (Berkeley and Los Angeles: University of California Press, 2013).
6. Barkun, *A Culture of Conspiracy*, 26.
7. See: Annette Hill, *Paranormal Media: Audiences, Spirits and Magic in Popular Culture* (London and New York: Routledge, 2010).
8. See: Christopher D. Bader, Joseph O. Baker, and F. Carson Mencken, *Paranormal America: Ghost Encounters, Ufo Sightings, Bigfoot Hunts, and Other Curiosities in Religion and Culture* (New York: New York University Press, 2017); Barkun, *Culture of Conspiracy*.
9. John W. Hoopes, "Introduction," *SAA Archaeological Record* 19, no. 5 (2019): 8.
10. *Media Matters* Staff, "Tucker Carlson Guest Kirstie Alley Says Scientology, not Professional Therapy, is the Most Effective Treatment for Depression," *Media Matters* (May 19, 2021), www.mediamatters.org/fox-nation/tucker-carlson-guest-kirstie-alley-says-scientology-not-professional-therapy-most.
11. Aylin Woodward, "Tucker Carlson Invited a 'Poultry Enthusiast' onto Fox News to Ridicule CDC Guidelines About not Kissing Chickens Amid a Salmonella Outbreak," *Business Insider* (May 22 2021), https://news.yahoo.com/tucker-carlson-invited-poultry-enthusiast-200831039.html. The Centers for Disease Prevention and Control (CDC), the public health agency of the United States.
12. Samson Amore, "Tucker Carlson Calls BLM's Existence 'A National Humiliation'," *The Wrap* (May 24, 2021), www.thewrap.com/tucker-carlson-blm-is-a-national-humiliation/.

13. Julene Barnes and Helene Cooper, "U.S. Finds No Evidence of Alien Technology in Flying Objects, but Can't Rule It Out, Either," *The New York Times* (June 3, 2021), www.nytimes.com/2021/06/03/us/politics/ufos-sighting-alien-spacecraft-penta gon.html.

14. Jack Brewer, "UFO Disclosure and Transparency: Good for Thee, Not for Me," *Blogpost. The UFO Trail* (June 7, 2021), http://ufotrail.blogspot.com/2021/06/ufo-disclosure-and-transparency-good.html.

15. Alice Stewart, "A Joe Rogan Debate between Trump and Biden is Just What We Need," *CNN* (September 15, 2020), www.cnn.com/2020/09/15/opinions/joe-rogan-moderate-trump-biden-debate-opinion-stewart/index.html.

16. See: Charlotte Ward and David Voas, "The Emergence of Conspirituality," *Journal of Contemporary Religion* 26, no 1 (2011): 103–21.

17. See: Bader et al., *Paranormal America*.

18. See: Henry Jenkins, Sam Ford, and Joshua Green, *Spreadable Media: Creating Value and Meaning in a Networked Culture* (New York: New York University Press, 2013).

19. Mark Allen Peterson, "Media Anthropology and the Digital Challenge," in *The Routledge Companion to Media Anthropology*, eds. Elisabetta Costa, Patricia G. Lange, Nell Haynes, and Jolynna Sinanan (Abington: Routledge, in press).

20. See: Andrew Peck, "A Problem of Amplification: Folklore and Fake News in the Age of Social Media," *The Journal of American Folklore* 133, no. 529 (2020): 329–51.

21. "3 Creepy Cases for Ancient Aliens," *Buzzfeed Unsolved Supernatural,* Buzzfeed Unsolved Network, YouTube (April 21, 2017), www.youtube.com/watch?v=BmUrJaOo1Lw.

22. Jason Colavito, "Review of Ancient Aliens S16E09 'The UFO Pioneers'," *jasoncolavito.com* (March 6, 2021), www.jasoncolavito.com/blog/review-of-ancient-aliens-s16e09-the-ufo-pioneers.

23. Patricia G. Lange, *Thanks for Watching: An Anthropological Study of Video Sharing on YouTube* (Louisville: University Press of Colorado, 2019).

24. Bill Nichols, *Speaking Truths with Film: Evidence, Ethics, & Politics in Documentary* (Oakland: University of California Press, 2016), 99–130.

25. The National Oceanic and Atmospheric Administration, an agency within the U.S. Department of Commerce.

26. Andrew David Thaler, "The Politics of Fake Documentaries," *Slate* (August 31, 2016), www.slate.com/articles/technology/future_tense/2016/08/the_lasting_dam age_of_fake_documentaries_like_mermaids_the_body_found.html.

27. This declaration by an anonymous fifth-grade biology teacher on a plane was reported by Thaler, "Politics."

28. See: Leighton C. Peterson, and Jeb J. Card, "Pseudoscience, Conspiracies, and the Case for Guerilla Archaeology," in *The Routledge Companion to Media Anthropology*, eds. Elisabetta Costa, Patricia G. Lange, Nell Haynes, and Jolynna Sinanan (Abington: Routledge, In press).

29. *Ancient Aliens Debunked*, directed by Chris White, VerseByVerseBT, YouTube (2012) 3:10:43, www.youtube.com/watch?v=j9w-i5oZqaQ.

30. Mathew Gildner, "Andean Atlantis: Race, Science and the Nazi Occult in Bolivia," *The Appendix* (June 5, 2013), https://theappendix.net/issues/2013/4/andean-atlan tis-race-science-and-the-nazi-occult-in-bolivia.

31. Tiwanaku is a major Middle Horizon early city in Bolivia, but Ancient Aliens enthusiasts call it Pumapunku, the name of one of the platforms at the site of Tiwanaku, after its renaming was popularized as the site name in von Däniken's *Chariots of the Gods?* in 1968.

32. Chris White, "Ancient Aliens Debunked," *Skeptic* (2012), accessed June 8, 2021, www.skeptic.com/reading_room/ancient-aliens-debunked/.

33. Christopher Heaney, "The Racism Behind Alien Mummy Hoaxes," *The Atlantic* (August 1, 2017), www.theatlantic.com/science/archive/2017/08/how-to-fake-an-alien-mummy/535251/.

34. See: www.amazon.com/Unearthing-Nazca-Season-1/dp/B073DRHRV2.

35. Matthew Thompson, "Tech Giants Criticised Over 'Conspiracy Theory' Videos on Gaia Streaming Service," *Leading Britain's Conversation* (February 10, 2021), www.lbc. co.uk/news/tech-giants-criticised-over-conspiracy-theory-videos-on-gaia-stream ing-service/.

36. Heaney, "Racism."

37. Les Carpenter, "The Curious Case of the Alien in the Photo and the Mystery that Took Years to Solve," *The Guardian* (September 30, 2017), www.theguardian.com/science/2017/sep/30/alien-photo-roswell-new-mexico-mystery.

38. For a full discussion, see: Heaney, "Racism."

39. See: Barkun, *Culture of Conspiracy.*

40. Anne Collins McLaughlin, "Explicitly Teaching Critical Thinking Skills in a History Course," *Science & Education* 26, no. 93–105 (2017), https://link.springer.com/article/10.1007/s11191-017-9878-2.

41. April Hunt, "Emory Class Looks at Fake Archaeological Stories to Understand Modern Thinking," in *Emory Report* (Atlanta: Emory University, April 3, 2018), https://news.emory.edu/stories/2018/04/er_archaeology_blakely/campus.html.

42. See: Jeb J. Card, "Steampunk Inquiry: A Comparative Vivisection of Discovery Pseudosciences," in *Lost City, Found Pyramid: Understanding Alternative Archaeologies and Pseudoscientific Practices*, eds. Jeb J. Card and David S. Anderson (Tuscaloosa: University of Alabama Press, 2016), 19–32.

43. This idea was propagated by Ignatius Donnelly and various theosophical movements and authors.

44. See: Graham Hancock, *Supernatural: Meetings with the Ancient Teachers of Mankind* (New York: Disinformation Company, 2006).

45. See: Joshua Cutchin, *Thieves in the Night: A Brief History of Supernatural Child Abductions* (San Antonio, TX: Anomalist Books, 2018); Jacques Vallee, *Passport to Magonia: From Folklore to Flying Saucers* (Chicago: Henry Regnery, 1969).

46. Graham Hancock, "Elves, Aliens, Angels, and Ayahuasca," *disinformation*, YouTube (October 26, 2010), www.youtube.com/watch?v=0qgMFO0KU-I.

47. See: Jeb J. Card, "America Before as a Paranormal Charter," *SAA Archaeological Record* 19, no. 5 (November 2019): 26–30, http://onlinedigeditions.com/publication/?m=16146&i=634462&p=1&pp=1&ver=html5.

48. Graham Hancock, "Response from Graham Hancock to the Society for American Archaeology," *blogpost* (November 25, 2019), https://grahamhancock.com/saa-archaeological-record-response/.

49. Card, "America," 26.

50. Stefan Milosavljevich, "Fundamental Objections to Graham Hancock," *Stefan Milo,* YouTube (June 22, 2020), www.youtube.com/watch?v=RwTkDkSbO-4.

51. The University of Sheffield confirmed the closure of their archaeology program in 2021. Geraldine Kendall Adams, "Outrage as Sheffield University Confirms Closure of Archaeology Department," *Museums Associations* (July 16, 2021), www.museumsassociation.org/museums-journal/news/2021/07/outrage-as-sheffield-university-confirms-closure-of-archaeology-department/#.

52. Stefan Milosavljevich, "Description," *Stefan Milo*, YouTube, accessed September 26, 2021, www.youtube.com/c/StefanMilo/about.

53. Stefan Milosavljevich, "How Long Have People Lived in America? – The Stone Age Explained," *Stefan Milo*, YouTube (October 9, 2018), www.youtube.com/watch?v=HV7LYwOqf9U.

54. The Solutrean hypothesis refers to a notion not largely accepted in archaeology of a migration across the Atlantic into Eastern North America before the more widely held models of sea and land movement from Siberia. Outside of academia, the notion became popular in alternative archaeology particularly among a swath of Eurocentric

audiences, including White Supremacists, and replicates a long history of early mainstream and later alternative archaeology emphasizing a Mound Builder Race before indigenous Americans, almost always labeled to be White. See: Jason Colavito, *The Mound Builder Myth: Fake History and the Hunt for a "Lost White Race"* (Norman: University of Oklahoma Press, 2020a).

55. Stefan Milosavljevich, "Does the Sphinx Water Erosion Hypothesis Hold Water??" *Stefan Milo*, YouTube (March 4, 2019), www.youtube.com/watch?v=lK2JM_nlkbM.

56. Stefan Milosavljevich, "How the Egyptians MIGHT have built the Great Pyramid," *Stefan Milo,* YouTube (February 22, 2019), www.youtube.com/watch?v=UeL3bfwu-Zk.

57. Jeb J. Card, *Spooky Archaeology: Myth and the Science of the Past* (Albuquerque: University of New Mexico Press, 2018), 263–65. Also see: Graham Hancock, *Fingerprints of the Gods* (New York: Three Rivers Press, 1996), 417–24.

58. See: Harry M. Collins, "Certainty and the Public Understanding of Science: Science on Television," *Social Studies of Science* 17, no. 4 (1987): 689–713.

59. Glenn Sparks and Will Miller, "Investigating the Relationship between Exposure to Television Programs that Depict Paranormal Phenomena and Beliefs in the Paranormal," *Communication Monographs* 68, no 1 (2001): 111.

60. See: Peterson, "Made Impossible."

61. Card, *Spooky*.

# 15

# RESPONDING TO TENSION

*Tessa Ratuszynska in conversation with Tammy Rae Matthews. Edited by Tammy Rae Matthews*

Tessa Ratuszynska is part of an open 360/ VR/ XR collaborative group based in Bristol, UK. In the project – called *The Othvrs*[1] – they and other artists boost representation of "othered" and excluded groups through organizing workshops and prioritizing flexible access funding to support and help participants learn skills and technology. In this conversation with Tammy Rae Matthews, they talk about the collaborative spirit of the collection and how their dedication to social equity has complemented their academic and practice-based work perspectives. They consider themselves to be a gender-nonconforming person but don't describe themselves as trans or nonbinary, using "they" pronouns in their academic work because they don't want it to be read through gender or biased by gender.

TRM: What is the value of exploring gender and other social justice issues through the i-doc?

TR: I've been interested in i-docs a long time, even though I make VR predominantly. At the moment, I'm doing a practice-based VR PhD, but because of COVID-19, I'm having to think about installations that don't involve touching and headsets, etc. So, it's definitely headed that way. In both VR and wider i-docs, the thing that I find most interesting is this: interaction has this amazing potential to hold audiences accountable, to involve audiences in a different way, to resist audiences just being passive and make them active. Reminding them that there is something that they can *do* beyond just watching a documentary. They can perform action in the real world as well, after they leave the space where they've experienced the documentary, be that financially, socially, whatever.

But it's this double-edged sword, I think. Because when you make a piece of work that somebody does get to interact with, that is somehow "work"

DOI: 10.4324/9781003174509-20

in itself to do or to experience. Sometimes that bit of "work" can be misconstrued as the other bit of "work"? Because you had to do something when you watched or experienced a documentary, like, you've done enough and that there's not more to be done? So, I'm interested in that tension.

I'm also interested in gamification or giving audiences agency inside work. If we're talking about a social justice issue, giving audiences agency inside works that are about someone's lack of agency. I think that's a really — maybe interesting is the wrong word — but an ethical tension there. I'm mostly thinking from a VR perspective. For example, the "refugee VR" experience, which is a common subject, and usually follows a set narrative; people having to leave their home because of a political conflict and having to create temporary or precarious housing or integrate into a new culture that is somehow hostile to them in some way. That narrative itself is very Westernized, and it doesn't acknowledge maybe, say, in the UK context, I've never seen a UK VR about a refugee experience that really acknowledges any kind of UK political involvement. It's more about generating "empathy" than any actual understanding of personal responsibility.

The benefit of making an i-doc, over just making a fiction piece of work about something, is that documentaries have these other things [than empathy] at their disposal. Nonlinear structures to deal with a subject that's too complex to narrow down to just one person's refugee experience, or this neoliberal idea of empathy. And the potential to create a piece of work to mobilize something that's much more beneficial, which would be solidarity or action. So, an i-doc can be a documentary that doesn't follow just this one journey but acknowledges that there might be multiple entry points to a story, or multiple perspectives, or that you can't just condense people's narrative to a soundbite. You might have to engage in this longer form, exploratory way to really engage with this nonfiction subject.

In thinking about the relationship between VR and maybe a decolonial practice — if you call it that. I'm going to badly paraphrase Sara Ahmed here in that great essay where she talks about what decolonial practice can look like in an institution.[2] That being the Black person or the person of color, having to explain to other people in the institution, how they experienced racism as it happens to them. And so, racism becomes something that happens to somebody's body because it's different rather than something that's created in an institution. That obviously puts the obligation on BIPOC to explain their experience, instead of putting the obligation on the system to understand the ways in which it creates whiteness as a default or whatever.

I think lots of VR also works on this premise. That you would go into a VR, especially lots of the "in the body of" VR experiences, you'll go in the body of somebody and have "an experience" of racism, of sexism, of having an abortion of being a refugee or whatever. This again puts the obligation on the othered person. So, rather than having a VR documentary about a trans person that might show you their life, show you how hard it is to be them really puts this onus on the fact that it's *their difference* that is making this life harder. That we – good people watching this documentary – have an obligation to make it easier *for them* – that's what I mean by neoliberal empathy. Rather, we could encourage users to just consider their own gender or consider how gender was assigned to them and formed around their body and how they interacted with their body. Gender isn't something that just happens to trans people. It's something that we all – have not even a responsibility – but an experience of, and that's something. I guess what I'm trying to say is privilege is something that's really hard to feel, obviously, because privilege is the definition of not having your sex or gender or race, etc. – not having that be a hindrance to your life in any way.

I guess, for me, the potential of VR is just having this slight separation from your body or thinking about yourself inside the VR can give you this window into yourself, inside your body, and onto your privilege, as it were. I consider myself a gender-nonconforming person, but I do not describe myself as trans. I'm conscious that as a cis-passing, straight-passing, white, middle-class person, I don't experience the kind of minoritization that a lot of trans and nonbinary people do. I'm read as a white woman, so that comes with a lot of power, even if I don't consider myself to be a woman.

TRM: How can practice-based research expand the field? And if you have any tensions with the questions, please feel free to comment on that.

TR: I am doing practice-based research, but I feel like I'm still really learning about what that is and what that means. But I guess particularly for me, VR is an embodied media and I guess there's lots of i-docs that would also count as that not just VR, but it's really hard to predict the effect of the work on the audience. You can design something, or you can imagine that making this space in VR is going to feel one way, and then when you put an audience in it, it has this opposite effect. Anecdotally, there was this time I did a VR documentary experience where the makers had LIDAR'd[3] out an environment and so the premise of the documentary was: you are really here, this is a very accurate representation of this space. But because of the way that LIDAR images *feel* to be inside of, they feel like a computer game! They feel totally computer-generated; you're used to seeing that kind of material in a computer game. And so, it doesn't *read as real*. And this changed the whole experience of the documentary. That feeling, it's sometimes very hard to imagine, the kind of mise-en-scène of VR is very hard to plan. So, that's why I think that VR in particular is something that has to be made and remade and experienced to be researched.

Also, I come from an installation art background, so I'm really influenced by installation art and also performance art practices and work. I think that the relationship's quite under written about in literature. Whereas interactive theater and VR, obviously, there's tons of books written about that relationship, and it is there, but I guess works where it's about making the space and what happens inside that space *is* the work. So, it can only happen in practice. It doesn't exist until it's there, if you see what I mean. That relationship is I think really interesting to me in VR. So, the liveness of it, I suppose, is something that has to be experienced in, in practice.

TRM:  How does decolonization appear in your work?

TR:  This is a question, I guess, I sense a tension in. I, I don't think I've ever used that word in regard to my work. And if I have, which I don't think I have, I would definitely use different words now. As a white person funded by an institution in Scotland, in Glasgow, in the United Kingdom. It's an incredibly white and colonial context. I think I would have to be doing a lot of work to ever make that statement. So, I just simply won't, but it is obviously an intention of the work to be anti-racist and to actively critique and move away from a lot of racist and colonialist ideas that are, and do exist in the VR genre.

Within making VR, there are a lot of tensions in well, the headset itself. There's lots written about how the VR headset itself is historically is a racist object, very exclusionary to people who aren't white, to people with disabilities or different ranges of mobility, so it's hard because you're making that work for inside that restrictive medium. Also, anything you make, especially if you put out online, because it's got that word "VR" and because of who feels ownership over that technology because of the marketing of the headsets and whatever, you are going to get a cis, white, male, probably, audience watching your work.

So, making with that knowledge, knowing that that's who's going to view the work, has tensions. I made a bit of work which was about queer clubbing. You'd want to be making that work for a queer audience, but you also know there will be that other audiences watching and so then you turn something – a queer club space – which is supposed to be about the premise of a queer club space; not performing to a cis, heteronormative gaze, and you end up compromising that. So, even though it's something I'm aware of, I'm not going to say that it's something I always perfectly manage. It's this kind of constant tension.

TRM:  Tell me a bit about your research. What are the main themes and objectives of your work overall?

TR:  Originally, I was really interested in making VR work about gender and the performance of gender, mostly using the 360° because I'm not a developer.

I was thinking about the 360° camera as potentially enacting this queer perspective where, because you're in this space that engenders certain performance, but you're not obligated to perform because your body is not really there, that the camera and maybe the technology could be inherently queer or could queer users perspective. I was working with football clubs in Glasgow, but because of the pandemic, I couldn't shoot that work anymore.

I guess my ideas evolved into the idea of space as having a direct influence on bodies and their performance. There were lots of figures coming out about the disproportionate exposure to COVID-19 and death rates in COVID-19 among different minoritized people in the United Kingdom. It clearly indicated that not everybody is experiencing public space in the same way, not everyone has access to space in the same way, or has the ability to avoid spaces in the same way. I was also influenced by obviously the Black Lives Matter protests and events, as well as a lot of disability rights activists talking about the ironies of RL[4] spaces that previously resisted having accessible online presences now having to move that way. Those all inspired me to maybe think about real-life spaces and digital spaces and how those are obviously designed around one kind of body, the free movement of one kind of body, and then thinking about spaces that are designed around other bodies. So, minoritized communities who make spaces that center their bodies' safety, their affirmation. That is what became my creative R and D (research and development), expanded performance fellowship project *Club XXY* (2021).[5] So now I'm at this point where I'm thinking about VR as maybe a more speculative tool to imagine space from other perspectives, predominantly a queer perspective, but outside or in opposition to constructs by which people are minoritized, I guess.

TRM: Who inspires you?

TR: Inspires me as in who I consider to be doing really amazing work in terms of translating nonfiction narratives into interactive artworks and also using that interaction to challenge audiences; I'm thinking of Danielle Brathwaite-Shirley.[6] I interviewed her for the same creative R and D project: *Club XXY*. She's a games designer and an artist. She makes work that's made using, but also designed for, the internet.

She uses kind of game, the infrastructure of games design to archive Black trans experience. Archive in terms of that these experiences or lives need to be held in some way. That they have been historically erased and or turned, you know, used in medical histories or turned toward other archival narratives like white colonial museum narratives, for example, and not treasured or explored as joyful or, like used in some other way.

She decided to make work that she described as an archive, but it stands quite apart from what you might think of as an archival institution space. And she makes this archive on the internet. She makes work as a Black trans person for Black trans people and with Black trans people in mind. During our interview, she was describing how she does that at all points in her making. It's not just about talking to other Black trans people, but it's in the interaction design. It is in the kind of images that are used as the textures on the surfaces, on the buildings, on the trees; she works from the foundation up with that in mind, which I also think is a really important practice. Obviously, I experience these works as a white person, and Brathwaite-Shirley is not making the work for me, and there are parts of her craft, where she holds space for Black trans joy, that can't exist if I, or another non-Black, non-trans persons are there trying to observe it. Because it would require too much education, because non-Black trans people's presence in that space makes it not a safe space and a space where that joy can't be expressed without performing to whiteness/non-Blackness/cisness, etc. Her work challenges you on entry to be explicit about your identity and your intentions within the space.

We were talking before: there is this white Western neoliberal attitude that you should be able to witness others' pain – that you might watch a documentary, feel for the other, and even come away as a better person because you did that. Brathwaite-Shirley actively resists this. Her games are not spaces where non-Black, non-trans people can come to educate themselves.

TRM:   What is the significance of queering VR? Do you see any tensions in this question?

TR:   Yes; lots of tension. There's lots of interesting ways that VR feels fertile ground for, as I said before, exploring ideas about the body and the queering potential of separating in some way the user from their body. Also, this idea of relinquishing that power and control a director might have traditionally to guide an audience through a story. Once people are inside of VR, they can look wherever they want. They don't have to follow the story that you've set up for them. They also can and will try and break the device, not the device, the headset, but trying to see the edges of what you've done basically. So, I think that in a way is inherently queer. You have to relinquish that control and that position of power.

But probably there are overwhelmingly more problems than there are potentials. I guess my use of the word "queer" would be as a critique of hetero-patriarchal ideas or ideals, but inherent in that is also racist, colonialists, extractive, consumerist concepts. VR as a technology is so related to military technology. So, that's a history that has to be acknowledged. It's also massively embedded with big corporate interests, consumerist companies – the biggest! So, you might say that negates the whole idea in itself. especially if Facebook continues to price out any other headset manufacturer or platform. Facebook headsets make you sign in with a Facebook account, which really makes impossible any anonymity. If queer practice or a queer way of making requires an openness and transparency about technology or and the accessibility of the technology to be picked up and used by anyone, this isn't possible within a Facebook-owned device – how the headset records your data and who uses that.

TRM:   I've been long been interested in the intersection between neurodivergent studies and queer studies. How do you think your work advances the field of disability studies?

TR:   I am also super interested in that intersection, and Crip Theory[7] as that space where Queer Theory and Disability Studies meet, but Crip Theory also includes race and gender studies and activism practice, which I think is also really important to what we're talking about. So, I think there's a lot there. I like the way that my research is going now, thinking about space and its influence on bodies.

When thinking about VR, I find disability studies as a critique, so amazing at breaking that down; how much of the spatial world has an implication of bodies and has assumed stuff about bodies and also illustrates what societally is implied in what a body should be or what a body should do. So, I'm really interested in disability studies for that reason. From an anticapitalist perspective, a lot of disability activists and theorists make this really interesting point: the idea of "inclusion" as perhaps being not necessarily the be all and end all. That we can actually go beyond inclusion. That there's a potential of bodies, or neurologies, to resist this capitalist idea that all bodies have to be useful or need to contribute, or need to be "included" so that they can produce for society.

I think neurodivergence is valuable as a perspective because there is this idea of a typical neurology or neurotypical ideal, but it's maybe the least lived up to in all of the ideals. So, whiteness or femininity or, or even ablebodiedness are things that some people might be able to enact without struggling at all and that happens a lot. But probably being neurotypical is something that massive amounts of the population can never actually attain continuously across their lifetime. And yet it's something that organizes so much of what our working lives and public lives. So that, as a perspective, is really interesting.

I would not say my work in any way advances disability studies though. Other artists, other people, academics working in disability studies, and disabled artists really inspire me and have really shaped my work. Obviously, I've worked with Jane Gauntlett and Jane Gauntlett's work is definitely placed there as breaking new ground in just VR in general, let alone discussing neurodivergence.[8] I've worked with her for a number of years, and then we've also worked with Unlimited, which is an organization in the United Kingdom that funds disabled artists to make work. So, I've met lots of artists through that, but in the same way as with queer artists, I don't really think that these artists were inspiring cause all their work is about disability or it teaches about disability, but just simply it's good, and often it's made from this outside perspective that is very critical of normative structures and values.

Obviously, it's important to think about access in practice and in the queer practice and in making work and VR work. I-docs as a media is possibly a form that allows the most integration of different methods of access. Different kinds of layering sound, subtitling, stuff that can integrate it into the form itself probably means that it's a medium that could really push that forward.

## Notes

1. See: www.theothvrs.com/.
2. See: Sara Ahmed, "The Nonperformativity of Antiracism," *Meridians* 7, no. 1 (2006): 104–26, www.jstor.org/stable/40338719.
3. Light Detection and Ranging.
4. Real life.
5. See: www.clubxxy.co.uk/.
6. Her work can be found at www.daniellebrathwaiteshirley.com/.
7. See: Robert McRuer and Michael Berube, *Crip Theory: Cultural Signs of Queerness and Disability* (New York: New York University Press, 2006), muse.jhu.edu/book/7696.
8. See: Jane Gauntlett, *In My Shoes: Dancing with Myself*, 360 Video (2016).

# 16

# IN THE LIGHT OF MEMORY

*Diego Cerna Aragon*

In November 2020,[1] Peru – which already had been one of the countries most affected by the pandemic and the global economic crisis – experienced a moment of extreme political instability, leading to the impeachment of then-president Martín Vizcarra.[2] This sparked a massive wave of civil unrest, as it was seen as a coup orchestrated by the opposition forces in the parliament.

As the crisis unfolded, the use of a particular tactic stood out: street projections (see Figure 16.1). These were light projections of political messages made by protesters over the surface of adjacent buildings. Ingenious demonstrators reached the house of Manuel Merino – Vizcarra's replacement in the presidential palace – to tell him that he was not their president, making clear that they wanted him out of office.[3] This tactic also targeted TV stations, which were deemed to be accomplices of the illegitimate regime for their negative portrayal of the people marching in the streets.[4]

Tragically, during the night of November 14, two young protestors – Inti Sotelo and Jack Bryan Pintado – were killed by the police.[5] The morning after, Merino stepped down from government after five catastrophic days in office. Activists continued to project statements, but now they had a different tenor. Projections were no longer a tool of protest. Projections now were a tool of memory: to memorialize the deaths of those who valiantly confronted an illegitimate regime.[6]

Luminous interventions have been gaining ground globally in recent years for multiple purposes. However, artists and activists in Latin America seem particularly keen to employ projections as a remembrance of historic political episodes. This has been the case in Chile, where the 2019 and 2020 protests employed projections to remember the cases of human rights abuses committed by their military and police.[7] Similarly, in Argentina, projections bring back the faces of the *desaparecidos* of the military dictatorship.[8] In Brazil, activists remember fallen fellows, recent victims of violent right-wing extremists.[9]

DOI: 10.4324/9781003174509-21

**FIGURE 16.1** Projection at Manuel Merino's house. Translation: "Not my president." Lima, Peru. November 13, 2020.

*Source:* Photograph by Ketty J. García Rondon

## From Light to Bytes

The affordances of projections certainly offer two prominent advantages. First, their portability. In contrast with other expressions such as graffiti and posters, the message of the projections is not fixed to the support (e.g., walls). So, as long as one can move the necessary devices around the city, the same message can appear in different spaces and/or at different times. The second advantage is their spreadability. Henry Jenkins, Sam Ford, and Joshua Green have defined media spreadability as "the potential – both technical and cultural – for audiences to share content for their own purposes,"[10] although, in this case, it is perhaps more adequate to employ the term users rather than audiences. The file containing the message to be projected can be shared with different users via any digital service.[11] Even more, with adequate equipment plus enough coordination, the message can appear in different places simultaneously. This literally annuls time and space concerns of mobility, achieving a synchronous and collective exercise of social memory.[12]

Nonetheless, there is an apparent contradiction between projections as a technique of (re)production of social memory and how memory is usually conceived. One of the inherent properties of projections is their ephemerality. Whereas graffiti and posters remain in their places until they are taken down, projections are only visible while the illuminating device is on. There is a tradeoff between immateriality and fixity. Paradoxically, the messages compelling us to remember fade when the light goes off.

Social media users have worked their way around this issue. The custom of capturing and posting remarkable moments or events have created – sometimes inadvertently, others purposely – an archive of these luminous manifestations, storing their message in a more stable form: bytes in a database. Here, the message acquires a second layer of spreadability. As publications are shared, the message reaches new persons: these memories are now available not only to those who witnessed a projection in a public space as it was happening but also to those who come across a post on social media (see Figure 16.2).

Certainly, these platforms have their own high dose of ephemerality. As any social media user knows, there is a propensity to quickly jump from one topic to another. Without any indexation or curatorial labor, these images would probably become hard to trace after a while. Fortunately, as previously mentioned, there are users dedicated to preserving them in social media accounts. The owners of these accounts not only posted the images they captured but also incentivized others to submit their own to be shared.[13] By storing, curating, and indexing these shareable images, these users create what we could name "spreadable archives."

Examples of these practices of archiving can be found in different platforms, although Instagram seems to be the preferred choice. For instance, Coletivo Projetação from Brazil is a longstanding collective that started in 2013 and does projections on a wide range of topics – from anti-racism to abortion legalization.[14] A much more recent initiative is La Nueva Banda de la Terraza from Colombia, which started in 2020.[15] Under their motto *#aisladosperonocallados* (#isolatedbutnotsilent), they started making projections as an alternative way of protesting during the COVID-19 pandemic.[16]

FIGURE 16.2    Instagram profile of project GRITA LUZ, Peru. Translation of the bio: "Collective civic projections. Follow the link and download images to project! If you have images, send them to gritaluz@gmail.com." The text in the three images at the bottom says "30 days, no one guilty." December 18, 2020.

*Source:* Photographs in the screenshot by Gritaluz

These archives are not free of complications such as ownership. These platforms are owned by corporations, and there are no publicly owned alternatives. As a consequence, the registers of all these messages invoking the public memory are ironically privately owned. They do not belong to the public and our access to them can change according to corporate decision-making processes. The luminous messages that moved across an open public space, once turned into digital images, now circulate through private digital infrastructure.

## Mediating Peruvian Memory

Besides these general technological issues, Peru has its own complex relationship with historical memory. After the period of internal conflict during the 1980s and 1990s, the transition government of Valentin Paniagua in 2001 organized a Truth Commission in charge of clarifying the crimes and human rights abuses committed during these decades. The commission produced a detailed report composed of nine volumes.[17] Given the evident impracticality of such work for dissemination purposes, an abridged version of the report was produced.[18] Still, this version was more than 500 pages long. An even briefer publication containing only the conclusions of the report was also produced.[19] Other alternatives, such as comics focusing on particular events, were also published.[20]

Written accounts of our collective memory are still necessary because they stabilize narratives.[21] Over the centuries, the book as a media form has been fundamental for the dissemination of information. People also share and discuss what they read. But, unlike the projections highlighted in this piece, with books information consumption happens primarily in a dialectical relation between one person and one object – either an actual book or any other artifact that takes its place.

Furthermore, the fact that Inti Sotelo and Jack Bryan Pintado died as a result of recent state-sanctioned violence complicates the production of official media memorializing them. Francisco Sagasti, the successor of Merino in Peru's presidency, asked for "forgiveness in the name of the state."[22] Moreover, his government promoted a museum exhibition to commemorate the protests.[23] Nonetheless, the issue remained highly controversial. A parliamentary commission integrated by Merino – who returned to his regular position as a congressman – questioned the organization of the exhibition in a public museum.[24] Furthermore, street memorial sites created by activists and common citizens have been repeatedly destroyed by far-right groups, which claimed to be "cleaning the communist trash."[25]

Projections in public spaces do not replace expressions in other media forms. What they offer are new possibilities for how memories can be told and retold. They move memories out of books or museum exhibitions and into the streets (see Figure 16.3). In this sense, it could be said that projections in these spaces make memory truly public. Moreover, their ephemerality also reminds us of the continuous labor that memory requires. Names, events, and ideas that are not mobilized are destined to wither.[26]

This point takes us to a final reflection about projections and their archiving as documentary practices, particularly in the Peruvian case. In so far as they are documenting "the real" – that is, crafting nonfictional narratives – the reply to the question about their documentary value seems to be affirmative. Nonetheless, a couple of contextual and sociotechnical characteristics of these practices compel us to complicate this otherwise straightforward answer.

The first set of issues arises from the context in which these practices took place. The political unrest in Peru confronted two opposite forces not only for the control of the government but also for establishing facts about reality – such as the causes of the death of the two young protestors, something disputed by right-wing media and politicians. The documentary practices were not limited to

**FIGURE 16.3**   Projection in the streets of Lima. Translation: "Justice for our brothers."
Lima, Peru. November 29, 2020.

*Source:* Photograph by Gritaluz

an ex post account of unanimously accepted facts, as a traditional understanding of a documentary may suggest. On the contrary, these practices were purposefully employed to stake a political claim about developing or overly recent events. In this sense, the practices here described not only documented "the real" but also participated in the making of reality. In other words, by documenting reality, reality was in the making.[27] This perhaps could also be said of most documentary practices but, in this case, the proximity between the events and the crafting of the narrative accentuated this feature and blurred the distinction between participating and documenting events.

Second, we should also consider how the sociotechnical relation between users and media shaped the act of documenting reality. This is especially the case with the spreadable archives. Even if the social media accounts that curated this content were managed by identifiable individuals or collectives, some also requested and accepted image submissions from other users. Users, therefore, were actively taking part in the events and their documentation, making it a participative – although controlled – process.[28] Furthermore, as social media users continued to produce and register these projections, making reference to "a documentary," as a well-defined and finished output carried on by an author, may not be adequate. Perhaps, instead of speaking of documentary work as a finished product, it would be more precise to define these types of initiatives as documentary processes; as a constant set of practices which remain open-ended.

These characteristics can defy conventional notions of what constitutes a documentary. However, the emergence of these documentary forms in the contemporary media landscape may just be a testimony of our current era of epistemological rifts. As global and national communities further fragment in what appears to be an inexorable process of social balkanization, the proliferation of narrative-making practices that attempt to shape reality seems only logical. Determining how these two phenomena cause or reinforce each other escapes the purpose of this chapter. However, despite the pessimistic diagnoses that these trends commonly provoke, it is also certain that oppressive narratives could not be subverted without the employment of some of these practices. Memory building is a continuous and collective endeavor. It is up to us to keep up this labor.

## Notes

1. A version of this essay was earlier published as Diego Cerna Aragon, "In Light of Memory: Surveying Recent Social Media Archives of Street Projections that Subvert Official Narratives in South America," *Immerse* (February 15, 2021), https://immerse. news/in-the-light-of-memory-bd8756592161.
2. Julie Turkewitz and Anatoly Kurmanaev, "Peru Chooses 3rd President in a Week Amid Street Protests," *The New York Times* (November 16, 2020), sec. World, www. nytimes.com/2020/11/16/world/americas/Peru-president-Francisco-Sagasti.html.
3. Protesters projected the phrase "no es mi presidente" (not my president) over the façade of Merino's house. See Ketty (@helloketty_pe), "Ahorita en la casa de Merino #Merinonomerepresenta #FueraMerino #MerinoNoEsMiPresidente https://t.co/ K6zVTGB7EP," *Twitter* (November 13, 2020), 10:10 p.m., https://twitter.com/ helloketty_pe/status/1327448773749051392.
4. Phrases such as "prensa vendida" (sellout press) were projected over media buildings. Carlos Caramantin (@carcaramantin), "Gran imagen. https://t.co/WENCF1MnLJ," *Twitter* (November 13, 2020), 9:11 p.m., https://twitter.com/carcaramantin/status/ 1327433873442136065.

5. Jacqueline Fowks, "Dos Fallecidos y Decenas de Heridos por la Represión Policial Contra las Protestas en Perú," *El País* (November 15, 2020), sec. Internacional, https://elpais.com/internacional/2020-11-15/al-menos-dos-fallecidos-y-decenas-de-heridos-por-violencia-la-policial-en-peru.html.

6. For example, see the projection of the text "se llamaba Inti como el sol y el sol nunca se apaga" (his name was Inti like the sun and the sun never fades out) made by artist Claudia Coca. Inti means sun in Quechua. Jacqueline Fowks (@jfowks), "Homenaje a jóvenes asesinados por la policía el sábado. Intervención lumínica en Miraflores de la artista visual Claudia Coca https://t.co/tQqRnai3rp," *Twitter* (November 16, 2020, 8:02 p.m.), https://twitter.com/jfowks/status/1328503859308867584.

7. Delight Lab (@delight_lab_oficial), "NO+NORMALIZACIÓN A LAS VIOLACIONES DE LOS DERECHOS HUMANOS. NO+IMPUNIDAD Y NEGACIONISMO," *Instagram Photo* (November 18, 2020), www.instagram.com/p/CHwV627BlrX/.

8. Espacio Memoria y DDHH exESMA (@espaciomemoria), "#ProyectamosMemoria. 19 Compartimos Algunas Imágenes de Las Muchas Que Nos Llegan de Todo El País," *Instagram Photo* (March 23, 2020), www.instagram.com/p/B-GV5pVgxK9/.

9. Projetemos (@projetemos), *Instagram Photo* (August 10, 2020), www.instagram.com/p/CDubwj4nmwp/.

10. Henry Jenkins, Sam Ford, and Joshua Green, *Spreadable Media: Creating Value and Meaning in a Networked Culture*, Postmillennial Pop (New York and London: New York University Press, 2013), 3.

11. For example, the bio of the Peruvian Instagram account GRITA LUZ (@gritaluz) said: "Follow the link and download images to project! If you have images, send them to gritaluz@gmail.com." "GRITA LUZ (@gritaluz)" (Instagram profile, accessed December 18, 2020), www.instagram.com/gritaluz/. My translation.

12. For an example of organized synchronous projections, see the *proyectorazo* led by the Space for Memory and Human Rights in Argentina. "Convocatoria: Proyectorazo / 24 de Marzo," *Espacio Memoria*, accessed December 18, 2020, www.espaciomemoria.ar/proyectorazo/.

13. For example, in its publication from March 2020, the Argentinean account Espacio Memoria y DDHH exESMA (@espaciomemoria) published multiple photos with a text saying: "We are sharing some images of the many that have been submitted from all over the country." Espacio Memoria y DDHH exESMA (@espaciomemoria), "#ProyectamosMemoria." My translation.

14. "Coletivo Projetação (@coletivoprojetacao)," Instagram Profile, accessed December 18, 2020, www.instagram.com/coletivoprojetacao/.

15. "@lanuevabandadelaterraza," Instagram Profile, accessed December 18, 2020, www.instagram.com/lanuevabandadelaterraza/.

16. Manuela Saldarriaga Hernández, "En Medellín, la protesta 2.0 se hace desde el balcón," *Cerosetenta* (blog) (April 21, 2020), https://cerosetenta.uniandes.edu.co/en-medellin-la-protesta-2-0-se-hace-desde-el-balcon/.

17. Comisión de la Verdad y Reconciliación, "Informe Final" (August 2003), www.cverdad.org.pe/ifinal/index.php.

18. Comisión de la Verdad y Reconciliación, *Hatun Willakuy: Versión Abreviada Del Informe Final de La Comisión de La Verdad y Reconciliación, Perú* (Lima: Comisión de la Verdad y Reconciliación, 2004), https://lum.cultura.pe/cdi/documento/hatun-willakuy-versi%C3%B3n-abreviada-del-informe-final-de-la-comisi%C3%B3n-de-la-verdad-y-0.

19. Comisión de la Verdad y Reconciliación, *Conclusiones generales del Informe Final de la CVR*, 2nd ed. (Lima: IDEHPUCP, 2013), https://repositorio.pucp.edu.pe/index/handle/123456789/111953.

20. Jesús Cossio, *Barbarie. Comics Sobre Violencia Política En El Perú 1985–1990* (Lima: Contracultura, 2010), https://lum.cultura.pe/cdi/documento/barbarie-comics-sobre-violencia-pol%C3%ADtica-en-el-per%C3%BA-1985–1990.

21. By the end of 2020, a group of activists, artists, academics, and participants of the protests published a book compiling photos, testimonies, and reflections about their experiences and the political moment that Peru was going through. See Musuk Nolte and Sandra Rodriguez, eds., *11/20* (Lima: KWY, 2020).

22. "Presidente Sagasti Pide Perdón en Nombre del Estado a los Jóvenes y Víctimas de Marchas," *El Peruano* (November 17, 2020), https://elperuano.pe/noticia/108229-presidente-sagasti-pide-perdon-en-nombre-del-estado-a-los-jovenes-y-victimas-de-marchas.

23. Enrique Planas, "La protesta llegó al museo: la muestra 'Generación bicentenario en marcha' se presenta en la explanada del LUM," *El Comercio* (December 11, 2020), sec. Arte, https://elcomercio.pe/luces/arte/la-protesta-llego-al-museo-la-muestra-generacion-bicentenario-en-marcha-se-presenta-en-la-explanada-del-lum-noticia/.

24. "Congreso cita a ministro de Cultura por exposición en el LUM sobre marchas contra Manuel Merino," *El Comercio* (December 7, 2020), sec. Congreso, https://elcomercio.pe/politica/congreso/manuel-merino-congreso-comision-de-relaciones-exteriores-cita-a-ministro-de-cultura-por-exposicion-fotografica-en-el-lum-sobre-la-generacion-del-bicentenario-en-marcha-alejandro-neyra-nndc-noticia/.

25. "Jack Pintado e Inti Sotelo: en dos meses hubo tres ataques al memorial de la Av. Abancay," *El Comercio* (January 15, 2021), sec. Sucesos, https://elcomercio.pe/lima/sucesos/jack-pintado-e-inti-sotelo-en-dos-meses-hubo-tres-ataques-al-memorial-de-la-av-abancay-noticia/.

26. One could almost rephrase the axiom by Jenkins et al. about contemporary media – "if it doesn't spread, it's dead" – and apply it to memories as well: memories that do not spread are dead. See Jenkins, Ford, and Green, *Spreadable Media*.

27. According to Aston and Gaudenzi, this is a defining characteristic of interactive media: "Our view is that interactive media creates a dynamic relationship between authors, users, technology and environment that allows for fluidity, emergence and co-emergence of reality. One of the things that we find to be new and exciting new about i-docs is the relations of interdependence that they create between the user and the reality that they portray." Judith Aston and Sandra Gaudenzi, "Interactive Documentary: Setting the Field," *Studies in Documentary Film* 6, no. 2 (June 1, 2012): 135, https://doi.org/10.1386/sdf.6.2.125_1.

28. In this sense, these practices are close to the definition of participative i-doc proposed by Aston and Gaudenzi. See Aston and Gaudenzi, "Interactive Documentary," 127.

# 17

# EXPANDING BOUNDARIES, INDIGENOUS, AND MIGRANT CARTOGRAPHIES

## Counter-Mapping the International Relations of the Odeimin Runners Club

*Debbie Ebanks Schlums, Adrian Kahgee, and Rebeka Tabobondung*

As a collective of Ogimaakwe – Indigenous and Caribbean women warriors, we proposed an a-colonial approach based on Anishinabek odeimin teachings.[1] Odeimin means "heartberry" – or "strawberry" – and it grows and thrives by sending out runners thereby creating a networked lattice of relations between individual plants. These plants are a metaphor for individuals and communities – one cannot survive disconnected from relations with one another. Furthermore, odeimin contains within it the idea of nourishment as physically and spiritually essential to the body. Inherent in this understanding is the notion that connected communities are also parts of the self. Pre-dating and parallel to Eurocentric humanist and post-humanist theoretical debates,[2] odeimin teachings circumvent a god-eye, human-centered view since no one entity – plant, animal, mineral, or spirit – dominates over another; instead, all are in relation. Similarly, Dolleen Manning expresses the connectedness of all in her Anishinabek conception of Mnidoo (spirit/mystery)-worlding:

> I expand the definition of consciousness beyond human/animal sentience by locating it in the world – a living agential co-responsiveness to the field itself; where the eye first opens. My trajectory introduces another dimension of experience or perhaps a different kind of sensibility, not as an entwined and reversible of-ness but instead as a with-ness.[3]

This framework converges with what Gwilym Eades and Yingqin Zheng refer to the odeimin as a "resisting practice,"[4] with the ethos of Marcus Garvey's self-reliant philosophy and strategy. We call this an "a-colonial" framework because this approach resists oppressive capitalist systems while taking a different path: one

DOI: 10.4324/9781003174509-22

outside of colonialism's hegemonic frameworks. By enacting and visualizing the connective runners, our first interactive film project investigated Indigenous cartographic traditions as a lived sense of space. Our next project builds on what we learned about how interactivity, relationality, storytelling, poetics, traditions, and histories intersect with and through analogue and digital platforms. Called *First International Relay*, this new project approaches i-docs through the detour of connectivity, whereby relationships are built and maintained via multiple platforms in the real, through the image, and by way of the spiritual, to produce an example of a potentially boundless a-colonial documentary practice.

## Indigenous, Process, and Performative Cartographies

In a seminar "Mapping for Awareness of Indigenous Stories in Cultural Heritage Collections," part of York University's Archive/Counter-Archive Summer Institute 2021 series, Stephanie Pyne referred to a series of collaborative multimedia mapping projects aimed at intercultural reconciliation and referred to the notion of performative cartography. As an Anishnaabekwe growing up with the land, Adrian understood this cartographic notion as an intuitive sixth sense. For her, performative cartography is rooted in culturally activated spaces from checking traplines with her father, to searching for morels and puffballs, to listening to stories that enlivened spaces with her ancestors from time immemorial, to dancing and attending ceremonies. Indigenous cartographies are diverse, just like Indigenous nations and cultures across Turtle Island. They regard Navajo sand paintings and mnemonic devices as maps. Ceremony, dance, wampum, and storytelling thus comprise forms of Indigenous cartographic traditions.

Similarly, Margaret Pearce and Renee Louis address Indigenous cartographic approaches and the need to move beyond Western cartographic traditions and language. They note that mapmaking, throughout all cultures, marks the spatial understanding of the environment from the "ontological and epistemological structures of that culture."[5] Thus, Indigenous cartography might also be viewed as process cartography, which Pearce and Louis describe as

> an incorporative, as opposed to an inscriptive, practice that emphasizes the process rather than on the artifacts that result from the process. Process cartography connects oral, written, performative, and experiential modes of mapping to transmit situated Indigenous cultural knowledge from one generation to the next.[6]

Furthermore, Indigenous mapping approaches, which Pearce and Louis term "depth-of-place" knowledge, extend beyond the Western notion of five senses to include spiritual experiences of place and the corresponding sensations of "intuition, place, time, and connection to the past, present, and future"[7] and point to the interrelatedness of all aspects of life extending throughout any given space. Here, Dolleen Manning's notion of Mnidoo-Worlding, based on Anishinaabe philosophy, is relevant in understanding the ways in which the meaning of "all our relations" extends through the human, the non-human (including spirit), and across time and space. Drawing on Maurice Merleau-Ponty, her argument lies in the notion that this "consciousness-ing" can be experienced:

> Ultimately, ceremonial reflexivity immerses the self in the perceptual field—exceeding subjective projection by rousing instead to this relational entanglement . . . . A world-mnidoo-self is not an experience of inert thingly silence, but of ancestors whittling axe handles, diminishing in one sense while increasing in another, consciousness cajoled from the competing and conversing of wood shavings-self and non-self-active, autonomous, living materiality.[8]

These methodologies of Indigenous, process, and performative cartographies, therefore, challenge Western cartographic approaches by situating the individual within the world and opening the door to the idea of mapping in a very interactive way, revealing place as a lived experience in relation to and with all others, rather than as a de-contextualized dot on an aerial view paper or satellite map.

An Indigenous cartographic approach underlies our work in the Odeimin Runners Club. Our first artistic collaboration, *Everything I Touch, I Change*, curated by Jaclyn Quaresma for an exhibition at the Durham Art Gallery, explores our understandings of human survival, connection to land and rematriation, as artists and scholars who are Indigenous, Black, and Persons of Color (IBPOC).[9] The films exemplify performative cartography as a means to thread the space–time of our territories, past–present–futures, and knowledges to help navigate current political and environmental instabilities facing our communities. This work was inspired by conversations we had regarding Octavia E. Butler's 1993 science fiction novel, *The Parable of the Sower*.

We introduce and link our territories through this project, not by pointing to a physical map, but through a sense of place that is alive and imbued with meaning beyond name and elevation and that embodies all of the senses including those that are more intuitive and less tangible. In the films, we also enact the spiritual framework of odeimin teachings upon which our collective was founded by beginning with the expression of our hearts – the emotions and feelings regarding our own stories and communities. These strawberry/heartberry teachings link us physically and metaphysically as women, as mothers, as artists, as storytellers, and as descendants from several nations. The method of filmmaking we used – process cinema – materially integrates our approach to place-making.

## Process Cinema and Counter-Mapping

Through Philip Hoffman and the Film Farm, we were introduced to process cinema, a method by which one shoots 16 mm film with a Bolex camera and then processes the celluloid film with flowers. In this method, the chemical reaction of the flowers causes the image to become visible. We also created what artist Karel Doing calls "phytograms." Doing describes phytograms as "a technique that uses the internal chemistry of plants for the creation of images on photographic emulsion" and draws on Indigenous epistemologies to explain the relationship the filmmaker has with the plants in its making.[10] Similarly, during a Film Farm workshop, Hoffman referred to the making of phytograms as "capturing the essence of the plant." Both descriptions parallel Indigenous and Caribbean conceptions of spiritual worlds connected to plant life we have come to know through our lived experience.

We adapted process cinema within our own IBPOC frameworks and protocols surrounding plants and plant medicines. For example, we laid down tobacco to honor and give thanks, along with asking the plant for permission before taking. We also practiced conservationist traditions respecting local ecologies by only harvesting a small amount of the plant. For instance, when Adrian picked trilliums for her film, she harvested the part of the plant above the green leaves rather than the whole plant. We chose plants from our territories that had relevance to our lived experiences in those spaces and gave thought to the plant's purpose or properties in terms of how the plants might be utilized or how they are used in our territories by our peoples. The ways in which we used phytograms aesthetically became an artistic cartographic expression that related to process cartography and "mapping as a means to transmit situated Indigenous cultural knowledge," as described by Pearce and Louis.[11]

For instance, Figure 17.1 shows Adrian's process in making phytograms with strawberry plants, dandelions, trilliums, cedar, sage, and other plant medicines from her territory as well as copper jingles from her regalia. If phytograms capture the plant's essence, she was curious about how that translated visually into the film. Her use of the strawberry plant connects conceptually back to the meaning of our collective, signifying the runners and interconnections of the odeimin teaching. Debbie worked with the sorrel plant as shown in Figure 17.2, which is indigenous to Africa and culturally traditional in her territory of Jamaica. Rebeka pushed the idea of revealing an essence by working with a mammoth tusk in her film. The images that resulted resembled live animal cells depicted in Figure 17.3;

**FIGURE 17.1** Making phytograms on 16 mm film.

*Source:* Photograph by Adrian Kahgee

**FIGURE 17.2**    Film still of phytogram from *The Traveller* by Debbie Ebanks Schlums.

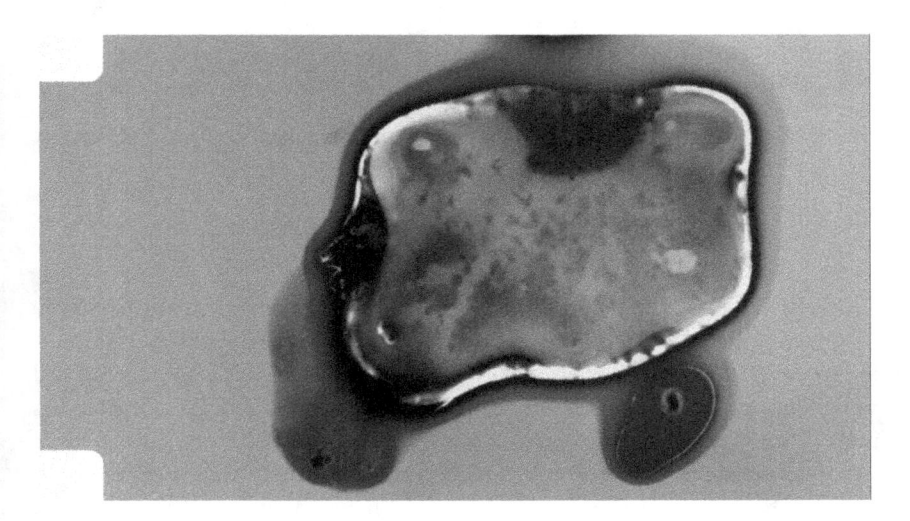

**FIGURE 17.3**    Film still of mammothgram from *Mammoth Bone* by Rebeka Tabobondung.

we termed these images mammothgrams. The phytograms surface in our films which are then accessed through an interactive metaphorical map that situates our stories. The map, shown in Figure 17.4, is a GIF constructed of multiple layers of phytograms, odeimin drawings, and conventional maps, complicating the single perspective, god-view, cartographic representation by embedding meaning into the representation of our respective territories. Both the process and the signifi-cance of the plants we selected have equal weight with the constructed images in conveying meaning through the works.

**FIGURE 17.4** Interactive webpage with GIF from *Everything I Touch I Change* by Odeimin Runners Club.

*Source:* By the authors

It is worth noting that our decision to use process cinema methods lies in the potential to move audiences beyond the voyeuristic, ethnographic, or anthropological representations wherein non-Indigenous people have used film to record Indigenous peoples and non-European cultures. In developing the films for this project, we worked against conventional and colonial forms of film narratives and instead performed cartography by injecting culturally informed gestures into the films to reflect our lived experiences, which are always already layered with depth of place knowledge and infused with the interrelations of other lifeforms and times as indicated by the phytograms and the mammothgrams. Process cinema's tactile nature further removes conventional voyeuristic practices because of the resulting film quality. The physicality of hand processing film with plants produces scratches on the celluloid film, physically and chemically embedding cultural and environmental knowledge into both the material and the resulting images, thereby visualizing Indigenous process cartography.

By performing cartography in the films within spaces in which Indigenous people have a lived experience since time immemorial – we are not just working with ourselves, but fostering relations with plants, animals, the land, and all our relations. Through dance, ceremony, or the clearing of land, we reveal hidden stories that speak to our individual experiences in our territories or where we are dwelling. These performances visualize our lived sense of space. In *The Traveller*, Debbie recognizes her presence as a guest but also honors a place of Black settlement and displacement on Saugeen Ojibway Nation Traditional Territory as she restores a site made for travelers and Freedom Seekers in marginal spaces.

In *Mammoth Bone*, Rebeka draws parallels to the dystopian world imagined in Butler's *Parable of the Sower* to that of Turtle Island upon which colonial cartographic traditions and structures have been imposed by intentionally removing our Indigenous process cartographies. Rebeka explores in the film her experience of stumbling across an unearthed mammoth tusk in relation to environmental change. She speaks to how we can survive with renewed Indigenous performative cartographies of ceremonies, lodges, offerings, and sacred sites.

Adrian's film, *Everything is Right Here*, explores the idea of removing colonial cartographic traditions imposed on the land, as indicated through fences, trespass signs, fields of dandelions, and barren farmland to unearth the Indigenous performative cartographies that are already deeply embedded in the land. The earth quite literally offers up these traditions to her in the form of an emergency survival blanket turned into regalia. She is asked to simply remember and give thanks. In all of these films, place-making through performance connects stories throughout time. We regard the integration of performative cartography with process cinema as our version of Indigenous and migrant process cartographies and also as manifestations of practice-based research (PBR), wherein different epistemologies – human, animal, spirit, and plant – came together to generate something new and old. As such these films are an example of the continuity of Anishinabe oral traditions as they intersect with migrant stories through performance and mapping.

In his *Film Farm Manifesto* on process cinema, Hoffman alludes to multiple connections between self and other and describes a method similar to process cartography:

> These images you make will be charged with your inner architecture. Do not be surprised if a person, animal, place, or thing shows you a way to go. These pathways can be provocative, treacherous, and joyful. They are places you have to go, one way or another, so you might as well start your trip.[12]

Linda Tuhiwai Smith underscores the role of connectedness across marginalized groups that call to mind odeimin teachings:

> The importance of making connections and affirming connectedness has been noted also by other minority group researchers. Connectedness positions individuals in sets of relationships with other people and with the environment. Many indigenous creation stories link people through

genealogy to the land, to stars and other places in the universe, to birds, and fish, animals, insects and plants. To be connected is to be whole.[13]

Thus, experimental film and process cartography converge in process cinema. Put differently, our work was not one of observing nature but of self-representation and working with and alongside the plants. Process cinema aligns with Anishinaabe odeimin teachings by providing a method by which to build relationships with plants (place) and seasons (time). However, odeimin teachings extend beyond such post-human discourse as actor network theory by acknowledging spiritual and cultural forms of knowing and relating beyond that which can be explained by the senses and deductive reasoning alone.

## Connecting Communities

*Everything I Touch I Change* was an opportunity to engage in PBR regarding the counter-mapping processes mentioned earlier. We are currently developing our next project, titled *First International Relay*, to apply and extend our research to our respective communities with funding from the Canada Council for the Arts. This project asks, how could we archive stories and make them available for our communities into the future? How do we protect personal and community stories while managing access from the wider public? As a broadly defined interactive documentary, *First International Relay* will place particular emphasis on revealing the intersections of Indigenous and Black Diasporic stories always already mapped on to the land.

Through artistic experimentation and community engagement, we plan to develop an interactive mediated platform to represent odeimin/strawberry runners, or "a-colonial" relations. Relationships existed prior to Contact and continue to exist between peoples across mainlands, islands, and continents. We ask, is it possible to recalibrate contemporary hemispheric relations outside of colonialism such that the settler position is one of being good guests with responsibilities to the hosts. Can we live more gently with the land and all the living beings that depend on it? In the spirit of reciprocity and sharing, we will visit each other's territories – Saugeen First Nation, Wasauksing First Nation, and Jamaica. Documenting these travels and relations will involve developing a deep and broad mapping method that weaves online interactivity with in-the-real engagement on the land.

The multipronged approach of *First International Relay* is important to how we view interactive documentary as a de-centered, democratized, land-based, community-engaged form of storytelling conducive to the continuity of oral tradition in Indigenous communities and cultural practices in migrant communities. According to Smith, establishing trust by clearly positioning oneself and maintaining relationships are key pillars on which Indigenous relationships are centered.[14] Indeed, our Collective views interactive documentary production as a dynamic *process* in which the aim is to build and maintain relationships rather than produce products as its primary goal. Instead, the mediated product is a means to establish and nourish relationships in the way that odeimin plants do before bearing fruit. Whereas many documentaries have an activist or social change agenda, the audience for our PBR and engagement model is primarily those communities we are engaging with. The terms of engagement with the broader public will ultimately be decided upon with the communities. The interactive platform will enable the building and maintaining of relationships through information flows that contribute to what Smith calls "international talking circles." Indeed,

> [b]uilding networks is about building knowledge and data bases which are based on the principles of relationships and connections. Relationships are initiated on a face to face basis and then maintained over many years without any direct contact. People's names are passed on and instructions are used to bring new members into the network.[15]

Smith's argument clearly supports the idea that silicon-based modes of interconnectedness simply extend traditional forms of relationship building and storytelling through digital interactivity. In a similar manner, *First International Relay* will be built on Indigenous and migrant notions of sharing knowledge and respecting each other's ontological and epistemological foundations. Such trust-building is rooted in the ways in which we follow cultural protocols, including how we introduce and position ourselves by stating who we are, where we are from, and how we are connected, a protocol that holds true for all of our communities. One way in which this protocol could be embedded in our platform is by requiring the community member's fulsome introduction according to their nation or community's custom when uploading content in order to situate participants first before uploading.

Figure 17.5 is an example of a common way of online story mapping we are investigating through the open-source platform called MapHub. The platform allows users to upload an content from anywhere in the world and is the seed of the *First International Relay* project. The final design of our web interface will push the aesthetics of mapping to reflect the process cartography of phytograms and of public engagement, especially regarding the question of community versus public access. We plan to learn from an online story-mapping platform with another open-source platform called Mukurtu CMS which hosts several Indigenous community archives and embeds protocols developed by a Waramungu community in Australia and hosted by Washington State University. The online mapping platform we are developing will have specific features that make Mukurtu CMS relevant to Indigenous communities such as embedding cultural protocols, community engagement, and the protection of cultural artifacts.

Our odeimin-guided methodology of process cartography and PBR extends to our conception of community engagement to include offline, in-the-real

**FIGURE 17.5**   Screenshot of Odeimin Runners Club experimental interactive story map.

*Source:* By the authors

interactive sensorial experiences in the form of a physical map. Margaret Pearce's *Coming Home to Indigenous Place Names in Canada*[16] is a model for what we are thinking about in terms of scale, community engagement, and process in following cultural protocols. In the process of creating the map, Pearce contacted each community to verify and request permission to publish the place names on the map. Where that permission was not granted,

> cartographic silence was recorded on the map. Silences are manifested in the withholding of translations, or a reticence in the way translations are worded, or sharing one type of feature while withholding all other types of names (for example, sharing river names but not other kinds of names). Silence tells outsiders we have heard enough, and that further elaboration is undeserved or unnecessary in this context.[17]

Pearce renews her engagement with the participating Indigenous communities across Canada at each exhibition of the map, when the protocol to ask for permission is repeated and updated. This lengthy procedure points to the importance of process rather than a product in which the latter is subject to change in relation to community.

Another important aspect of this map is the ability to physically "touch" the territory and recognize or learn the Indigenous place names on the map, noted by curator Patricio Davila. Such a large physical map would be an inviting space on which community members could document oral traditions. The map could also serve as a means to facilitate Indigenous protocols such that knowledge designated to remain within the community is safeguarded through physical community access. Another important aspect of a physical map is that it is arguably more inclusive to Elders, for instance, who may not engage in online environments but could view the territory and recall areas to which they have connection.

We are also considering methods of interaction to engage technically savvy youth and traditional cultural practices in order to link the online content of the digital map to the physical map in the community. One of these strategies is augmented reality (AR). Our intention is to support traditional artisans to create handmade AR markers that are painted, beaded, and/or sculpted, and then placed on the physical map. The AR marker would then link, via mobile devices, to the online stories connected to the physical map. Another method of interactive mapping we will integrate into the project is locative media, which echoes performative cartography by requiring the body to be present on the land. A user would experience a GPS-triggered sound walk accessed through an app such Echoes XYZ. By being present and connecting to land, users will have access to stories relative to that place and, in having such access, we feel they will embody the story more fully. This final level of interactive digital storytelling thus brings the de-territorialized virtual map and the abstracted physical map full circle to co-create on and with the land from which these representations are derived. The multipronged approach thereby makes room for the sharing of community members' stories from their subjectivity and encourages the expression of the multiple ways in which oral traditions are told, namely, through birch bark scrolls, beadwork, painting, dance, and oral storytelling. The interactive documentary is thus a sum of parts assembled by a distributed network of storytellers in which each person's story contributes to the story of an interconnected web of relations of family, clan, communities, friendships, and non-human relations. As such, this form of documentary echoes the ways in which Mnidoo-Worlding and odeimin runners exceed the self by extending into all other relations and expanding boundaries in both intangible and material ways.

Through Indigenous cartographic practices that include process and performative cartographies, and through interactive film and digital media, the Odeimin Runners Club place contemporary relations on a continuum rather than as "new encounters," outside the language of discovery and within a concept of time immemorial, activating and re-activating the long ties between Indigenous communities, between Black and Indigenous peoples on the mainland, and between the islands and the mainland. In pursuing an a-colonial path rooted in odeimin teachings, Odeimin Runners Club unapologetically grounds our cultural identities in the land of northern and rural Ontario and in Jamaica in relation to and with one another.

## Notes

1. A version of this essay was earlier published as Debbie Ebanks Schlums, Adrian Kahgee, and Rebeka Tabobondung, "Indigenous and Migrant Embodied Cartographies: Mapping the Inter-relations of the Odeimin Runners Club," *Interactive Film and Media Journal,* 2, no. 1 (January 2022).
2. See, for instance, conceptions of the posthuman posited by Donna Haraway, "Situated Knowledges: The Science Question in Feminism and the Privilege of Partial Perspective," *Feminist Studies* 14, no. 3 (1988): 575–99, https://doi.org/10.2307/3178066; Bruno Latour, *Reassembling the Social: An Introduction to Actor-Network-Theory* (Oxford University Press, 2005); Rosi Braidotti, *The Posthuman* (Oxford: Polity Press, 2013).
3. Dolleen Manning, "The Murmuration of Birds: An Anishinaabe Ontology of MnidooWorlding," in *Feminist Phenomenology Futures*, eds. Helen A. Fielding et al. (Bloomington: Indiana University Press, 2017), 162–63, http://ebookcentral.proquest.com/lib/york/detail.action?docID=5108586.
4. Gwilym Eades and Yingqin Zheng, "Counter-Mapping as Assemblage: Reconfiguring Indigeneity," in *Information Systems and Global Assemblages. (Re)Configuring Actors, Artefacts, Organizations*, eds. Bill Doolin et al., vol. 446, IFIP Advances in Information and Communication Technology (Berlin and Heidelberg: Springer Berlin Heidelberg, 2014), 79–94, https://doi.org/10.1007/978-3-662-45708-5_6, 6.
5. Margaret Pearce and Renee Louis, "Mapping Indigenous Depth of Place," *American Indian Culture and Research Journal* 32, no. 3 (January 1, 2008): 107–26, https://doi.org/10.17953/aicr.32.3.n7g22w816486567j, 110.
6. Pearce and Louis, "Mapping Indigenous Depth of Place," 110.
7. Pearce and Louis, "Mapping Indigenous Depth of Place," 114.
8. Manning, "The Murmuration," 170.
9. Our intentional use of the term "IBPOC," rather than the more common "BIPOC," projects an a-colonial present and future which foregrounds Indigenous peoples on Indigenous land while remaining in allyship with other racialized peoples.
10. Karel Doing, "Phytograms: Rebuilding Human – Plant Affiliations," *Animation* 15, no. 1 (March 2020): 22–36, https://doi.org/10.1177/1746847720909348, 24.
11. Pearce and Louis, "Mapping Indigenous Depth of Place," 110.
12. Philip Hoffman, "Your Film Farm Manifesto of Process Cinema," in *Process Cinema: Handmade Film in the Digital Age*, eds. Scott MacKenzie and Janine Marchessault (Montreal, Kingston, London and Chicago: McGill-Queen's University Press, 2019), 293.
13. Linda Tuhiwai Smith, *Decolonizing Methodologies: Research and Indigenous Peoples* (London and New York: Zed Books, 2006), 148.
14. Smith, *Decolonizing Methodologies*, 157.
15. Smith, *Decolonizing Methodologies*.
16. An online version of Margaret Pearce's *Coming Home to Indigenous Places in Canada* may be found here: https://umaine.edu/canam/publications/coming-home-map/coming-home-indigenous-place-names-canada-pdf-download/.
17. Margaret W. Pearce and Stephen J. Hornsby, "Making the Coming Home Map," *Cartographica: The International Journal for Geographic Information and Geovisualization* 55, no. 3 (September 1, 2020): 170–76, https://doi.org/10.3138/cart-2019-0012, 174.

# FILMS AND INTERACTIVE PROJECTS

Benson, Joel Kachi, dir. *In Bakassi*. Lagos: VR360 Stories, 2018. Virtual Reality.

Benson, Joel Kachi, dir. *Daughters of Chibok*. Lagos: VR360 Stories, 2019. Virtual Reality.

Benson, Joel Kachi, dir. *J. D. 'Okhai Ojeikere*. Lagos, n.d. Video.

Bollendorff, Samuel and Abel Ségrétin, dirs. *Journey to the End of Coal*. Paris: Honky-tonk Films, France, 2008. Interactive documentary. www.samuel-bollendorff.com/en/voyage-au-bout-du-charbon/ (archival only).

Braithwaite-Shirley, Danielle, dir. *BlackTransArchive*. London 2021a. Interactive Archive. https://blacktransarchive.com/.

Braithwaite-Shirley, Danielle, dir. *Pirating Blackness*. London 2021b. Interactive Docugame. www.blacktranssea.com/.

Branch, John, writer. "Snow Fall: The Avalanche at Tunnel Creek." *New York Times*. New York: New York Times Publishing Company, 2012. Multimedia Feature. www.nytimes.com/projects/2012/snow-fall/index.html#/?part=tunnel-creek.

Braun, Guilluame, Bruno Choinière, Thibaut Duverneix, and Philippe Lambert, dirs. *A Journal of Insomnia*. Montreal: National Film Board of Canada, 2019.

*Buzzfeed Unsolved Network*. Buzzfeed (2018-present). YouTube Channel. www.youtube.com/channel/UCKijjvu6bN1c-ZHVwR7-5WA.

Carabalí, Angela and Thibault Durand, dirs. *Pregoneros de Medellín*. April 2015 at Medellín, Colombia: Carabalí Grupo Creativo, 2015. Interactive documentary. https://pregonerosdemedellin.com.

Chang, Anita, An-Chi Chen, Kainoa Kaupu, Hauʻoli Waiau, and Shin-Lan Yu, dirs. *Tongues of Heaven*. New York: Third World Newsreel, 2013. DVD.

Chang, Anita and Michella Rivera-Gravage, dirs. and prods. *Root Tongue: Sharing Stories of Language Identity and Revival*. Lost Angeles and Hayward, CA, Taiwan: 2016-present. Web documentary. https://root-tongue.com/.

Cizek, Katerina, dir. *Highrise*. Montreal: National Film Board of Canada, ongoing. Interactive and web documentary. highrise.nfb.ca. *Out My Window* is a part of this project.

Colinart, Arnaud, Amaury La Burthe, Peter Middleton, and James Spinney, creative dirs, and Béatrice Lartigue, Fabien Togman, and Arnaud Desjardins, artistic dirs. *Notes on*

*Blindness.* Paris and London: Ex Nihilo, ARTE France, and Archer's Mark, 2016. Virtual Reality. www.notesonblindness.co.uk/vr/

Court, Marie and Rosemarie Lerner, dirs. *Proyecto Quipu.* Peru and London: Chaka Studio, 2011. Interactive documentary. https://interactive.quipu – project.com.

Falcone, Rachel and Michael Premo, dirs. *Sandy Storyline.* New York 2013. Interactive Documentary. www.sandystoryline.com.

Fernandez, Alberto, Cesar Vallejo, and Charo Marcos, dirs. *Guadalquivir.* Madrid: RTVE, 2013. Interactive Documentary. http://lab.rtve.es/guadalquivir/.

Florin, Fabrice, dir. *Moss Landing.* Cupertino, CA: Apple Multimedia Lab, 1989. Interactive video database. www.convivial.com/project/early-interactive-works/ (archival only).

Funari, Vicki, prod. and Jesikah Maria Ross, dir. *Troubled Waters: Tracing Waste in the Delaware River.* Philadelphia, PA. 2014. Multi-authored interactive documentary. https://troubledwaters2014.tumblr.com/.

Gaudenzi, Sandra and Sandra Tabares-Duque, coordinators. *Corona Haikus.* Facebook, Ongoing. Facebook Public Group. www.facebook.com/groups/226094118756231/.

Gauntlett, Jane, dir. *In My Shoes: Dancing with Myself.* London 2016. 360 Video.

Handal, Alexandra Sofia, dir. *Dream Homes Property Consultants.* Berlin: Ciné-Dérive, Cinema and New Media Production House, 2007–2016. Interactive documentary. http://dreamhomespropertyconsultants.com.

Harris, Jonathan, dir. *Sputnik Observatory.* Interactive Database. New York: Jonathan Harris 2009. http://number27.org/sputnik.

Irigaray, Fernando, dir. *Calles Perdidas: El Avance del Nacotráfico en Rosario.* Rosario, Argentina: DocuMedia Periodismo Social Multimedia, Universidad Nacional del Rosario, 2014. Interactive documentary.www.documedia.com.ar/callesperdidas/.

Jones, Leonie, dir. *The Battle of Coral Balmoral.* Sydney: Meanjin Entertainment, 2016. DVD.

Jones, Leonie, dir. *The Battle of Coral Balmoral.* Sydney 2020. Interactive Documentary. www.fsbcoral.org.

Kiln.it, Francesca Panetta, Lindsay Poulton, Alex Purcell, Stephen Moss, Nabeelah Shabbir, and Lily Brazier, dirs. *First World War: The Story of a Global Conflict.* London: The Guardian UK, 2014. Interactive documentary.www.theguardian.com/world/ng-interactive/2014/jul/23/a-global-guide-to-the-first-world-war-interactive-documentary.

Köppen, Uli, Tanja Pröbstl, Francesca Panetta, and James Burke, organizers. *Corona Diaries.* Cambridge, MA: Nieman Foundation, 2020-present. Online database. https://coronadiaries.io/about.html.

Kraus, Berni and United Visual Artists, dirs. *The Great Animal Orchestra.* Paris: Foundation Cartier, 2016. Interactive Documentary. www.legrandorchestredesanimaux.com/en.

Kumar, Aashish, dir. *Body, Home, World – South Asian American LGBTQ+ Journeys.* New York: Embers Films, 2021-present. Interactive documentary. http://bodyhomeworld.com/.

McLaughlin, Cahal, dir. *Prisons Memory Archive.* Belfast 2006-present. https://prisonsmemoryarchive.com/

Meitin, Alexander, artist. *Living Rivers/Rios Vivos.* 2019. Interactive map gallery exhibition.

Miller, Elizabeth, Kim Grinder, and Juan Caroly Zaldivar, prods. and dirs. *SwampScapes.* Miami 2018. Online film and virtual reality. www.swampscapes.org/.

Milosavljevich, Stefan, dir. *Stefan Milo,* YouTube Channel (2018-present). www.youtube.com/channel/UCZ9jWH_8tJ-Nmaj8dSQdEYA.

Panetta, Francesca and Lindsay Poulton, dirs. *6x9*. London: The Guardian UK, 2016. Virtual Reality. www.theguardian.com/world/ng-interactive/2016/apr/27/6x9-a-virtual-experience-of-solitary-confinement#gvr-howto

Peterson, Matt, dir. *Scenes from a Revolt Sustained*. New York 2014. Online documentary. https://revoltsustained.tumblr.com/

Peterson, Matt and Malek Rasamny, dirs. *The Native and the Refugee*. New York and Beruit: Ongoing. Mutiplatform Documentary. https://thenativeandtherefugee.com/

Ratuszynska, Tessa, dir. *Club XXY*. Glasgow 2021. 360 web-doc. www.clubxxy.co.uk/.

Ratuszynska, Tessa, Fi Nicholson, Ilsa Badenoch, and Freya Campbell, artists. *The Othvrs*. Bristol, UK (2018-present). 360/VR/XR collaborative. www.theothvrs.com/

Ryan, Kathleen M., dir. and David Staton, prod. *Pin Up! The Movie: An Interactive Documentary*. Longmont, CO: TaylorCatProductions, 2021. Interactive Documentary. www.pinupthemovie.com.

Serra, Andrià, Ferran Clavell, Ramon Vallès, and Santiago Torres, dirs. *Guernika, Pintura de Guerra*. San Joan Despí, Spain: TV3 – Televisió de Catalunya, 2007. Interactive Documentary.

Sheldon, Elaine McMillion, dir. *Hollow*. 2013. Interactive Documentary and DVD. http://hollowdocumentary.com/ (archival only).

Szalat, Alex, Joël Ronez, and Susanna Lotz, dirs. *Gaza/Sderot*. Paris and Tel-Aviv, ARTE France, Bo Travail, 2008. Interactive Documentary. http://gaza-sderot.arte.tv/ (archival only).

White, Chris, dir. *Ancient Aliens Debunked*. VerseByVerseBT. YouTube (2012) 3:10:43. www.youtube.com/watch?v=j9w-i5oZqaQ

# INDEX

Printed in the USA
CPSIA information can be obtained
at www.ICGtesting.com
LVHW021127170924
791293LV00002B/436